Dictionary of Fortifications

Dictionary of Fortifications

An illustrated glossary of castles, forts, and other defensive works from antiquity to the present day

Jean-Denis Lepage

Pen & Sword
MILITARY

First published in Great Britain in 2022 by
Pen & Sword Military
An imprint of
Pen & Sword Books Ltd
Yorkshire – Philadelphia

Copyright © Jean-Denis Lepage 2022

ISBN 978 1 39907 224 3

The right of Jean-Denis Lepage to be identified as Author of this work has been asserted by him in accordance with the Copyright, Designs and Patents Act 1988.

A CIP catalogue record for this book is available from the British Library.

All rights reserved. No part of this book may be reproduced or transmitted in any form or by any means, electronic or mechanical including photocopying, recording or by any information storage and retrieval system, without permission from the Publisher in writing.

Typeset by Mac Style
Printed in the UK by CPI Group (UK) Ltd, Croydon, CR0 4YY.

Pen & Sword Books Limited incorporates the imprints of Atlas, Archaeology, Aviation, Discovery, Family History, Fiction, History, Maritime, Military, Military Classics, Politics, Select, Transport, True Crime, Air World, Frontline Publishing, Leo Cooper, Remember When, Seaforth Publishing, The Praetorian Press, Wharncliffe Local History, Wharncliffe Transport, Wharncliffe True Crime and White Owl.

For a complete list of Pen & Sword titles please contact

PEN & SWORD BOOKS LIMITED
47 Church Street, Barnsley, South Yorkshire, S70 2AS, England
E-mail: enquiries@pen-and-sword.co.uk
Website: www.pen-and-sword.co.uk

Or

PEN AND SWORD BOOKS
1950 Lawrence Rd, Havertown, PA 19083, USA
E-mail: Uspen-and-sword@casematepublishers.com
Website: www.penandswordbooks.com

Contents

Synopsis vi
Acknowledgements vii
Conversion Table viii
Introduction ix

Part I   A Short History of Fortification   1

Part II   Siege Warfare   21

Part III   Dictionary   35

Bibliography   337

Synopsis

This dictionary is an attempt to give an explanation in both words and illustrations to the technical language and specialized terms developed in military architecture.

The book is divided into three parts, in order to have a complete understanding of the development of military architecture and activities involved in defensive warfare from prehistoric times until today.

The first part recounts in chronological outline the many aspects of the historical evolution of coastal, permanent and semi-permanent fortifications.

Part Two discusses the technical development of siege warfare, siege machines and tactics.

Part Three represents the bulk of the book. Listed in alphabetical order, it includes the definition and description of terms of fortifications. Some important entries can take the form of a short article giving basic information about a fortification. To enhance comprehension, some entries are further explained by an illustration, a sketch, a ground plan, a cross-section, a map or an artistic impression. The reader can orientate himself rapidly to browse through related entries following a theme by use of the cross-references indicated by (q.v.).

The book features a bibliography for further reading.

It is intended for the general reader – the reader with an interest but little specific knowledge in the subject of military architecture. It is an attempt to sum up the enormous amount of evidence and documentation about fortifications, stimulate interest, provide sufficient information and inspiration and point up new areas for further investigation.

Acknowledgements

I would like to gratefully thank the following people for their friendly help in putting together this book: Jeannette Aty à Stuling, Nicole Lapaux, Jan-Reijer à Stuling, Jacques Jouy, Rudi Rolf, Ben Marcato and Eltje-Jakob de Lang.

Conversion Table

1 millimetre (mm)	0.039 inch (in)
1 centimetre (cm)	0.393 inch
1 metre (m)	1.093 yards
1 kilometre (km)	0.621 miles
1 kilogram (kg)	2.204 pounds (lb)
1 tonne (t)	0.948 long ton (UK)

Introduction

Fortification is one of the oldest military sciences, and humans have constructed defensive works for thousands of years. Like all other human activities, fortifications have evolved in a variety of increasingly complex defensive designs, always in direct response to the development of offensive weapons. From their rudimentary beginning, fortifications have become one of the foremost military arts, gathering complexity and creating its own jargon – a language sometimes confusing and contradictory, somewhat difficult to understand and rather particular to describe and to write about. The purpose of this book is to present the complex issues of fortifications to a wider public in an accessible form, both in text and illustrations. It is an introduction and explanation of the terminology of its architectural and technical features in order to convey a precise meaning in a convenient and hopefully pleasant fashion.

This work is intended to be a book of reference, a complete, many-sided history of fortifications as a whole arranged in dictionary/glossary form.

For practical reasons, I have placed geographical limits to this work. The focus is on Europe, with attention paid to the Middle East and the Mediterranean basin (which are the roots of European fortification and civilization), and to America (which is Europe's offspring). There are many over-simplifications and numerous omissions, I am afraid, and for this I apologize, making only the excuse that with so massive a subject, the references have to be selective.

The objective of this work is to provide a reliable source of information and reference. It is also intended to stimulate the interest of the general lay reader and provide him with a basic tool for further research.

Jean-Denis G.G. Lepage
Groningen
February MMXXII

Part One

A Short History of Fortification

Fortification Before the Introduction of Firearms

Generality

Fortifications are defensive constructions, protected positions, reinforced buildings, screening elements and shielding structures designed and constructed to strengthen a place against attack. The term is derived from the Latin words *fortis* (strong) and *facere* (to make).

Fortification – the art of building defences – is an activity almost as old as the human race itself. From ancient antiquity to modern times, the use of fortifications has always been a vital necessity to protect settlements, communities, villages, towns and cities.

Antiquity

It is commonly assumed that permanent fortification was developed at the same time as the inception of agriculture and the creation of the first human sedentary settlements in the Near East. When people began to settle in permanent villages, to domesticate animals, grow their own food and stock their surpluses, they became targets for predatory animals and particularly fellow-human marauders, raiders and thieves. There is naturally no certitude about this, but much evidence supports the thesis that early forms of fortifications would have first appeared when and where organized civilization started, notably in Mesopotamia, Assyria and Egypt. Initially, these fortifications were presumably very basic, consisting for example of elementary thorny hedges, simple fences and uncomplicated enclosures. Gradually, more effective elements were introduced, combining obstacles made of wood (palisades or brushwood fences), earthworks (ditches and earth walls) and stone or adobe masonry. In Ancient Mesopotamia and Egypt, due to many factors such as improvement of agriculture by irrigation, growth of population, development of trade and conquest by war, the first empires and large cities appeared. Those imperial cities were enclosed by elaborate constructions of masonry, for example stones, adobe clay and bricks, sometimes constituting gigantic, spectacular and impressive defences.

The evolution of fortification always resulted from improvements made in weaponry, and throughout history there has been a continuous duel and a perpetual swing in the balance of the superiority of attack or defence. Simple fortifications using a ditch, earth wall and timber palisade never disappeared: European prehistoric Celtic hillforts were the predecessors to castles, which emerged in the Middle Ages.

From the unknown start of fortification until the introduction of firearms in the Late Middle Ages and Renaissance, fortification existed in many variations of size, shape, design, thickness, height, tracés, groundplan, complexity and quality of building materials, but it was always characterized by height, thickness and solidity. For centuries, defensive works presented a very high vertical profile in order to resist climbing and to create elevated observation and combat emplacements favourable for the defenders owing to that dominating position. Obviously, verticality and height – using the force of

Temple of Ramses III located near Luxor in Ancient Egypt.

gravity – were extremely useful for dropping and shooting down projectiles onto a group of attackers at the base of a wall. Sturdiness and thickness of walls offered stability and permitted defenders to resist the battering ram and underground mining.

Fortifications were continuously expanded and developed, often including a ditch and always a high wall topped with a walkway protected by crenelated breastwork. At intervals along the walls, high towers and turrets were added for the purpose of flanking defence. Entrances to castles, fortresses and fortified cities were few, and always included strong gatehouses featuring solid gates and doors, drawbridges, combat emplacements and often outworks (advanced defensive structures).

Egyptian frontier defences included outposts such as the Old Kingdom settlement at Buhen near the Second Cataract in Nubia. The cross-section shows Bouhen's dry ditch and two stone walls with towers.

Assur was the capital of the Assyrian Empire (modern-day Iraq) from *c.* 2025–608 BC. Assur was established on the River Tigris and included an inner city with houses, palaces, gardens, temples and many other buildings, which were enclosed by two impressive defensive walls with towers, gatehouses and moats.

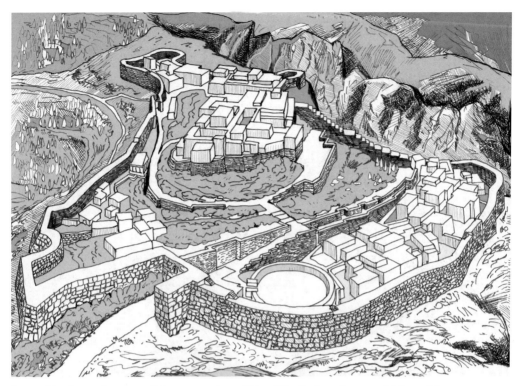

Located in the north-eastern Peloponnese about 90km (56 miles) south-west of Athens, Mycenae was one of the major centres of civilization. At its peak in 1350 BC, Mycenae was a fortified military stronghold including an acropolis (citadel) and a lower town covering an area of 32 hectares.

The Lion Gate was the main entrance of the Bronze Age acropolis of Mycenae in southern Greece. Constucted during the thirteenth century BC, it was made of enormous stones and included a defensive bastion.

Simple fortifications combining one or more ditches, a breastwork, a palisade, an earth wall and a gatehouse in the form of a wooden tower were always used throughout recorded history.

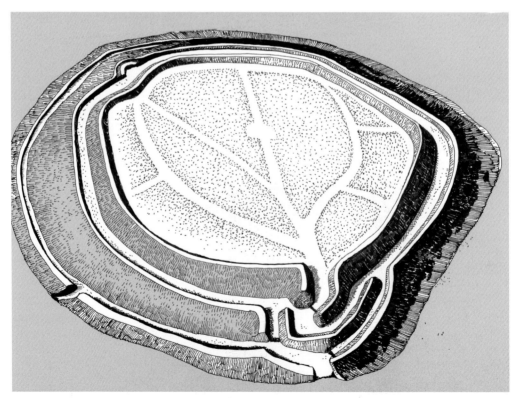

A hillfort or *oppidum* was a fortified settlement established during the Bronze and Iron Ages in Celtic Europe. Defences included ditches and earth walls topped with palisades.

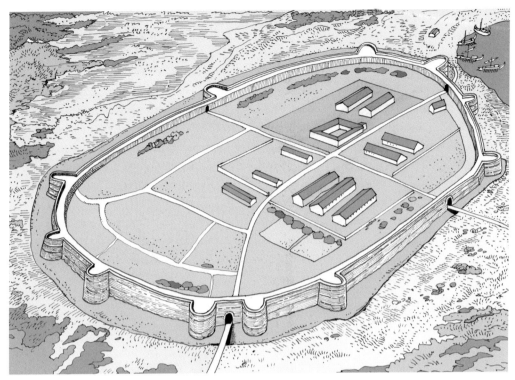

The Roman Empire reached its greatest extent in the early second century AD. In the north it reached England, and Pevensey Castle in East Sussex was one of the Roman 'Saxon Shore' forts. These were defensive ports and fortresses constructed to control and protect the English coasts from Saxon pirates and raiders.

The Roman Empire was accomplished through military conquest. Once the Empire was established, Rome gave it two centuries of peace, but beyond the borders enemies were lurking. Consequently, the Romans built defences, called *limes*, to keep them at bay, including natural elements (rivers, mountains, forests, marshes, deserts) and man-made fortifications.

Middle Ages

When the Roman Empire collapsed many, of the Romans' skills (notably that of masonry and fortification) were lost to the Barbarian invaders who settled in Europe during the so-called Dark Age (the early medieval period from *c.* AD 475–1000).

Vertical walls, strong towers and sturdy gatehouses developed in Antiquity were gradually revived in medieval Europe. The Middle Ages saw the development of private castles of all sizes, the growth of existing towns and the creation of new settlements, and thus the reintroduction and development of urban fortifications including a combination of ditches, palisades, earth and stone walls, towers and gatehouses. All over Europe, minor barons, wealthy lords and powerful kings walled themselves in behind elaborate fortresses that were meant to be defensive in numerous independent counties, small duchies and large realms frequently living in autarky. The fortifications of castles, cities and settlements were continuously improved, modernized and enlarged to match the development of weapons and siege machines. The Crusades in the twelfth and thirteenth centuries formed an important part of the transformation and expansion of European society, when Western Crusaders were confronted by the advanced Byzantine and Muslim civilizations. In the late Middle Ages, some castles had become imposing and sophisticated fortresses where feudal lords gathered their courts and knights, and administrated and ruled their domains, principalities and kingdoms.

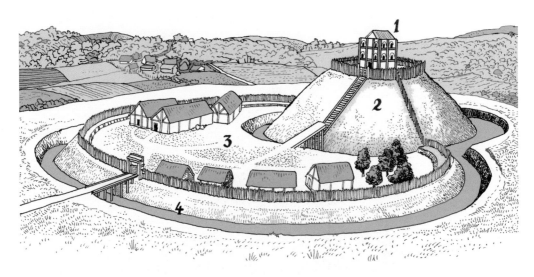

Motte-and-bailey castle. 1: Tower; 2: Motte; 3: Bailey; 4: External ditch and palisade.

The castle of Loches on the Indre River in central France was built in the ninth century and featured one of the first massive stone keeps.

The construction of the castle of Cochem in the Rhineland-Palatinate in Germany started in the 1050s. The castle became an imperial property in 1151 and was continuously enlarged by the German emperors throughout the Middle Age.

A typical medieval castle was characterized by high and thick vertical walls. No two castles were the same, but the main basic features often included the following: 1: Moat (dry or filled with water); 2: Gatehouse with drawbridge; 3: Tower; 4: Curtain or wall; 5: Wall-walk with battlement on top of the wall; 6: Timber hoarding; 7: Postern (sally port); 8: Pepper-pot turret; 9: Inner yard; 10: Keep.

Fortifications Since the Introduction of Firearms

Transitional Fortification

Medieval fortifications were gradually made obsolete by the progressive development of gunpowder and siege cannons in the fifteenth century. However, it must be pointed out that firearms did not render medieval castles and urban walls obsolete overnight. Adaptation to fortifications was as slow as the progressive evolution of firearms.

After a short period of transition characterized by the use of lowered and squat structures, broad and deep ditches, earth rampart artillery platforms (bulwarks) and low, roundish, thick-walled, casemated artillery gun towers, a new system of fortification evolved at the beginning of the sixteenth century in Italy. This system, called the bastioned fortification, was destined to dominate the art of fortification for some three centuries.

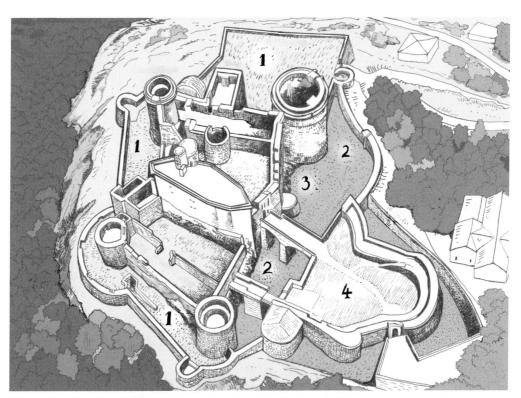

The medieval castle of Bonaguil, located at Fumel in the Lot-et-Garonne department in south-west France, was built in the thirteenth century and adapted to the use of firearms at the end of the fifteenth century with the addition of gun platforms (1), the deepening of the ditch (2) defended by a flanking *moineau* (3), aka *caponier*, and the construction of a large advanced artillery work called a barbican (4).

Bastioned fortification

The introduction of the low-profiled bastioned fortification in the early sixteenth century had two important features. First, it resisted quite well the attackers' projectiles, and second, it allowed the emplacing of numerous well-protected defensive guns, which could use reciprocal cross and flanking fire.

The medieval verticality of old was thus definitively replaced with horizontality and defence in depth spreading over large areas. Natural gravity was no longer needed, being replaced by the powerful force of exploding black powder.

Although relatively simple at first, the bastion system of fortification became increasingly complex with numerous tracés, designs and many added outworks and advanced works. The new manner of fortification was efficient, flexible and adaptable to suit varying situations and natural conditions. There was, however, one crucial disadvantage: the very high cost involved. Indeed, conceiving, designing, building and maintaining a bastioned enceinte (main line of fortification) was so expensive that only rich free cities, wealthy dukes and powerful lords, princes, kings, emperors, senior prelates and popes could afford modern artillery and bastioned fortifications.

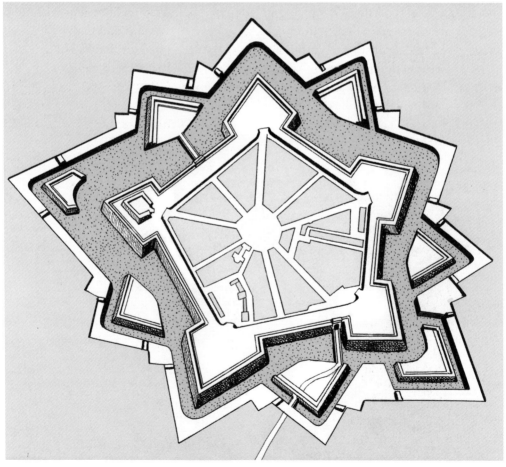

Bastioned fortifications (Rocroi, France).

The bastion system clearly announced a new era. It sounded the death knell of the private feudal castle and marked the end of the self-financed medieval urban enceinte. Its adoption caused the end of local wars between rival barons and marked the start of the monopoly of the state in matters of war and national defence.

The new bastioned system (in numerous shapes, sizes and styles) was widely adopted and quickly became the norm across Europe and in the colonies founded by the European nations in the newly discovered continents.

In the seventeenth and eighteenth centuries, warfare was marked by dynastic wars and a large number of sieges, in which fortification and artillery played a central role. Against this background, fortification became a sophisticated military science developed by specialized engineering personnel with a technical jargon of its own.

The bastioned system remained in use until the end of the Napoleonic Wars at the beginning of the nineteenth century.

Revival of the Tower

Significant improvement in artillery had occurred during the eighteenth century, the French Revolution and Napoleonic Wars (1789–1815) demonstrating the superiority of attack over defence. After 1815 it became clear that bastioned fortifications with their intricate arrangements of bastions, outworks, advanced positions and empty glacis no longer fared well against the disrupting effects of concentrated artillery. The bastioned tracé was originally and essentially a flanking system. It had been designed in the sixteenth century to protect the curtain walls by covering fire from the flanks of the bastions, but since the flanks themselves, as well as the curtains, could now be engaged at a greater distance by enemy artillery, there was little justification for the tracé. During

British Martello Tower.

Dutch *Torenfort* (Muiden).

the course of the eighteenth century, a bastioned enceinte had become vulnerable and was practically always doomed to surrender.

As a first response there was a revival of thick artillery towers in different designs such as the British Martello tower, the French *lunette* and *tour modèle*, Dutch *torenfort*, large Maximilian tower and the tower-fort in Sweden and Russia.

Polygonal Fortification

A new system of military architecture gradually evolved in the nineteenth century. Known as the Polygonal fortification, or Prussian method because it was developed in Germany, this new scheme finally brought an end to the long reign of the bastioned fortification. The new system was characterized by simple structures and detached forts, in fact large gun batteries presenting a straight front (without bastions) with faces as long as necessary. They were made of strong masonry covered with thick layers of earth. They were bristling with guns placed in thick, masonry, multi-storey towers, in numerous casemates and also mounted in open and compartmented emplacements protected by thick earth parapets. These detached autonomous forts, deployed in wide circles and yet mutually supporting each other, replaced the continuous bastioned enceintes. Once again the main disadvantage was that they were extremely expensive to build and maintain, swallowing up gigantic state funds. In the second half of the nineteenth century, they suddenly became outdated due to tremendous advances in artillery techniques and new powerful explosives.

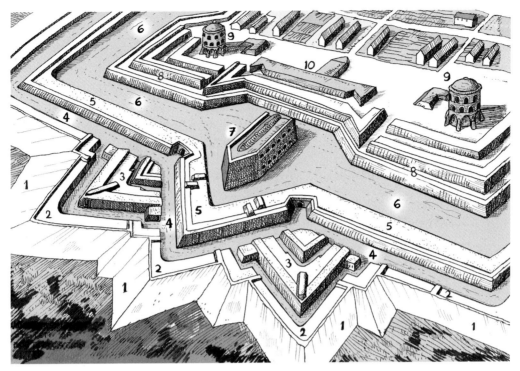

Polygonal front as advocated by Montalembert: 1: Glacis; 2: Covered way; 3: Advanced lunet; 4: Advanced ditch; 5: Envelop; 6: Main ditch; 7: Caponier; 8: Main wall; 9: Artillery tower; 10: Bombproof barrack.

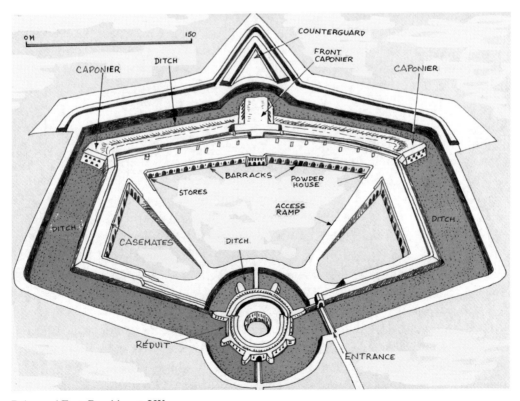

Polygonal Fort, Brockhurst, UK

Ferro-concrete fortification

By the late 1880s, all existing fortifications around capitals, cities, ports or other defended locations had become obsolete. As a response, polygonal forts could be adapted and reinforced. Facilities moved under the surface, with deep passages, underground galleries and tunnels connecting subterranean bombproof barracks and quarters, magazines and machine rooms, while observatories and weapons were emplaced in concrete casemates and armoured turrets.

However, in many cases new rings of modernized forts had to be built, which again considerably increased the gigantic cost of national defences.

The First World War

The First World War (1914–1918) was not fought around permanent ferro-concrete forts as expected, but surprisingly in non-permanent field fortifications and trenches. In 1914 the Germans had developed extremely powerful 42cm super-howitzers that crushed the modern Belgian concrete forts around Liege, bringing many war leaders (a bit too rapidly, as it turned out) to the conclusion that permanent fortifications were useless and unreliable. By the end of 1914, the whole front in Belgium and north-eastern France had unexpectedly paralyzed into a stalemate. From then until early 1918, the conflict evolved into a horrific war of attrition with a dramatic revival of field and semi-permanent trench fortifications spreading from the North Sea to the Swiss border. This trench warfare was punctuated by massive frontal infantry attacks preceded by intense artillery bombardments. These were rarely successful, only causing terrifyingly high casualties, as illustrated by appalling butchery at Verdun and on the Somme in 1916. Solutions to the deadlocked struggle included increased artillery fire and an improvement in infantry assault tactics, as well as the development of tracked assault vehicles (tanks) and supporting aviation. Because of those novelties, and also owing to the massive and decisive involvement of the forces of the United States, there was a return to mobile warfare between August and November 1918. Ultimately, the Allies achieved a decisive victory over the exhausted German forces.

Interwar, 1918–1939

After the First World War, the traditional art of fortification in the form of the classical fort had been completely and finally discredited by the continuously improved might of artillery and machine guns, and the nascent but very promising power of aircraft and armoured tracked vehicles. The era of large, enclosed, compact and expensive forts was definitively over.

They were replaced with relatively small and dispersed concrete pillboxes, shelters and bunkers featuring strong and thick walls and roofs. Well camouflaged, and often partly buried underground, concrete bunkers were designed and constructed to constitute lines of defence or clusters of resistance. In addition, anti-tank and anti-personnel passive obstacles (including explosive mines, barbed wire, ditches and concrete blocks) were

This concrete battery (bloc 4, featuring three embrasures for 75mm guns) was part of Fort Fermont near Longuyon in the Meurthe-&-Moselle department. Fort Fermont included seven advanced armed combat blocs connected by underground galleries (fitted with an internal electric railway) to subterranean garrison quarters, power plant, ammunition and supply stores, kitchen, infirmary and two entrance blocs placed at the rear.

installed in a kind of prepared battlefield. In the 1920s and particularly in the 1930s, with the threat of a new conflict growing, practically all nations constructed lines of scattered concrete bunkers and modernized their coastal fortifications. The French Maginot Line – intended to defend the frontier of France from German aggression – was without doubt the best example of this form of underground ferro-concrete combat defence. However, all nations convinced by the validity of the 'prepared battlefield' were fated to be disappointed when the Second World War broke out in September 1939.

The Second World War

The Second World War (1939–1945), the most widespread and deadliest war in history, was actually a series of conflicts characterized by numerous campaigns, enormous battles, various strategic, transoceanic, continental and intercontinental movements, rapid advances and huge mobile offensives entailing gigantic military means and involving millions of combatants.

Advances in modern warfare (motorization, tanks, airplanes, paratroopers) had made large-scale permanent military architecture obsolete in many situations. However, permanent fortified lines of defence were still constructed, the best example being the German Atlantic Wall, which was intended to repulse any Allied attack on the western façade of the European continent.

The depicted pillbox type FW3/28 was designed in 1940, when Britain feared a German invasion. It could house one QF 2-pdr anti-tank gun. Top: Front view. Bottom: Plan.

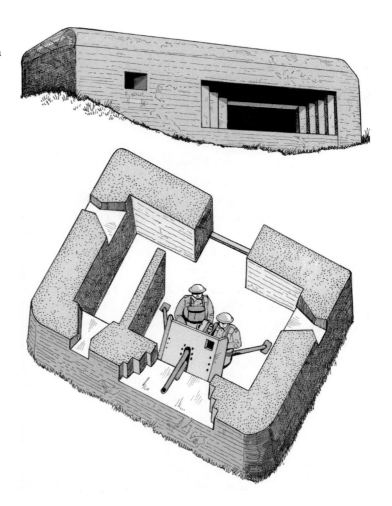

German coastal bunker (Atlantic Wall) near Calais, France.

Besides, in all theatres of the war, field and semi-permanent fortifications remained widely in use for defensive actions, as protection against attack from the air and as means of slowing down an enemy offensive while reserve forces were rushed to the spot under attack. Field fortifications, anti-tanks obstacles and wide minefields played an important role, particularly in open terrain.

Fortifications after 1945

After 1945, with the development of nuclear bombs and intercontinental ballistic missiles, most forts and permanent fortifications became obsolete and were discarded. However, being very expensive to demolish and dismantle, many were relegated to the role of storage spaces, as well as military, police or fire brigade training grounds. Some were just left to rot, while others were sold to private owners. Only a few nuclear-proof shelters, launching silos and secret command centres buried deep inside mountains were created and built for military use.

However, field fortifications and reinforced field fortifications kept – and still keep today – much of their value in conventional warfare, particularly in low-intensity conflicts

Joux Castle is located in an imposing mountainous landscape in the upper valley of the River Doubs near Pontarlier, France. It still displays an interesting summary of military architecture including the following:
1: Original early medieval castle.
2: Medieval enceinte.
3: Artillery tower (sixteenth century), enceinte and ditch.
4: Bastioned front with bastions and ditch (seventeenth century).
5: Polygonal fort with masonry casemates and compartmented earth artillery emplacements (late nineteenth century).

and guerrilla wars. Indeed, entrenchments, breastworks, walls of gabions, trenches, sandbags or even simple earth screens can still provide a good level of protection against small-calibre projectiles.

There is only one unchanging feature of fortification – at least when used in conventional warfare: what matters in the last analysis is less the quality of the work itself than the determination of the garrison inside.

Today, a considerable number of fortifications survive, and there has been renewed interest in military architecture throughout the world. Associations and societies have sprung up seemingly everywhere to safeguard remaining monuments, castles, forts and buildings, and to promote an ever-widening interest for those witnesses of the past. Many vestiges that have endured centuries of warfare and the slow but damaging effect of weather are now popular and impressive tourist destinations and prominent local landmarks – priceless historical testimonies of times gone by.

Located in southern Bavaria (Germany), Neuschwanstein was constructed in the nineteenth century by King Ludwig II of Bavaria. The castle, although featuring architectural elements of the Middle Ages, is less a medieval fortress than an idealized expression and an idyllic symbol of nineteenth-century neo-Romanticism.

Part Two

Siege Warfare

Siege Warfare Before the Introduction of Firearms

Generality

Developed in Ancient times by most ancient civilizations (notably by the Assyrians, the Greeks and the Romans), the art of conducting sieges was widely used throughout history, as victory in wars frequently depended on the seizure of strongholds, castles, fortresses and fortified towns.

To achieve the capitulation of a fortified place, the besiegers had several means available.

First of all, a conflict did not always entail risking the lives of combatants, and a siege could be forestalled by diplomacy and compromise. Furthermore, through intimidation, bravado, blackmail or the capture of hostages, as well as menace, ruse, deception, corruption, treachery, surprise or forgery, a siege operation could be quickly and victoriously concluded. When these means failed, the besiegers were obliged to take the place *manu militari* (by force of arms).

For the attacking party, a siege was a large-scale undertaking demanding time, plenty of troops, skilled engineers and many workers, ammunition, machines, tools, accommodation, enormous supplies, comprehensive logistics and considerable organization. For the besieged, it was the start of a period of suffering, fear and great uncertainty. For both sides, determination and good preparation were thus of crucial importance. The outcome of a siege depended to a great extent on many factors such as physical courage, individual bravery, inspired leadership, logistical preparation and stores of supplies, as well as good morale, determination and pugnacity on both sides.

The actual methods by which a castle, town or stronghold could be besieged and eventually taken (or repulsed) did not show any major changes throughout Antiquity and the Middle Ages. The most notable differences were seen in the amplitude of means and number of men involved, the quantity of weapons deployed and advances in the field of ballistics with the appearance of new siege machines.

Ultimately, it was the development of gunpowder and the gradual introduction of firing weapons in the late Middle Age and during the Renaissance that made radically new methods of siege warfare necessary.

Basically, there were two main ways by which a stronghold, castle or town might be taken.

The first method was attrition. This encompassed blockading the defenders and waiting until they were worn out and exhausted by starvation, isolation, sickness and epidemics, internal quarrels and discouragement.

The second approach was assaulting the defences by sheer force, a method that was divided into several phases.

Throwing machines

The attackers started putting pressure on the besieged by blockading them and sealing off all access to the outside world. Archers and later crossbowmen were then deployed behind wooden protective screens to shoot their arrows and bolts, while hurling siege machines bombarded the defenders with devastating effect. Many throwing machines were designed and used for hurling various kinds of projectiles (such as large arrows, rocks and stones) before the introduction of firearms. The catapult was an ancient nevrobalistic or torsion weapon. Its propelling power was provided by the elasticity of twisted sinews and ropes. It was composed of a solid timber framework holding a pivoted arm tightly strained on a rotating roller fitted with twisted ropes. The trebuchet, probably introduced during the Crusades, was another hurling machine using the energy of a counterweight.

Used by the ancient Romans the *cheiroballista* was a large crossbow shooting bolts (large arrows).

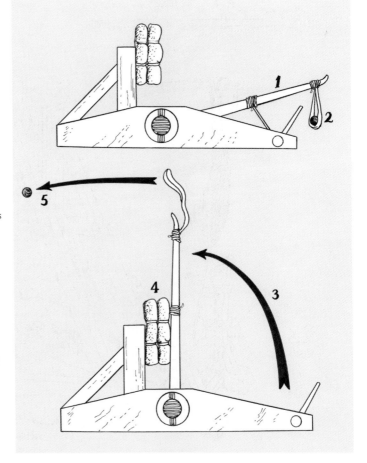

The pivoted arm catapult (1) was winched down. The missile, usually a heavy piece of rock (2), was then loaded in a kind of spoon or sling. A system allowed the unlocking of the mobile arm, which, owing to the strong tension of the twisted rope, was released upwards with great strength (3). The rotating movement of the arm was violently stopped by a transversal beam fitted with a strong padded cushion (4), resulting in the projectile being propelled in a high curving trajectory (5).

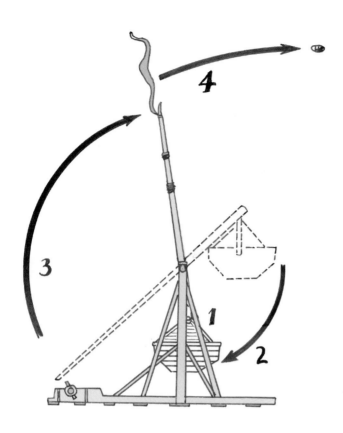

The propelling energy of the trebuchet was provided by a solid, heavy weight (1) that was fixed to the short arm of a huge pivoted beam resting on a strongly built framework. The missile was loaded in a sling, placed on the end of the long arm, which was winched down to the ground (2) and then released. Under the weight of the counterpoise, the arm went up (3) with great strength, the sling opened by centrifugal force and the missile was then swung away with a high parabolic trajectory (4).

Escalading

The besiegers could also attack the top of the wall by utilizing several methods, including by climbing and assaulting the top of the wall by throwing grappling hooks attached to a rope or by using large scaling ladders. This was naturally extremely dangerous, and often the attackers would use protected assault devices such as the sambuca (a mechanically raised assault ladder above a roofed structure fitted with wheels) or build a belfry (a rolling assault tower high enough to overtop the attacked wall). A belfry was made of timber and fitted with wheels, and moved by means of capstans, pulleys and ropes manoeuvred and winched by a party of men or drawn by oxen.

Helepolis.

Belfry.

Belfry (cross-section).

Ramming and mining

The attackers could also make a breach by destroying a part of the defences. In the case of a simple palisade, the attackers would try to dislodge the wooden beams or set them on fire. In the case of a strong masonry wall, they would attempt to collapse the wall by ramming (using a battering ram), mining (digging an excavation under the wall's foundations) or by sapping and boring (picking off, tearing out and dislodging the stones at the base of the wall).

Battering ram.

Battering ram. The device is shown here placed inside a protective 'cat' (rolling shed).

Mine.

Defenders reactions

Assaulting a stronghold using a ladder, belfry, ramming, undermining or sapping were time-consuming, very complicated, dangerous and difficult, even impossible, particularly when the target was surrounded by a moat – a broad ditch filled with water – or built on a hard and rocky crag. Those attacks were very dangerous operations because the defenders did not meanwhile remain idle. They could launch a sudden and devastating raid (known as a sally or sortie) against the enemy. Sorties, raids and counter-attacks were important for the morale of the besieged, while tactically a successful sortie might turn the tide of a siege.

The defenders dropped stones and rocks, threw incendiary materials, projected spears and javelins, and shot down arrows on the exposed attackers.

The latter responded by using strong movable timber protective galleries or mobile sheds fitted with wheels and covered with solid roofs. These wooden rolling sheds – just like the timber belfry and all other siege machines – were vulnerable to fire, and thus were often revetted with fresh rawhides, grass or wet turf in order to resist incendiary projectiles.

The last phase of the siege was the assault, either on top of or in the ruins of the breached wall. This was a confused and bloody hand-to-hand battle, a crucial confrontation for both parties and often the turning point of the siege.

Siege Warfare with Firearms

Powder and Cannons

At the end of the Middle Age, early guns and portable firearms progressively played a more important role in conflict, particularly in siege warfare. Although primitive and unreliable, the new fire weapons were far more effective and less cumbersome than ancient and medieval hurling machines. Gradually, siege warfare was dominated by the deadly clash of artillery, unless a small and stealthy party could infiltrate inside the target and open the gates to the rest of their comrades. Indeed, everything previously said about surprise, menace, pressure, treason, blockade and attrition was still applicable.

It was in the actual breach-making and storming of a castle or citadel that firearms brought radical changes.

Underground mines (now filled with explosives) were used by attackers to smash walls, and destroy gates and towers, while heavy cannons (grouped in siege batteries) could make a breach by delivering an uninterrupted series of hammer blows until the masonry collapsed.

Gates and doors could still be smashed by a ramming party, but gunpowder allowed for extensive and swift destructive possibilities in the form of new explosive devices (known as petards) that could destroy wooden doors and even sections of stone walls.

Mons Meg is a large medieval siege bombard, built in 1449 and exhibited today at Edinburgh Castle in Scotland. It has a length of 15 feet (4.6m), a calibre (barrel diameter) of 20in (510mm) and weighs 15,366lb (6,970kg).

Renaissance gun.

Early handgunman.

Siege fortifications

Of course, the besieged also used firearms. In the actual storming of a place, the advantages of firearms lay with the defenders, as the discharge of guns and arquebuses made uncovered approaches very dangerous. The assailing party reacted by developing types of siege fortification mostly made of earth, and accordingly resorted to digging – usually at night. Henceforth, shovels, pickaxes, spades and wheelbarrows became weapons of war too.

Attacking methods consisted of bringing artillery as close as possible to the defensive walls by digging approaches – a network of trenches in zigzagging patterns in order to avoid enfilading fire. Trenches and saps were dug to connect gun batteries, temporary fortlets, sconces and redoubts. These field fortifications made of piled earth and palisades were built to serve as command posts, supply-magazines and places where assaulting parties could regroup and the wounded be gathered.

The first phase of the siege was an artillery duel. The besiegers bombarded the defenders with mortars, while cannons tried to make a breach in the walls. The defenders replied with counter-fire, aiming to hinder as much as possible workers digging approaching trenches and to destroy breach batteries. As always, the defenders could launch a surprise counter-attack (or sortie) to disorganize the attack and drive back the besiegers.

Siege gun emplacement.
1: Timber platform; 2: Fascine; 3: Gabion; 4: Stormpole.

Assault

When the breach was made (either by bombarding the walls or exploding subterranean mines under the enemy fortifications), assault parties stormed in a rush and fought in a bitter hand-to-hand combat in the smoking ruins. As previously mentioned, the final assault was a crucial and bitter battle for both parties, and was usually the turning point of the siege. A repulsed assault often cost many casualties, and could cause the collapse of the attacking party. On the other hand, a successful assault could result in pillage, rape, destruction, fire and the massacre of the defenders. To avoid this terrible predicament, the defenders often chose to negotiate an honourable capitulation before the situation reached that point.

Vauban's Methods

In the seventeenth and eighteenth centuries, warfare was characterized by dynastic conflicts and a predominance of sieges, in which fortification and artillery played a central role. Strategy was dominated by carefulness, with most risks being calculated in advance. Eighteenth-century royal rulers and their strategists frequently preferred controllable and codified siege warfare rather than the hazardous chances of a bloody and uncertain battle on the open field. Consequently, besieging a fortified place became a complicated military science, elaborated and carried out by expert and specially trained engineering officers who developed a particular technical terminology.

In the seventeenth century, the French engineer Sébastien Le Prestre de Vauban (1633–1707) designed a systematic method of laying siege, using existing elements of field fortifications or approaches (parallels, saps and batteries). Parallels were trenches excavated by the besiegers alongside the attacked front, enabling them to get closer and closer to their objective in comparative safety.

The parallels were also used for general communication, as emplacements for guns batteries, as regrouping places for assault parties and as a starting point for underground mining.

When the breach was made, the next step was the decisive hand-to-hand assault, unless negotiations were opened beforehand.

Obviously not all sieges progressed with the clockwork precision and strict geometry as described by Vauban, each besieged place presenting its own natural particularities. Nevertheless, Vauban's method of laying siege constituted undeniable progress. The business of conducting sieges became as formal and preordained as a game of chess. This considerably reduced the attackers' casualties and frequently (at least in the eighteenth century) led to negotiations followed by the capitulation of the defenders after an honourable resistance.

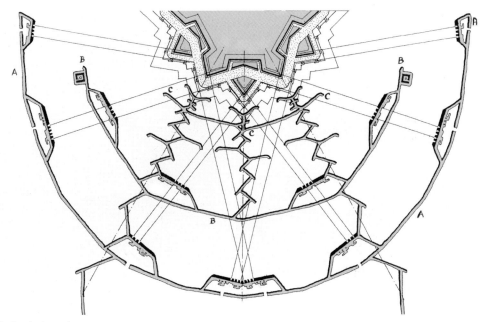

Vauban's siege theory.
AA: first parallel with gun batteries.
BB: second parallel with redoubts.
CC: third parallel with *cavaliers de tranchée*.

Sieges in modern times

The method of laying siege designed by Vauban remained in use (with a few changed details and improvements) for many years. It was still employed throughout the eighteenth century, and during the Napoleonic Wars (1802–1815).

The nineteenth and twentieth centuries also saw a number of important sieges, such as Sevastopol during the Crimean War (1853–1856), Vicksburg and Port Hudson during the American Civil War (1861–1865) and Port Arthur during the Russo-Japanese War (1904–1905).

Trench warfare that developed during the First World War was in essence a huge attritional siege with opposing static entrenched belligerents.

Although the Second World War was characterized by large-scale movement and offensive battles, there were several notable sieges, for example of Malta, Leningrad, Stalingrad, Tobruk and Bastogne.

Sieges in the late nineteenth century and throughout the twentieth century included the common phases of the past: blockade, attrition, bombardment and assault. However, what had changed were the distances involved, the scale, firepower and amplitude of combat, the magnitude of destruction and number of casualties, notably civilians caught up in a destructive vortex. Since the Industrial Revolution, casualties and the scale of destruction have intensified enormously due to the development and lethality of new weapons – notably extremely powerful explosives, armoured vehicles, machine guns, long-range artillery, strategic bombardment aviation and nuclear bombs and missiles.

Siege of Berg-op-Zoom in the Netherlands, from 12 July to 16 September 1747. The map shows the French siege works (parallels and saps) for attacking the Dutch defences.

Part Three

Dictionary

Military architecture has developed a peculiar jargon and a large number of specialized terms in order to express and designate the many aspects and intricate techniques involved. The following dictionary is intended to give an explanation in both words and illustrations to this technical language.

Note: q.v. is the abbreviation of Latin *quod vide* – literally meaning 'which see'. It serves to indicate that more facts on a term are available elsewhere, thereby directing the reader to other entries for further related information.

A

Abatis: A defensive obstacle consisting of rows of felled trees lying lengthwise and parallel to each other, with boughs and sharpened branches pointing outwards in the direction of the attackers' approach. When more time was available, the branches were cut and set in the ground (possibly in combination with a ditch), with their trimmed and sharpened branches facing the enemy. Acacia trees, for example, with their long and sharp barbs, provided a dangerous obstacle. Indeed, practically any thorny and spiky vegetation was appropriate, proving almost as effective as barbed wire. Abatis had already been used by the Ancient Romans, when they were known under the designation *cervi* or *cippe* (q.v.).

Abri d'intervalle: In the Maginot Line (q.v.), a stand-alone shelter providing accommodation for units whose task it was to help defend the intervals between the permanent combat works.

Abutment: An additional structure built to support the lateral pressure of an arch or span. See Buttress.

Acropolis: In Ancient Greece, the acropolis ('upper city') was a citadel (q.v.) often placed on a commanding eminence and reinforced with high walls for defensive purpose. The acropolis served as a refuge and stronghold, and contained military and food supplies. It was also a sacred place containing the temples and shrines of the gods, and an administrative centre with a royal or municipal palace. Nearly every Greek city-state had an acropolis, but the best known are those of Athens and Corinth. See Arx, Alcazar, Castle, Keep and Rocca.

Admiralty scaffolding: Also known as beach scaffolding or obstacle Z.1, these were anti-tank and anti-landing ship barriers constructed by the British in the summer of 1940 when under threat of a German invasion. Essentially, obstacle Z.1 was a fence of scaffolding tubes 9ft (2.7m) high, placed at low water so that tanks could not get a good run at the beach. Admiralty scaffolding was deployed along miles of vulnerable beaches in southern England.

Advanced armour: In nineteenth-century fortification, an outer ring of armour made of cast iron to provide additional protection for a gun turret. See Armoured turret.

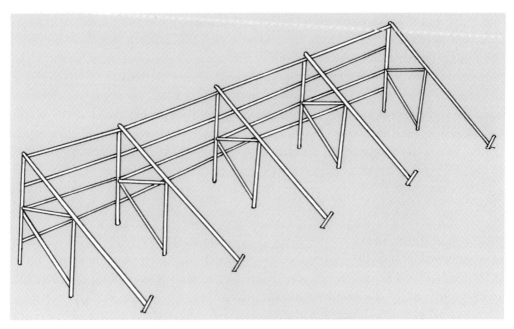

Admiralty scaffolding.

Advanced ditch: A defensive excavation at the base and ahead of a glacis (q.v.) opposite the covered way, adding another obstacle to an attacking enemy party. See Ditch.

Advanced glacis: See Glacis.

Advanced post: A small work constructed forward of the main line intended to warn of or delay a surprise attack.

Advanced works: Projecting combat positions which occupied a portion of terrain ahead of a main defence line. They were designed to force the besiegers to begin a siege from a greater distance and to cover parts of the ground not easily seen from the main wall. In bastioned fortification (q.v.), a clear distinction existed between outworks (q.v.), placed in the main ditch inside the perimeter of the covered way, and advanced works, which were placed ahead of the main ditch outside the main centre of resistance. Advanced works formed external fortified positions which were in direct defensive connection with the main enceinte (q.v.), outworks and counterscarp (q.v.). For this reason, their gorges (rear) were always open. They significantly augmented the defensive perimeter and therefore obliged the besiegers to increase the development of approaches and thus the number of workers and troops. They also safely set the combat zone further ahead of the main enceinte. A siege was actually a succession of battles and combats, beginning in the detached works (q.v.), then in advanced works, continuing in the covered way and the places of arms, then in the outworks and finally the main enceinte. Advanced works could be temporary, being hastily pushed out just before or during a siege. But some were permanent, built at the same time as the fortress and constantly maintained. Others were semi-permanent, which meant that they were overhauled, reoccupied and rearmed only in periods of war when the threat of a siege was likely.

Regarding efficiency of advanced works, the greatest theorists of fortifications had controversial opinions. Some were favourable to their use, arguing that they compelled the attacker to begin his siege operations at a distance. Outworks and advanced works, supported by other works behind and alongside them, multiplied the obstacles in the attacker's way so that the difficulties in gaining ground never ceased. Repeated complexes of fortification of this type often extended 300 yards ahead of the central enceinte and constituted powerful obstacles to a siege. Hornworks (q.v.) and crownworks (q.v.) involved the occupation of a piece of ground which might otherwise prove useful to the enemy; they could cover the entrance to a town or could be used to fortify a new suburb. They could also form a bridgehead when a town was established on two banks of a river. Nevertheless, other experts were radically opposed to their employ, objecting that they were useless, being much too expensive to build and to maintain, and that they dangerously scattered the defender's forces. Hornworks were strongly criticized because of the limited number of guns their half-bastions could contain and because of the long vulnerable wings where guns and crews were dangerously exposed to enfilading fire (q.v.). Critics observed that the purpose of hornworks and crownworks was more to terrify or deter the enemy rather than actually strengthen the defence. Advanced works were also unpopular, because defenders posted there could feel left alone or sent to sacrifice their lives, so they were often tempted not to fight tooth and nail, soon retreating after a few rounds had been shot at them. Furthermore, once conquered, advanced works provided the besiegers with captured guns, space and material to carry on the siege. As for the other advanced works, *flèches*, redans, lunettes and *tenailles* (q.v.), most theorists and military engineers agreed that they had little resisting power as they had insufficient room to mount many guns, that enemy batteries of superior strength

In the seventeenth and eighteenth centuries, the age of formalism, advanced works were codified. The most commonly used were: the crownwork (1); the hornwork (2); the double hornwork (3); the hornwork reinforced with a *tenaille* (4); the *flèche* or arrow (5); the redan (6); and the detached lunette (7). Other less-common advanced works included various forms of single *tenaille* (8); the double *tenaille* (9); the swallow's tail (10); and the bishop's mitre (11).

could easily defeat them, and that they could be outflanked and attacked in reverse. They could thus at best confuse the enemy and play only a delaying role in the first phase of a siege. See *Fort d'arrêt*.

Adobe: Adobe (or cob or mudbrick) is a natural building material made from sand, clay or silt, mixed with water, and some kind of fibrous or organic material (sticks, straw, dung). Shaped into bricks using frames and dried in the sun, adobe structures are extremely durable. The material was used in the Late Bronze Age and Iron Age, from the eighth century BC on, for the construction of houses and fortifications in the Middle East, North Africa, South America, south-western North America and southern Europe.

Adulterine castle: In the Middle Age, a castle (q.v.) or a fortified house built by a vassal (subordinate land holder) without the permission of his suzerain (feudal overlord), without the so-called licence to crenellate (q.v.). Building an illegitimate/adulterine castle was often regarded as an act of open rebellion.

Agger: This Latin term (meaning 'heap') designated two things:

1) A fortified urban enclosure (e.g. Agger Servi, aka the Servian Wall, built around Rome between 378 and 350 BC).
2) An attack platform, a terrace or an embankment erected by a Roman besieging force.

Usually constructed by piling up rubble, stone, rocks, brushwood and earth, and often buttressed by a timber framework, the construction of the *agger* demanded a large labour force and a lot of time. The embankment had two main purposes: a) securing easy access to the fortress for the assaulting party; and b) making a smooth path for bringing siege machines (e.g. battering rams and ballistae) to the upper part of the wall, where it was thinner and weaker than at the base. A spectacular example of siege *agger* would be the dirt ramp (265ft long and 100ft high) built by the Romans at the siege of Masada in the Judean Desert in 73 BC during the First Jewish–Roman War.

Air-raid shelter: Long-range bomber aircraft appeared in the 1930s, after which the protection of both civilians and vital workers producing the weapons of war became a necessity. Air raid shelters, also known as bomb shelters, are structures for the protection of the civil population as well as military personnel against enemy attacks (bombing) from the air. During the Second World War (1939–45), some air-raid shelters had a makeshift character, including cellars, underground metro stations, quarries, tunnels etc. Others were purpose-built shelters, similar to bunkers in many regards as they were made of concrete – some even with a capacity of several thousand people. Some were underground, while others were huge monolithic structures towering ten storeys high and topped with anti-aircraft gun emplacements and radar installations. See Anderson shelter, *Flakturm*, *Hochbunker*, *Luftschutzraum*, Morrison shelter, Stanton shelter.

Alcazar: An alcazar (sometimes called a zuda) is a Moorish fortified palace often functioning as a citadel (q.v.). The term derives from the Arabic word *al qasr*, meaning palace or fortress. Many cities in Spain have an alcazar (Segovia, Madrid, Toledo,

Seville). In Portugal this was called *alcacer*, as in the city of Alcacer do Sal. The palace, headed by an alcaide (governor), was often adapted by Christians after the Reconquista. See Ksar.

Alexandria front: A form of Napoleonic bastioned fortification designed in the 1800s by the French General François de Chasseloup-Laubat (1754–1833) at Alessandria near Milan, Italy.

Alcazar at Segovia, Spain.

Allan Williams Turret: A Second World War British, small prefabricated metal turret placed on top of a concrete or brick-lined cylindrical pit 1.2m (4ft) in diameter sunk into the ground. The armoured turret, which rose only 13in from the ground surface, was mounted on a ball race that enabled a complete 360 degrees traverse. It was manned by a single soldier armed with a rifle, a light Bren machine gun or a Boys anti-tank rifle. The weapon could be fired either through a front slot (which was further protected by a shutter) or through a circular top hatch for anti-aircraft fire. This opening was also the

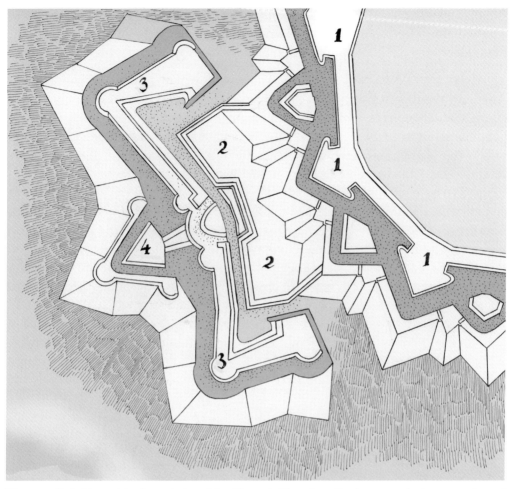

The so-called Alexandria front designed by General Chasseloup-Laubat comprised a succession of defensive lines, including a classical bastioned front (1) protected by a large hornwork (2) with short wings, an advanced envelope (3), an advanced ravelin (4) and a glacis.

only way in and out for the occupant, who had to be someone who did not suffer from claustrophobia. The turret proved rather ineffective. The pit was prone to flooding, the view was limited and it was difficult to rotate the cupola while tracking targets, firing and reloading at the same time. With all its disadvantages, the British Army did not like this design, so most were placed at RAF airfields. It is estimated that about 200 (perhaps 300?) of these turreted pits were installed around airfields in Britain in 1940. After the war, the steel turrets were reclaimed for their metal, so extant examples are extremely rare. The turret was designed by A.H. Williams in conjunction with Colonel V.T.R. Ford and Lieutenant Williamson, and built by Rustproof Metal Windows Company in Saltney, Chester, where the turrets were produced. See FW3.

Allure or **alure:** A gallery or a passage along the parapet of a medieval castle. Often a synonym of wall-walk (q.v.).

Alternating staircase: A staircase used for communication between different floors of a tower or keep (q.v.). The staircase reversed its turn from right-to-left to left-to-right from floor to floor. This design was used to break the flow of the enemy's advance once they had gained entry to the keep. See Stair.

American West forts: Forts in the United States during the conquest of the West, and during the Indian Wars, greatly varied in function, type and size. Originally they were lightly fortified military posts intended to maintain peace among the tribes, as well as between Native Americans and white emigrants. Others were small trading posts or enclosures built by commercial companies. Conflict started when white settlers encroached more and more upon native lands, and as westward expansion continued, and when the US government failed to protect tribal territorial rights and uphold treaties, wars between the white invaders and Native Americans intensified. In response, the US government began a series of frontier campaigns to 'tame' the Indians, force them on to reservations and convert them to a 'civilized' life. Frontier forts both for infantry and cavalry were established, but were regarded more as police and law-keeping posts than pure military positions. They were made from materials available in the area. In forested areas, wood was used, and the typical frontier fort was generally composed of a rectangular perimeter enclosed with a palisade (q.v.), with blockhouses (q.v.) at the corners. Other materials were used, such as adobe (q.v.), and stone wherever available. Inside the perimeter there were officers' quarters, barracks, stables, storehouses and

American West fort.

headquarters buildings, grouped around a central parade ground. Some forts, particularly in the Great Plains, did not have walls surrounding them at all because attacks were generally unlikely. Known as open forts, their security depended on offensive tactics such as patrolling and scouting the surrounding country.

Ammunition store: For obvious security reasons, ammunitions stores were restricted areas always placed at a safe distance from living quarters and active armed emplacements. In the fortifications of the twentieth century, complexes of concrete bunkers including roads, tracks or paths were set up to enable communication. A concrete platform was often built in front of the ammunition store so that supply trucks could park. However, scattering units presented disavantages; indeed, if the ground was churned up, if roads and tracks were destroyed or impracticable, in case of bombardment for example, the guns in the active casemates could no longer be supplied. In design, ammunition stores were generally simple; they were not equipped with gaslock, sophisticated ventilation systems or caponier (q.v.), but they were always guarded. In some case they could be used to shelter equipment, materiel or supplies – even wounded soldiers in an emergency situation. Very often, the internal layout of an ammunition bunker was designed in order that the doors leading to the stores were placed laterally inside the corridor; in other words, the entrances to the ammunition stores opened into a gallery that led to the main exit/entrances on either side, so if the main entrance was directly shot at, the projectiles could not reach the ammunition.

Small-calibre ammunition was packed in boxes and cases, whereas heavy shells were stored on shelves and transported by means of rails placed in the ceilings. Ammunition was also stored in non-standardized concrete bunkers or masonry stores deeply concealed under the ground. See Arsenal, Citadel and Powderhouse.

Anderson shelter: A British air-raid shelter made of galvanized corrugated steel sheet, named after Home Secretary Sir John Anderson, who was responsible for civil defence in 1938. Issued by the authorities in December 1938, the shelter was 6ft high, 4ft 6in wide and 6ft 6in long, and could accomodate between four and six people. To complete construction, it was intended that 15in of soil be distributed over the roof of the shelter. More than 2 million of the shelters were put up during the Second World War. Although flimsy, miserable to use, damp, cold and unpleasant because their thin walls made the occupants all too exposed to the noise of bombardment, Anderson shelters proved surprisingly effective during the Blitz – the sustained strategic bombing of Britain by Nazi Germany between September 1940 and May 1941.

Anti-aircraft gun emplacement: Given the vertical nature of anti-aircraft fire, guns could not be placed in roofed casemates (q.v.) but were instead installed in open platforms called gun pits (q.v.). The gun had to have a free and unobstructed field of fire, without tall buildings and high vegetation around it. As a rule, anti-aircraft gun positions were always dug deep in the ground, kept as small as possible, camouflaged and built flush with the ground in order to present a low profile, both for concealment and to offer less of a target. See Gun pit and *Bettung*.

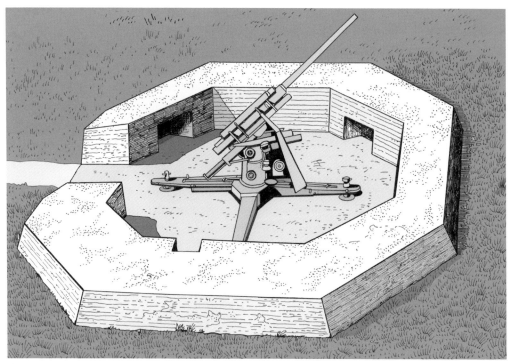

German *Bettung* with 88cm AA gun.

Anti-personnel mine: A form of explosive device designed for use against unprotected infantrymen. Like booby traps (q.v.), anti-personnel mines were/are always concealed. They explode when knocked, stepped on or disengaged by a wire. In addition to the obvious ability of mines (and booby traps) to kill or injure, their presence has other important effects. These include the ability to demoralize soldiers, as mines and booby traps kill or maim comrades; to increase the need for logistical (mostly medical) support; to keep soldiers continually stressed, suspicious and unable to relax because it is difficult for them to know which areas, buildings or objects are safe; to make soldiers cautious instead of aggressive and confident; to create no-go areas (real or imaginary) after a mine or booby trap has killed or wounded someone; and to create confusion and disorientation. Anti-personnel mines and booby traps are indiscriminate weapons. They do not differentiate between friend and foe, and they can harm civilians and other non-combatants (during and after a conflict) who are unaware of their presence. Therefore, it is important to keep an accurate record of their location so they do not harm friendly troops and can be cleared when the conflict is over.

Anti-personnel obstacles: A wide variety of such obstacles could be constructed. See Abatis, Barbed wire, Booby trap, Caltrop, *Cervi*, *Cippe*, Ditch, Fakir's bed, Fraise, Flooding, Monk and Wolf's pit.

Anti-tank ditch: An excavation intended to oppose tank progression. The profile of the excavation, its width (about 4.5m) and depth (about 3m) varied, but were always calculated so as to be impracticable to any armoured vehicle. The anti-tank ditch was either a simple V-shaped excavation dug into the ground or a permanent and costly installation made of concrete. An anti-tank ditch could also be filled with water. Rivers, canals and other waterways were often used as anti-tank ditches. In hilly terrain, a continuous tank barrier could be created by cutting into the slope, making an almost vertical wall which could not be negotiated by armoured vehicles. The cratering of roads or tracks was also an effective route-denial measure; sited around a bend, camouflaged, sown with anti-tank and anti-personnel mines and covered by automatic and anti-tank fire, a crater (either dug by hand or created by high explosive) meant the enemy having to deploy dismounted infantry and engineers to clear the obstacle before the route was made safe for the resumption of progression.

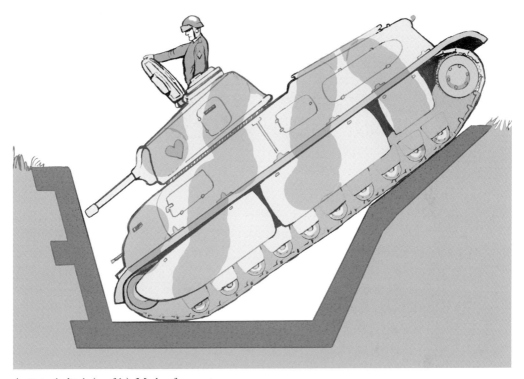

Anti-tank ditch (profile). Made of concrete.

Anti-tank hedgehog: Concrete mobile anti-tank obstacle originating from the Czech arsenal. The hedgehog comprised three steel bars or rails bolted together. The device was generally 1.4–1.8m high and weighed about 300kg. Like an overscaled caltrop (q.v.), it was an efficient obstacle as it always kept its function even when tipped over.

Anti-tank mine: High-explosive device placed slightly underground and camouflaged, which exploded violently when a vehicle drove over it. Some were detonated by a wire or when the magnetic field varied when the large metallic mass of a tank entered its vicinity. They damaged the tank's most vulnerable parts: the undercarriage and caterpillar tracks. See Mine.

Anti-tank obstacle: Anything designed and used to hinder the progress of armoured fighting vehicles. Natural obstacles were/are used, including ditches, moats, steep-banked rivers, canals, dense woodlands, ridges and railway enbankments. A whole range of man-made permanent anti-tank obstacles were also designed. Permanent anti-tank obstacles and flooding (q.v.) had a major disadvantage, as they gave away the location of the forward edge of the main defensive front. See Anti-tank ditch, Anti-tank hedgehog, Anti-tank mine, Anti-tank rail, Anti-tank wall and Belgian gate.

Anti-tank obstacles (Second World War, British).
1: Cylinders made from a section of sewer pipe 3–4 ft (91–120cm) in diameter filled with concrete, typically to a height of 4–5ft (1.2–1.5m), frequently with a dome at the top.
2: Hairspin, a section of rail welded at around a 60° angle.
3: Hedgehog, vertical lengths of rail placed in sockets in the road.

Anti-tank rail: Defences used in the French Maginot Line (q.v.). These effective anti-armour obstacles were formed of rails or steel girders firmly set in a concrete base. The rails were pointed, and intended to break or at least damage the tracks of a tank should it try to cross. Installed in rows of growing height, rails constituted a strong obstacle. A German version of this obstacle was called the *Eisenbahnschienen*. A variant was composed of prefabricated concrete beams called concrete poles (in German, *Betonpfähle*).

Anti-tank wall: A heavy permanent linear obstacle often made of reinforced concrete. The anti-tank wall was a good obstacle tactically as it required violent means to breach or destroy it. However, it was very costly to build and gave away the location of the forward edge of the main defensive front. It could also easily be bypassed.

Approach: Approches or *attaques* were a network of screening earthworks dug and established by a besieging force in order to create cover near the defence works. See Siege work, Battery, Circumvallation, Countervallation, Parallel, Sap, Trench and Part 2 (Siege Warfare).

Apron: The apron (also called batter, plinth or talus) was a thick, compact and sloping mass of large stones added to the lower part of curtain walls and towers. It could have different forms: triangular, angular, almond-shaped or similar to a bridge-fender, the prow of a ship or a bird's snout. The apron increased the stability of the construction and rendered sapping, mining and ramming more difficult. Another advantage was that when the defenders dropped stones upon attackers from the machicoulis (q.v.), they could splinter and ricochet on the apron with a shrapnel effect, causing further injuries to the enemy. The apron also inhibited the use of scaling ladders, which could not be placed upon the angled slope; if placed on the nearest level ground, they would either be too short or would be resting at such an oblique angle that they would inevitably be weakened to the point of collapse if several attackers tried to ascend at the same time. See Talus and Plinth.

Marten's tower, Chepstow Castle, Wales.

Arc of fire: The area of ground covered by an individual weapon, usually expressed by scope or number of degrees of field of fire a projectile weapon has when firing through an aperture from the wall of a fortification, such as an arrow slit, gun port, crenel or embrasure.

Armour: Protective covering used to prevent damage from being inflicted to an individual, vehicle or structure through use of direct contact weapons or projectiles, usually during combat. Using a great variety of materials (e.g. hides, linen, leather, mail and full metal plates of bronze, iron or steel), armour has been used to protect soldiers, war animals such as horses (the application of the latter being called barding) and war machines such as warships, armoured fighting vehicles and fortifications. Advances in metallurgy in the second half of the nineteenth century allowed the use of armour in innovative ways in new fortification design. In 1875, laminated armour using rolled iron was first used in casemates to provide protection against field guns. Rolled iron gave way to cast iron providing protection against siege guns. However, cast iron was not altogether suitable for protection against high-explosive shells, and its use was discontinued in the 1880s. Beginning in 1885, steel replaced cast iron for the construction of armoured turrets (q.v.), eclipsing turrets, armoured cupolas and casemates (q.v.), armoured doors etc.

Armoured casemate: Gun chamber protected by metal plates. See Casemate.

Armoured cupola: Small turret for observation and occasionally a light machine gun. See Cloche.

Armoured door: Doors of bunkers and other shelters were very often armoured in the twentieth century. The usual design was a trapdoor to minimize the size and expense. If the door was on the surface and exposed to the blast wave, its edge was normally counter-sunk in the frame so that the blast wave or a reflection could not lift the edge. Bunkers generally had two doors, with a main entrance and an emergency exit.

Armoured fort: The tremendous improvement of artillery in the late 1880s resulted in the burying of everything possible and reinforced concrete replacing masonry. Fortification thus entered into the age of concrete and metal armour. Forts built between 1885 and 1914, and obsolete masonry polygonal forts (q.v.) that were modernized, had their ditch defended by a coffer (q.v.), replacing the vulnerable caponier (q.v.), and their glacis covered by a thick and impassible network of barbed wire (q.v.). Infantry parapets and traverses and open artillery emplacements were all removed. Armament was placed in concrete casemates and armoured steel turrets (some being retractable or 'disappearing') to deliver the fire necessary to deal with an enemy at a distance and flank the immediate vicinity of the work from assault. Ammunition magazines, stores, workshops, headquarters, telephone exchanges, infirmaries, machinery to move the turrets, barracks and accomodation for the garrison were protected with concrete, buried under the ground and connected by passages, tunnels, posterns and galleries. Indeed, all was subterranean, illuminated by electricity produced by internal combustion engines, which also powered all the machinery necessary for living in and operating the fort – notably the ventilation system and the hoists supplying guns with rounds. Fortress troops literally became troglodytes. After 1885, military architecture had entered a new era. Needless to say, it was a very costly era, as such sophisticated forts with all their refinements cost a fortune to build and maintain. See Disappearing gun, *Casemate de Bourges*, Armoured turret and Eclipsing turret.

Armoured turret: Observation or armed emplacement protected by armour. An obvious solution to the problem of protecting a gun from overhead fire is to house it under an armoured cupola or in a turret (much as in a modern warship). By the end of the nineteenth century, a number of such products were designed. The German Schumman-Gruson chilled iron cupola was demonstrated in 1885 and patented in 1886. It was immediately adopted by Austria-Hungary, Belgium, Germany, Italy and the Netherlands. Turret and cupola systems were produced by the French company Schneider and the Czech firm Skoda. Occasionally, an armoured gun turret (q.v.) used in static permanent fortification was a discarded warship or tank turret with the original guns. The main disadvantage of this kind of equipment was the high cost involved in purchasing and maintaining. Revolving armoured turrets could be jammed by a direct hit from heavy siege artillery, thereby leaving the fort defenceless. Nevertheless, armoured turret and cupola systems were adopted in almost all modern forts around the world. The various systems were largely found wanting when the test of war came in 1914.

A further refinement was the retractable or disappearing turret. See Eclipsing turret.

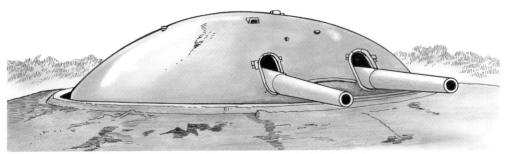

Armoured turret with twin 105mm gun at Fort Spijkerboor, the Netherlands.

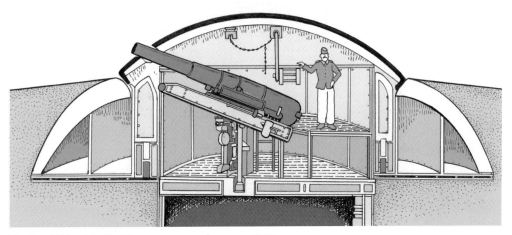

Profile of Schneider/Le Creusot armoured turret *c.* 1900.

Arresting fort: An isolated stronghold, independent fort or advanced fortified position intended to delay an enemy attack. See Advanced work and *Fort d'arrêt*.

Arrow: A small outwork made from two jutting-out faces. It was often placed in the salient angle of the glacis and connected to the covered way by a narrow sunk passage. See *Flèche*.

Arrow headed bastion: A bastion (q.v.) with *orillons* (q.v.). See Ears.

Arrow loop: Also called arrow slit, a long, narrow and usually vertical opening in a wall or merlon, through which archers and crossbowmen could shoot. See *Balistraria* and Loophole.

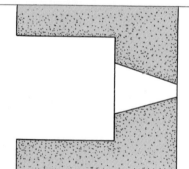

Top: Cross-section.
Bottom: Plan.

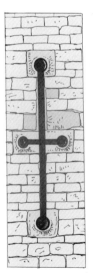

Various shapes of arrow loops.

Artillery park: The place where the artillery was encamped or collected, including the guns and the carriages, ammunition, appurtenances, equipment and personnel necessary for working them. See Arsenal, Remise.

Artillery tower: A tower specifically adapted to fire weapons, generally fitted with casemates (q.v.). See Tower.

Ulm, Germany.

Wawel Castle, Cracow, Poland.

Arsenal: A storing place for weapons and ammunition. The arsenal was an essential building, a vital logistical base in a fortified town, fort or citadel. Its shape, dimensions and capacity depended on the importance of the place. In the seventeenth and eighteenth centuries, the arsenal was often composed of a central yard with buildings around it. These included vast magazines on the ground floor, where guns, carriages, wheels and carts were stored. Small arms (muskets, swords etc) and equipment were generally stored on the upper floors in armouries. The highly dangerous gunpowder was seldom stored in the arsenal, but instead kept apart in special powder-houses (q.v.). The arsenal was completed by various premises and workshops for masons, smiths and carpenters, who built, repaired and maintained military equipment, artillery and fortifications. The arsenal was meant to provide everything the local garrison needed, but also to be able to supply armies on campaign. The siting of arsenals was thus of enormous strategic importance, and they were often located in frontier fortresses.

In a military harbour, the arsenal was a huge fortified and restricted zone including shipyards, rope- carpenter- and sail-workshops where warships were constructed, repaired, armed and supplied. See Submarine bunker.

Arx: In a Roman town, a citadel (q.v.) defending the town, and a safe place to which the population could take refuge, was known as an *arx*. The *arx* was frequently built upon an area of elevated ground, such as a hill with precipitous sides, chosen for purposes of defence. It was not only a fortified place, but was also the administrative and religious heart of the city. Like the Greek acropolis (q.v.), the Roman *arx* contained temples, offices and other government buildings, and formed the nuclei of large cities of classical antiquity. See Keep.

Ascent: The staircase or inclined ramp used to reach the rampart walk. In Roman fortification this was called the *ascensi valli*.

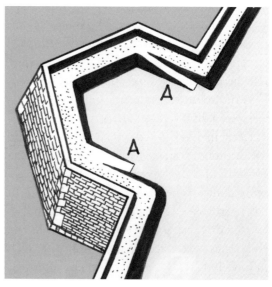

Ascent (A).

Asparagus: The so-called 'Rommel's asparagus' – in German *Holzpfahl* or *Rommelspargel* (q.v.) – was a simple Atlantic Wall (q.v.) obstacle designed in 1944 by Field Marshal Erwin Rommel himself. It consisted of a 2.5–3m-long tree-trunk or stake on top of which was placed an anti-personnel mine. The 'asparagus' were used in groups, particularly on the beaches of the English Channel and the Atlantic Ocean to disrupt amphibious landing. They were also planted into the ground in open areas in the hinterland (meadows, fields etc) to oppose glider and airborne troops. These were called *Luftlandesperre* (*L-Sperre* in short, airborne landing obstacles). Each pole was spaced about 25–30m apart. They were connected to each other with barbed wire or cables which detonated mines.

Atalaya: Spanish term for a watchtower (q.v.), often placed on an elevated point. Isolated or built in rows, they had a vigilance/warning function against raiders and pirates from North Africa.

Atlantic pocket: See *Festung*.

Atlantic Wall: The *Atlantikwall* was an extensive system of Second World War coastal fortifications built along the western coast of Europe by the Germans between 1941 and 1944. Extending from the Franco-Spanish border in the south to Norway in the north, it was intended to defend against an anticipated

Asparagus.

Allied invasion of the continental mainland from Great Britain. On 23 March 1942, Führer Directive Number 40 called for the official creation of the Atlantic Wall. After the Saint-Nazaire raid on 28 March 1942, Adolf Hitler ordered naval and submarine bases to be heavily defended. Fortifications remained concentrated around ports until late 1943, when defences were increased in other areas. The Organisation Todt (q.v.), which had designed and constructed the Siegfried Line (q.v.) along the Franco-German border, was the chief engineering group responsible for the construction of the Atlantic Wall's major fortifications. Thousands of forced labourers were impressed and employed to construct these permanent fortifications. The Atlantic Wall primarily consisted of a juxtaposition of defensive 'hedgehogs', a girdle of infantry positions, machine-gun and mortar nests, anti-tank gun emplacements, medium and long-range coastal artillery batteries, observation posts and radar stations. In addition, the Germans held several armoured divisions as a mobile strategic reserve.

Early in 1944, Field Marshal Erwin Rommel was assigned to inspect and improve the Atlantic Wall's defences. Under his direction, the number of bunkers and general strength of the Atlantic Wall was increased by additional reinforced concrete pillboxes built along the beaches, or slightly inland, to house machine guns, anti-tank guns and light artillery. Minefields and a multitude of obstacles (anti-personnel, anti-tank and anti-landing craft) were established on the beaches themselves, and underwater obstacles and mines were placed in the waters just off shore. By the time of the Normandy invasion in June 1944, the Germans had laid almost six million mines in northern France. More gun emplacements and minefields extended inland, along roads leading away from the beaches. In likely landing spots for gliders and parachutists, the Germans emplaced mined poles known as asparagus (q.v.). Low-lying rivers, marshes and estuarine areas were flooded as well. Rommel firmly believed that Germany would inevitably be defeated unless the Allied landing could be repulsed on the beaches.

Atlantic Wall map.

In reality, the much-vaunted Atlantic Wall, against which the invading Allies were intended to dash themselves into ruin, was only a figment of Hitler's imagination. However, owing to Rommel's frantic efforts to create a strong defensive system, the Atlantic Wall was relatively strong along the Dutch, Belgian and French coasts facing the English Channel and the North Sea. But it was only in the Pas-de-Calais (the northern part of France facing the Strait of Dover) that the Wall existed in anything like its intended form. This heavily fortified section was avoided, and instead the Allies landed in the less-defended Normandy. The defensive German *Atlantikwal* was never completed, and it failed to stop the invasion on 6 June 1944 that marked the start of the liberation of Europe from the Nazi yoke.

Attrition: Blockade, sustained pressure and continued attacks intended to wear down and weaken the enemy. See Siege, Trench warfare and Part 2 (Siege Warfare).

Auxiliary fort: A Roman permanent fortified camp intended for non-Roman soldiers. Locally recruited auxiliaries and hired foreign mercenaries from all parts of the Empire included infantrymen, archers and light cavalry. Auxiliary forts were much smaller than the legionary fortresses (q.v.), covering on average about 5 acres as opposed to the 50 acres of a legionary fortress. On the other hand, they were much more numerous, over 200 of them being recorded in Britain, for example at mid-Glamorgan, Gwynedd and Caernarvon in Wales, Strathclyde in Scotland and Housesteads in northern England. See Legionary Fortress, *Castellum* and *Numerus*.

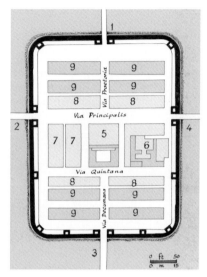

Auxiliary camp (Roman). 1: North Gate; 2: West Gate; 3: South Gate; 4: East Gate; 5: Headquarters; 6: Commander's residence; 7: Supply stores; 8: Workshops and stables; 9: Barracks.

Avant poste: French for advanced post. In the Maginot Line (q.v.), these were positions which might consist of one or several blockhouses and obstacles placed ahead of the main front.

B

Bailey: The enclosed courtyard associated with a fortified mound or motte-and-bailey castle (q.v.). Eventually, the term came to designate the main yard or court of any castle. The medieval bailey, also called the *basse-cour*, contained various buildings: residential and domestic quarters, stables, stores, a forge, chapel, hall, well or cistern and all other facilities required for the daily life of a small community.

Bailiff: In the Middle Ages, an officer in charge of allotting work to peasants, organizing repairs to castles and carrying out other jobs in a medieval castle. He was also the sovereign's representative in a district.

Balistraria: A *balistraria* – often referred to as a loophole (q.v.) – was a vertical aperture in a Roman fortification through which a defender could shoot arrows or throw javelins. In Middle Ages castles, it was a very narrow, long vertical aperture through which a crossbowman crould shoot his weapon. See Arrow loops and Loophole.

Ballistarium: A platform used to support a throwing machine (*onager* or *ballista*, for example) which was used to defend a Roman fort.

Balloon: A large bag of lighter-than-air gas (often hydrogen) attached to a steel cable anchored to the ground in order to deny low-level airspace to enemy aircraft. Widely used during both World Wars of the twentieth century, it was an immobile obstacle gently moving in the wind. This passive weapon forced enemy aircraft to higher altitudes, decreasing surprise and bombing accuracy, and the cable presented both a psychological and material hazard to enemy pilots.

Bangalore: An explosive charge placed on the end of a long, extendible tube. It was used by combat engineers to clear obstacles (e.g. a minefield or barbed wire) that would otherwise require them to approach directly, possibly under fire.

Banquette: A raised narrow platform (sometimes stepped) behind the parapet, sufficiently high to enable the defenders standing upon it to fire over the crest of the parapet yet be protected. Also known as a fire-step (q.v.).

Bar: The gatehouse (q.v.) or barrier to a fortified town. Hence Temple Bar and Holborn Bar in London.

Barbed wire: Barbed wire was invented and patented in 1874 by the American Joseph F. Glidden, originally as a farm-fencing device intended to restrain cattle. Barbed wire is a series of artificial metal thorns, made of sharpened wire barbs twisted at intervals around a central strand. It was first adapted to military purpose by the end of the nineteenth century, but its full significance was not appreciated until the First World War. Quite cheap and easy to install, it was nevertheless dangerous and brought spaces under control. Barbed wire can be used to make a fence enclosing a base, camp or airfield, but also around a PoW camp, prison or concentration camp, which has made it symbolic of oppression and denial of freedom. On the battlefield, it can be placed in line to form a dangerous obstacle intended to stop or hinder infantry progression, or channel an attack to defiled and defended areas. Barbed wire fully exploits the lethality of automatic weapons by holding targets in the line of fire and by keeping them away from the gun and its crew. It also has the advantage of not obstructing view. Depending on the requirements and available resources, wire obstacles may range from a simple fence in front of a defensive position to elaborate patterns of impassable barriers, random thick tangled masses (held by screw pickets or poles fitted with eyelets), concertinas (large stretching coils) or low entanglements which consist of irregularly placed stakes that have been driven into the ground with only some 15cm (6in.) showing (the barbed wire is then wrapped and tightened on to these stakes).

The effectiveness of any wire obstacle is greatly increased by placing booby traps and concealing anti-tank and anti-personnel mines in and around it. Barbed wire can also be electrified, which makes it very dangerous and lethal. On the battlefield, barbed wire can be crushed by tanks, destroyed by heavy artillery bombardment or explosive, or discreetly breached by a party using wire-cutters. Several soldiers can also lie across the wire to form a bridge, over which the rest of the soldiers can pass.

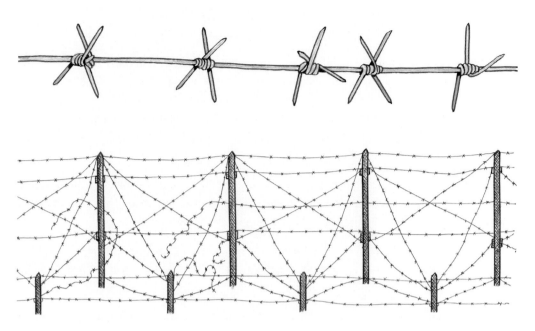

Top: Close up; Bottom: Fence with poles.

Barbette: Artillery is said to fire '*en barbette*' (or '*a barba*') when a gun is placed so as to fire over a simple parapet (q.v.) without the use of a porthole or embrasure (q.v.). The term is also employed to designate the platform upon which a gun may be emplaced.

Barbette.

Barbican: An advanced or exterior work protecting the gatehouse to a city or castle. Originating from Arabic military architecture, it was brought back to Western Europe by the Crusaders. It could be a simple palisade (q.v.), an earthwall with stockade or a thick masonry work. It could have various forms, for example a large round tower, a strong rectangular building or enclosure with towers and turrets, or an oval or horseshoe shape. It could also be a walled passage projecting from the front of the gatehouse, which had large spaces in the roof, or no roof at all, so that defenders could fire upon any attackers trapped inside. Erected on the far side of the ditch, at the exterior end of the bridge, it concealed the gatehouse (q.v.), worked as a filter and provided an additional external line of defence as it was fitted with  combat emplacements, its own ditch and a portcullis and drawbridge, in addition to those in the main gatehouse. The barbican also enabled the gathering of a party to prepare for a sortie (q.v.) or to protect a retreat. The barbican always had an open gorge (q.v.) so that, if captured, attackers were exposed to the defenders' fire from the gatehouse.

Montmartre Gate, Paris.

In the fifteenth century, the barbican was adapted to the use of firearms and often became a powerful bulwark (q.v.) or a formidable artillery tower with strong masonry, ramparted walls, *terre-plein* fitted with gun emplacements behind thick parapets and storeys furnished with gun casemates. The barbican's shape was still varied, but it was often a large U-shaped work projecting into the moat ahead of the gatehouse. As medieval traditions still remained strong, it was not uncommon for the work to be fitted with machicolations and crenellations. See *Demi-lune* and Ravelin.

Barmkin: The small walled yard attached to a Scottish pele tower (q.v.).

Barra: Either a bar (q.v.), barbican (q.v.) or tower (q.v.) at one end of a bridge.

Barracks: Quarters accommodating soldiers. The Roman barracks built in camps and forts was a wooden or masonry building, generally housing a century – a unit of eighty men. Larger rooms were for the centurions (officers), and the legionaries shared quarters, with eight men to a room. In Western Europe, before the introduction of barracks in the eighteenth century, soldiers were billeted in civilian homes in garrison towns, the unfortunate inhabitants being obliged to provide food and sleeping accommodation for one or more men. Campaigning soldiers were often accommodated piecemeal in the loft of an inn, in livery stables or in damp and frequently insanitary bivouacs and tented camps. This method was uncomfortable and hard work for the troops (as it always took some time to assemble them), and understandably very unpopular for civilians. The introduction of barracks in the eighteenth century paralleled and exemplified the rise of standing armies. Barracks enabled a strict control of the men by the NCOs, as all soldiers were – or at least were supposed to be – supervised, correct, present, ready and armed at any time when needed.

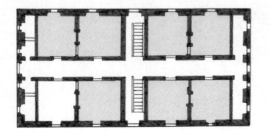

Montdauphin, France, 1700.

Barricade: A light and (often temporary) structure or barrier (q.v.) placed across a street or road as obstruction in order to block, control or force the flow of traffic. It can also forbid the passage to a protected, forbidden or hazardous area. In military terms, a barricade designates any improvised field fortification (q.v.), most notably as a roadblock. In modern times, the barricade is a common feature during political turmoil, riots, revolts, revolutions and civil wars, often in urban areas, where it can be made of improvised looted materials including pavement slabs, timber, stones, felled trees, overturned vehicles or anything else available.

Barrier: Any obstacle preventing forward movement.
1) A strong gate built to defend the entrance of a passage into a fortified place. Also a movable pole placed at a checkpoint or guardhouse.
2) A gate tollhouse in medieval cities for the collection of taxes.
3) A network of fences and obstacles, a line of fortified cities or a girdle of forts intended to protect a disputed border. See Atlantic Wall, Berlin Wall, Maginot Line, Ligne Morice, Wellington Barrier, West Bank Barrier.

Barrière: Also called the Wellington Barrier, this was a network of twenty-five fortified cities (notably Antwerp, Liege and Huy) in Belgium stretching between the Scheldt and along the Meuse rivers. It was intended to create a buffer region that would prevent future French aggression in northern Europe after the Napoleonic Wars. The *Barrière* scheme was partly financed by Britain and supervised by Arthur Wellesley, 1st Duke of Wellington – hence its name.

Barrière de Fer: The *Barrière de Fer* (Iron Barrier), also designated the *Système Séré de Rivières*, was a large programme of modern fortifications designed by Engineering General Séré de Rivières. Built between 1874 and 1914, the scheme was intended to defend important French cities (such as Paris and Lyon) and the eastern border of France against any future Prussian aggression. The Iron Barrier included large clusters and lines of detached polygonal forts, notably around the cities of Metz, Belfort, Langres and Verdun. See *Feste*.

Bartizan: A small overhanging or corbelled turret projecting from the corner or the top of a tower or wall, or projecting from the angle of a fortification. It was used as a watchtower or a defensive position. Bartizans were also used as strengthening buttresses or simply as decoration on later residential palaces. See *Echauguette*, Pepperbox tower, Sentry box and *Poivrière*.

Bartizan.

Bascule bridge: A form of drawbridge (q.v.) using a counterweight.

Base aéroterrestre: The concept of a *base aéroterrestre* (air-ground base), successfully tested by General Wingate's British Chindits and by Colonel Cochran's USAAF Air Commandos against Japan in Burma in 1944, was further developed by the French during the First Vietnam War between 1946 and 1954. In a first phase, it consisted of capturing a zone held by the enemy (such as the elusive Communist Viet Minh) by dropping paratroopers. Once the area was seized, an airfield was installed, other troops were brought in by airplane and a *camp retranché* (q.v.) was constructed. From this heavily fortified base, which was exclusively supplied by air, ground operations and offensives were launched and possibly decisive pitched battles fought. Thereby, the French (owing to their superior firepower and their domination of the sky) hoped to break a deadlock that had lasted for years and to defeat their Viet Minh enemy, win the war and keep Indochina in the French colonial empire. These tactics worked relatively well at the Battle of Na San in late 1952. However, when the Viet Minh received massive Chinese support and developed powerful anti-aircraft artillery that could break the vital air bridge, the concept of an air-supplied offensive base established in enemy-held territory was successfully countered, leading to the disastrous and humiliating defeat of Dien Bien Phu in early 1954.

Basse-court: From the French *basse-cour*, the outer or lower enclosed yard or court of a castle. See Bailey.

Bastei: A bastei (or basteja) was a large artillery tower designed by the German artist Albrecht Dürer (1471–1528) in his book on fortification, *Etliche Unterricht zu Befestigung der Stett, Schloß und Flecken*, published in 1527. Dürer's bastei was a U-shaped tower with

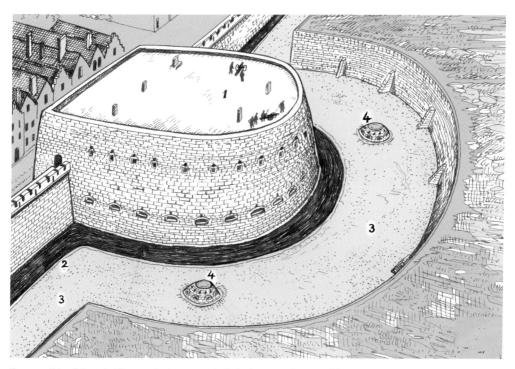

Designed by Albrecht Dürer, the bastei included a large wall tower (1), a wet ditch and a broad and deep dry ditch (3), in which small and low defensive turrets (4) were placed.

a diameter of 130m and massive walls with a height of 40m. It was to be surrounded by a 35m-wide ditch flanked by small caponiers (q.v.). Numerous guns were placed on a top platform and in vaulted casemates (q.v.). The dimensions and the cost that would have been involved in the construction of such monster towers precluded any materialization of the artist's fantasy. However, Dürer's influence could be felt in several huge comtemporary artillery works like the *Blauwe Toren* (the Blue Tower) in Antwerp, the basteja of Krakow in Poland or the English coastal forts built by King Henry VIII. See Transitional fortification.

Bastide: Fortified settlements (about 300 of them) newly founded between *c.*1220 and 1370 in southern France. Bastides were created by order of the kings of France and of England who were fighting over possession of the rich province of Aquitaine. Bastides were given a square or rectangular plan, inspired by the ancient Roman urbanism. The space inside the new villages was divided into regular living parcels, with a church and market square in the middle. Bastides were usually fortified with a masonry enceinte, flanking towers and gatehouses. See *Castelnaux* and *Sauveté*.

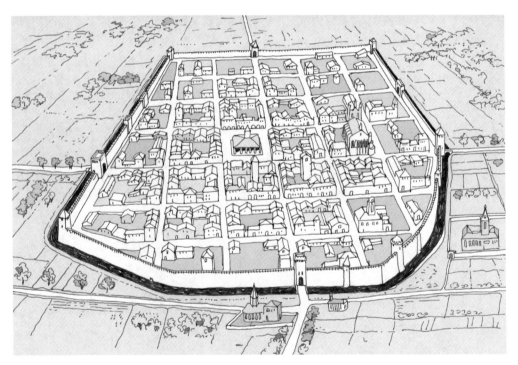

Mirande, France.

Bastille: An advanced work in French medieval fortification protecting the gate of a castle and more particularly of a city. The bastille had the same function as a barbican (q.v.) but it was frequently larger, totally enclosed and manned with its own garrison. The Bastille of Paris, also called the Castle Saint Antoine, which originally defended the Saint Antoine gate in the east of the city, was the most famous. Built between 1370 and 1380, it was a typical block-castle with thick walls and eight towers 24m (78ft) high.

The Bastille, aka Castle Saint Antoine, in Paris, France.

The Bastille lost its military role in the fifteenth century and was then used as a political state prison, often regarded as a symbol of monarchic oppression. It came to fame owing to its storming on 14 July 1789, which sparked the French Revolution. See *Châtelet*, Barbican, Block-castle and Bridgehead.

Bastion: A salient work placed along the curtain of the fortress with two essential characteristics. First, it had a pentagonal outline that was formed by two faces turned outwards to the enemy; both faces joined at the jutting-out salient. They were connected to the curtain (q.v.) by two sections of wall called flanks. The meeting point of the face

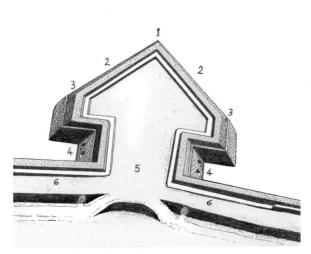

The main parts of a bastion: 1: Salient ; 2: Face; 3: Shoulder; 4: Flank; 5: Gorge; 6: Adjacent curtain (wall).

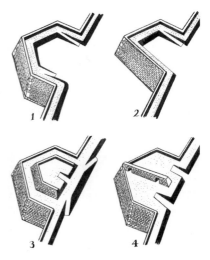

Bastions had various shapes: 1: Void bastion; 2: Half-bastion; 3: Bastion with Cavalier; 4: Traversed bastion.

and flank was called the shoulder. The gorge was the open space at the rear turned to the inside of the city or fort. The surface enclosed by those five lines was called the *terre-plein*. Second, it had a ramparted profile constituted of two revetments (q.v.) – masonry walls holding a thick mass of earth, a backfill, which absorbed artillery fire like a cushion.

The bastion was rather low above the ground in order not to be an easy target, while the depth of the moat prevented escalading. In addition to being solidly constructed and so difficult to damage or destroy, bastions offered defenders excellent combat emplacements for crossfire and enabled them to return in equal measure a besieger's artillery fire. The distance between two bastions – thus the length of the curtain – was dictated by the firing range of the contemporary arquebus and musket. Each bastion lay within musket shot of each other, which made it possible to cover all areas in front of the fortification.

Bastioned curtain: See Reinforced order.

Bastioned fort: A fort (q.v.) built according to the bastioned system (q.v.).

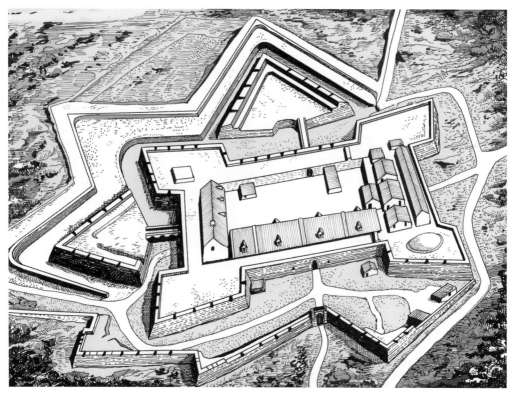

Fort Ticonderoga, Lake Champlain, New York State, USA.

Bastioned front: The basic elements of a bastioned front were one curtain (q.v.) and two half-bastions (q.v.). This geometrical unit could be repeated at will with various salient angles to enclose a city, a sconce (q.v.) or a fort. Curtains and bastions – protected by a thick parapet (q.v.) – were built at the same low level, forming a wide passageway along which artillery, munition carts and troops could be rapidly deployed. At the same time they constituted a broad combat emplacement suited for both infantry and artillery. The flanking (q.v.) capacity of the bastioned front allowed mutual fire from and onto any part of the enceinte, thus leaving no dead angles or blind spots (q.v.) to benefit the attacker.

The basic elements of a bastioned front included two half-bastions (1); a section of wall named curtain (2); a deep ditch (3); a ravelin or *demi-lune* (4); a covered way (5); places-of-arms (6); and a glacis (7).

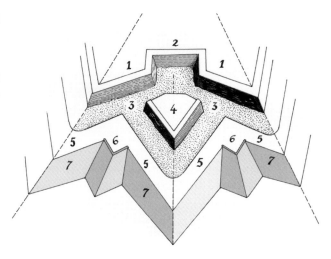

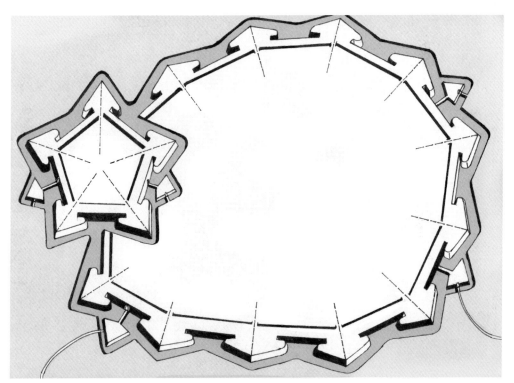

The same bastioned front could be repeated at will with various lengths and different angles to constitute a citadel (left) or enclose a whole town.

Bastioned system: The great merits of the bastioned system (invented by Italian engineers *c.* 1500) were its flexibility, ease of construction and adaptability to suit varying conditions – important characteristics which quickly led to its adoption as an international method of defence. The bastioned tracé, a circuit of low and thick walls punctuated by protruding bastions, presented many advantages. It gave a fortress not only the necessary solidity to withstand enemy bombardment, but also the ability to bring as much firepower as possible to bear on the attackers, combining the destructive power of artillery itself with an aggressive form of mutually flanking defences. Bastions, cavaliers, *demi-lunes* (aka ravelins) and all other elements of the system were so designed and positioned that cannons mounted on each of them could provide cover not only to the full length of the rampart walls and ditches, but to the neighbouring works and surrounding area as well. The full area could be swept by flanking crossfire, leaving no blind spots and denying attackers any cover. The overall effect of flanking fire from bastioned works restored the balance in favour of defence as rapidly as cannons had reversed it at the end of the fifteenth century. The only disadvantage of the bastioned system was the very high cost involved. It therefore marked the end of an era, the disappearing of the private castle and private local wars, and announced the monoploy of the state in matters of national defence.

The bastioned system ensured that war rarely extended beyond a series of sieges. Because the new fortresses could hold many men, an attacking army could not ignore a powerfully fortified position without serious risk of counter-attack. As a result, when a

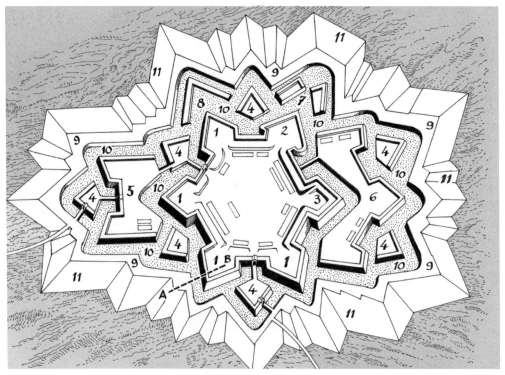

Bastioned system. 1: Bastion; 2: Bastion with ears; 3: Void bastion; 4: Ravelin (*Demi-lune*); 5: Hornwork; 6: Crownwork; 7: Tenaillons; 8: Counterguard; 9: Covered way with places-of-arms; 10: Ditch; 11: Glacis.

campaign was launched, virtually all towns had to be taken, which was always a difficult operation, sometimes a long, drawn-out affair, potentially lasting several months to years. Many battles in the seventeenth and eighteenth centuries were fought between besieging armies and relief forces sent to rescue the besieged.

The bastioned system, which remained in use until the early decades of the nineteenth century, had a significant impact on European urbanism. Its bastions, ditches, outworks, advanced works and glacis required enormously wide restricted militarized areas, which for centuries hindered the development and growth of cities.

Bastioned tower: This typical work, designed by the French engineer Vauban, was meant to provide flanking fire and protect the main wall. Because of its relatively small dimensions, the bastioned tower was not an easy target for enemy mortars and was not vulnerable to enfilade (q.v.) and ricochet fire (q.v.). It was usually provided with two casemated floors: the casemates in the lower tier flanked the ditch, whilst the upper ones covered and commanded the detached bastion placed in front of it.

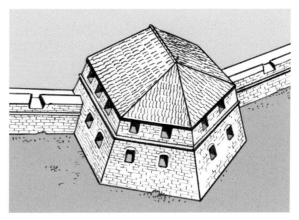

Bastioned tower.

The top of the tower was either arranged as an artillery platform or fitted with a roof to protect men and guns from bad weather and enemy fire. The casemated, totally masoned bastioned tower was, however, much more expensive to build than the earth-filled or solid bastion (q.v.), and – although fitted with ventilating flues and vents intended to clear the choking smoke from the guns in the casemates – the crucial problem of ventilation remained unsolved. Bastioned towers were used by Vauban at Besançon, Landau, Belfort and Neuf-Brisach, but they never caught on with other fortress builders.

Bastionet: A small bastion (q.v.) or a roundel (q.v.) casemated or open at the top, often placed in the salient of the ditch of a detached work.

Bastista: In medieval Italy a fortified village, generally built for defensive purpose on top of a highand steep crag. Aka Batista or Bautista. See Village *perché*.

Bastle house: Fortified dwellings and farmhouses built along both sides of the Anglo-Scottish border, in the areas formerly plagued by the so-called Border Reivers from the late thirteenth century to the end of the sixteenth century. Bastle houses were characterized by thick stone walls, a ground floor devoted to stable-space, living quarters on the floor above the ground, windows in the form of narrow arrow slits and roofs usually made of stone slate.

Batardeau: A cofferdam, embankment or small dike constructed across a ditch intended to retain water in a wet ditch or moat (q.v.), to separate dry and wet ditches or to isolate

Batardeau.

running sea or river-waters from standing moat-waters. The batardeau was often built in masonry crosswise in the ditch, and thus formed a dangerous weakness in the defensive system. To prevent its use as a means of crossing the ditch by enemy troops, it was usually made impassable by topping it with a sharp knife-edges or *dos d'âne* (q.v.) and fitted with a monk (q.v.) A batardeau could be hollow and fitted with a gallery in which sluices and watergates could be placed in order to regulate the height of water in the moat.

Battered plinth: This term refers to the base of a wall provided with a widening slope. This added stability to the construction, strengthened the bottom of the wall against undermining and sapping and provided a ricochet surface for projectiles such as rocks being dropped down from machicolations (q.v.) that would bounce off horizontally and crush the attackers. See Apron.

Battering ram: The ram was a strong beam, often with a metal point at one end. It was a basic and favourite siege weapon in Antiquity and the Middle Ages. The device was operated by a party of men utilizing a backwards and forwards movement against a gate or masonry wall in order to create a breach (q.v.). The violent impacts worked by direct percussion but also by vibrations, which loosened stones. In order to protect the men moving the battering ram, the device was attached by ropes or chains to a solid structure on wheels (called a cat or rolling shed), which was covered by a fireproof material such as dung, earth, clay, seaweed, green grass or freshly skinned animal hides. See Part 2 (Siege Warfare).

Battery: A battery was an artillery emplacement specially arranged to receive guns of the same type firing in the same direction and towards a common objective. If permanent, the battery could be completed by a barracks for the gunners, a store, powder-house and fortified enclosure, in which case it could grow to the capacity of a redoubt (q.v.) or a fort (q.v.). The word also designates the guns themselves.

Battlement: A battlement (also called crenellation) is a defensive combat element placed on top of a parapet (q.v.) for the protection of the wall-walk (q.v.). Parts of the battlement were cut out at regular intervals to allow the discharge of arrows or other missiles. These indented void parts are called crenels (q.v.). The standing solid parts between the crenels are called merlons (q.v.), behind which defenders could seek cover. A parapet wall with battlements is said to be crenellated or embattled. See Breastwork, Hoarding and Machicolation.

Top: Seen from inside, with the wall-walk (1) and the parapet or breastwork composed of void crenels (2) and solid merlons (3). Bottom: Seen from outside.

Bawn: A bawn (from the Irish *bahun*, meaning enclosure) was the defensive wall surrounding an Irish towerhouse.

Bay: A section of trench (q.v.) placed between two adjacent traverses used as a passage. See Chicane.

Beachhead: A temporary defensive position established around the site of a beach landing, which is used as a secure base for subsequent operations.

Beach obstacles: Devices intended to hinder, damage, sink or even destroy landing craft approaching a beach. Beach (aka anti-landing) obstacles were laid in such a fashion as to deny access to the shore, lying underwater or just below the surface of high tide. Some were discarded anti-tank obstacles (q.v.), while others were hastily improvised devices. Their intrinsic destructiveness was reinforced by a variety of mines (q.v.), booby traps (q.v.) and explosives intended to both damage craft which struck the obstacles and to deter any attempt at removal. They were on the whole simple, cheap, rapidly erected and extremely dangerous. Obstacles were efficient only when they were set up in great density, which meant gigantic numbers of them – demanding great effort, the means and time. Beach obstacles suffered heavy pressure from violent up and down tidal streams, sank in loose sand and were dislocated by storms. Salty seawater caused wood to rapidly rot and metal to rust. They had thus to be permanently controlled and maintained. See Admiralty scaffolding, Atlantic Wall, Belgian Gate, Czech hedgehog, Mined raft, Mined pole, Naval mine, Nutcracker mine, Square mine, Strand bars, Strand beams and Tetraeder.

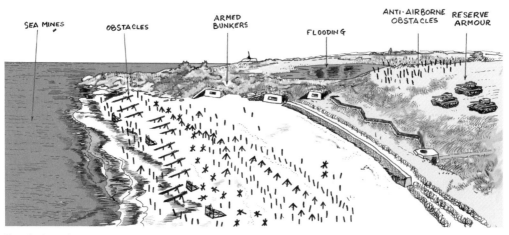

Beach obstacles.

Belgian Gate: The so-called Belgian Gate (aka Element C, called by the Germans *Rollbock* or *Cointet-Gitter*) was a mobile anti-tank obstacle designed by the French Colonel Léon-Edmond de Cointet de Fillain in 1933. De Cointet de Fillain proposed his invention to the French Army but the device was refused because of its high cost, though a number were built, purchased and used in the Maginot Line as roadblocks.

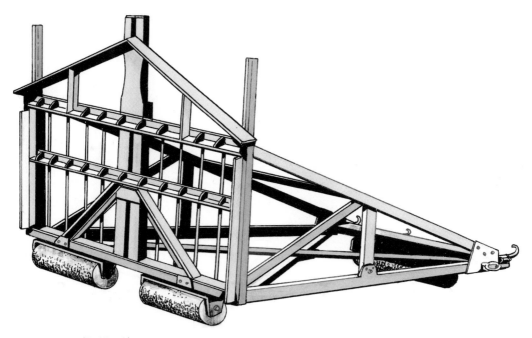
Belgian gate (Rollbock).

The designer was more fortunate in Belgium, where his patent was purchased – hence the name *Element Cointet* or *Grille Belge* (Belgian Gate). The device was composed of a 3m-wide and 2.5m-high strong metal gate firmly fixed on a 3.3m-long carriage moved by three rollers. The obstacle was fully made of strong and thick steel bars, and thus extremely robust and effective, but also quite expensive. It was rather heavy (1,400kg) and not easy to manoeuvre (it could only be moved by a towing vehicle or a pair of horses). In the Atlantic Wall (q.v.), captured Belgian Gates were used by the Germans mainly as anti-landing craft obstacles.

Bending tunnel: Underground mine (q.v.) given a zigzagged or curved plan in order to help prevent the explosive force of the charge placed in the chamber at the end of the mine from travelling back along the length of the gallery. Described as *sinuosi cuniculi* by the engineer Francesco di Giorgio Martini in his book *Trattati*.

Benes Line: A line of strongholds, bunkers, artillery emplacements and obstacles modelled on the French Maginot Line (q.v.). The Benes Line – named after President Edvard Benes (1884–1948) – was established in 1937 by Czecholovakia along its border facing Nazi Germany, stretching from Ostrava to the Giant Mountains at Krkonose. After the Munich Agreement and the dismantling of Czecholovakia in 1938, the defensive line fell into German hands without a fight. Although unfinished, it provided valuable information about the French defences.

Bent entrance: An entrance of a fortification involving one or more sharp changes in direction. If an enemy force gained entry, they then had to turn because of the shape of the entry, which exposed their unshielded side to the fire of the defenders. See *clavicula*.

Bergfried: German for a twelfth- and thirteenth-century high and square keep (q.v.). Called *Bergfried* in Germany and *Berchfrit* in Austria, this large tower was generally used as both dwelling place and combat emplacement. Varying in shape, often square but also rectangular, pentangular and infrequently circular, some *Bergfrieden* were reinforced on their most vulnerable face by a *Schildmauer* (q.v.), a high and thick wall screening the habitation parts. Examples can still be seen in the castles at Wassenburg, Bruck, Kinzheim and Andlau.

The castle of Bruck is situated near Lienz in the Tyrol, Austria. Built at the end of the thirteenth century, the castle has a high square *donjon* (*Berchfrit*), a residential house (*Palas*), a crenellated enceinte, a shield-wall (*Schildmauer*) and an outer enclosure. Today, the castle of Bruck houses a Tyrolean museum.

Bereitschaftsraum: In German First and Second World War concrete bunkers, the *Bereitschaftsraum* was a troop-chamber, a quarter including standardized chairs, stools, tables and cupboards for the crew's personal gear, and narrow folding three-tier bunks suspended by chains attached to the ceiling.

Berlin Wall: The Berlin Wall (*Berliner Mauer* in German) was a barrier built by the German Democratic Republic (GDR, communist East Germany) entirely encircling West Berlin, separating it from East Germany, including East Berlin. The Berlin Wall's purpose was to avoid illegal emigration and escape by Eastern Germans to the West. It became an infamous symbol of the Cold War. After its erection in 1961, and for more than a quarter of a century, the Berlin Wall was succesful in achieving its goal, stopping almost all escapes. Around 5,000 people attempted to break out, with estimates of the resulting death toll varying between 98 and 200. The Berlin Wall had a high concrete wall (illuminated at night by floodlights), barbed wire, anti-tank obstacles, electrified

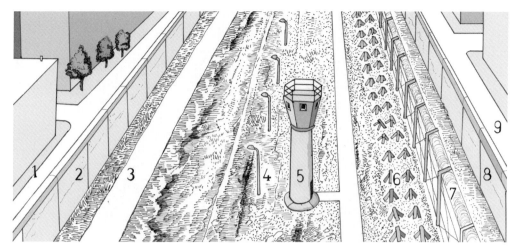

Cross-section of Berlin Wall (*c.* 1978). 1: West Berlin; 2: Concrete wall; 3: Patrol road; 4: Lighting system; 5: Watchtower; 6: Obstacles; 7: Wire fence; 8: Concrete wall; 9: East Berlin.

fences, minefields covered by warning sensors and watch towers guarding a wide area known as the 'death strip'. It was watched over and patrolled by soldiers and armed policemen. There were only a few gateways with checkpoints for carefully controlled contact between the two Germanies. The Berlin Wall was erected in the dead of night and for twenty-eight years kept East Germans from fleeing to the West. Its destruction, which was nearly as instantaneous as its creation, was celebrated around the world. It was dismantled in the winter of 1989/90 by crowds of Germans in a celebratory and euphoric atmosphere. Its enthusiastic destruction paved the way for German reunification, which was formally concluded on 3 October 1990. See Iron Curtain and Checkpoint.

Beobachtungsglocke: Also called a *Kleinglocke* or cloche (q.v.), this was a small, roundish, non-movable, bell-shaped armoured observation cupola (q.v.) fixed on the top of a German bunker. Access was only possible from inside the bunker by means of a ladder or a narrow staircase. The cupola was pierced with narrow spy-holes, which could be fitted with optical magnifying devices (e.g. binoculars, tank-periscope).

Berm: A cleared and bordering space or path (a few metres wide) between the ditch and base of a rampart on the scarp. It served as a communication and patrol path all around the fortress. In case of heavy bombardment by an enemy, the berm stopped (a part of) the debris from the rampart falling into and filling the ditch.

Bettung: German term for an open gun pit (q.v.). See Anti-aircraft gun emplacement.

Biehler fort: A German standard polygonal fort (called *Biehlersches Einheitsfort* or *Schemafort* in German) designed by the Prussian engineer Hans Alexis von Biehler. This typically polygonal fort included barracks placed in the gorge, numerous artillery emplacements protected by traverses (q.v.) and a dry ditch defended by a caponier (q.v.). About seventy detached Biehler forts were built in the period 1870–1890 as defences around German cities such as Cologne, Strasburg, Posen, Thorn, Königsberg, Ingolstadt, Metz, Küstrin, Spandau, Ulm, Mayence and Magdeburg. See Polygonal system.

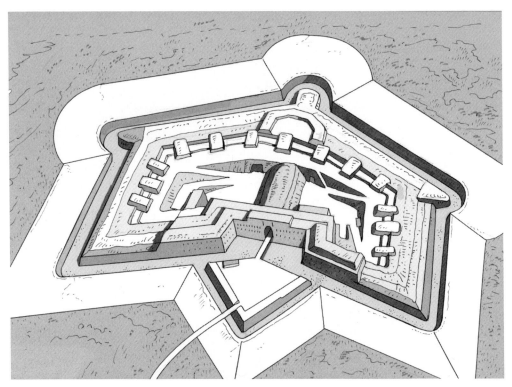
Biehler fort.

Bishop's mitre: An advanced work (q.v.) in the form of a *tenaille* (q.v.). Also called a priest's cap, it differed from the *queue d'aronde* or swallow's tail (q.v.) due to its two slightly spreading wings (q.v.).

Bison: The Bison was an armoured fighting vehicle produced in Britain during the invasion crisis of 1940–1941. Based on a number of different truck chassis, it featured a fighting compartment protected by a layer of concrete. Various sorts of Bison were used by the Royal Air Force to protect airfields, and by the Home Guard. Effectively a mobile pillbox that could be driven to defensive positions when and where needed, they would certainly have been quite adequate to defend against the lightly armed German paratroopers who were anticipated to attack airfields. It is not clear how many Bisons were produced, but estimates vary between 200 and 300. An extant example (a Thornycroft Tartar 3-ton, 6x4 truck) is on display at the Bovington Tank Museum in Dorset.

Bivallate: A hillfort (q.v.) defended by two concentric walls and ditches. See Multivallate.

Bivouac: Temporary camp without tents specially built by mountaineers, campers and campaigning soldiers.

Blast pen: An embankment on two or three sides that is open from the front (and in some cases also from the rear to cater for jet efflux or to permit entry of aircraft) to admit and store aircraft. Blast pens, protecting aircraft against bomb blasts and splinters

Blast pen.

during enemy air attacks, are also designed for storing or parking missiles, specialist vehicles etc. Also called a hardened shelter.

Blast wall: Screen intended to resist and protect from the destructive pressure of the wave of highly compressed air caused by an explosion. Blast walls are made either of a thick earth cover or of concrete, and are systematically placed before a door or in front of an access. See Parados and Traverse.

Blind arch: A curved symmetrical structure built inside a masonry wall as support and reinforcement.

Blind arch.

Blindes: Planks, boards and beams intended to provide protection and cover, for example placed over a trench in order to support a covering of hurdles or sandbags.

Blind spot: Dead angles or blind spots are areas below and beyond which a part of ground could not be seen, and thus could not be fired at.

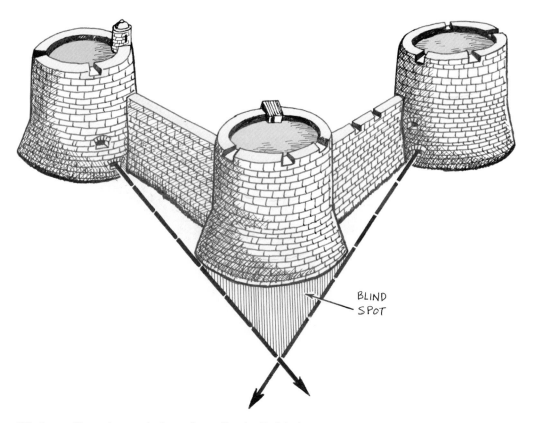

Blind spot. Shown here at the base of a medieval cylindrical tower.

Bloc: In the French Maginot Line (q.v.), a general term for a reinforced bunker. There were three main sorts: armed combat *blocs*, defended entrance *blocs* (for men on foot and ammunition) and observation *blocs*. See *Ouvrage*.

Blockade: An act, effort or means to seal off by force a place to prevent food, supplies, war materiel or people from entering or leaving. A tactic known as 'investment', blockade is one of the methods used in siege warfare, consisting of isolating and waiting until starvation, thirst, disease, discouragement or internal quarrels oblige the besieged to surrender. Blockade was typically coupled with attempts to reduce the fortifications by means of siege engines, artillery bombardment, mining (q.v.), sapping (q.v.) or the use of deception or treachery to bypass defences. See Part 2 (Siege Warfare).

Block-castle: A castle without a keep (q.v.) whose walls and towers were constructed at the same level, creating a massive core, and fitted with broad wall-walks to form a large summit combat terrace. This disposition, that left only a small and narrow bailey in the middle of the castle, enabled easy communication, and allowed defenders to deploy their hurling machines (later firearms). Typical of the late fourteenth century, the Bastille (q.v.) in Paris, the castle of Tarascon in southern France and Nunney Castle in Somerset (Britain) were examples of block-castles.

Blockhaus: A military fortified construction made of masonry or square logs or concrete used as a shelter, an observation point or a combat position. In the Maginot Line (q.v.), a *blockhaus* was a type of stand-alone infantry combat position armed only with machine guns. See *Ouvrage*, Bunker, Blockhouse and Pillbox.

Blockhouse:
1) A small, isolated fort in the form of a single building, often made of square logs. It was intended to serve as a defensive strongpoint against any enemy who did not possess any heavy siege artillery. In the nineteenth century, standard patterns of blockhouses were constructed for defence in frontier areas, particularly South Africa, New Zealand, Canada and the United States. Blockhouses may be made of masonry where available, but were commonly made from very heavy timbers, sometimes logs arranged in the manner of a log cabin, as the name derives from the German *Block* (beam) and *Haus* (house). There were usually two or even three floors, with all storeys being fitted with embrasures or loopholes, and the uppermost storey was often roofed.
2) A wooden rectangular or square roofed tower placed at the corner of a fort, having the same flanking function as a bastion (q.v.). See American West forts.
3) In forts built before the end of the nineteenth century, a blockhouse could be similar to a *corps-de-garde* (q.v.), a rifle casemate controlling the entrance of a fort or fortified place.

Blockhouse.

Bocage: See Hedgerow.

Bolwerk: Dutch term originally designating an additional artillery emplacement made of earth. It eventually gave the words bulwark (q.v.) and boulevard.

Bombel's wall: Named after Jean-Baptiste de Bombel (a military engineer of French origin, serving the Dutch United Provinces in the seventeenth century), the so-called Bombel's wall was a wall with a roundish shape placed inside the salient of a bastion in order to increase firepower. The only surviving example is to be found at the fortress of Naarden near Amsterdam.

Bombing trench: An auxiliary trench used in First World War trench warfare (q.v.). It was dug behind the front line at a suitable distance to allow grenades to be thrown from it into the forward trench. Its purpose was to permit raiding or attacking parties entering the first trench to be swept with grenades.

Bombproof: Any structure sufficiently thick and strong to be impenetrable by bombs and shells.

Bonnet:

1) A small earthwork placed above a parapet in order to shield the *banquette* from enfilade fire.
2) An outwork positioned ahead of the salient angle of a bastion or *demi-lune*.

Booby trap: A booby trap is a device designed to kill or severely injure non-protected enemy personnel. A booby trap is always in some way concealed so that it cannot be seen, or disguised to look harmless. Typically, a booby trap is hidden inside, behind or underneath another object, and often designed to be triggered by the targeted victim. Most, but not all, military booby traps involve an explosive, but a booby trap is distinct from a land mine (q.v.) and anti-personnel mine (q.v.) by the fact that it is often an improvised device, whereas an explosive land mine is manufactured for its specific purpose. However, mines and booby traps have the same effect: they are intended to demoralize soldiers as they kill or maim comrades; they keep soldiers continually stressed, suspicious and unable to relax because it is difficult for them to know which areas, buildings or objects are safe; they slow down troop movement as soldiers are forced to sweep areas to see if there are more of them; they make soldiers cautious instead of aggressive and confident; they create no-go areas (real or imaginary) after they have killed or wounded someone; and they cause fear, confusion and disorientation. See Obstacle, Anti-personnel mine and Mantrap.

Borg: Dutch term for a nobleman's fortified country house in the province of Groningen in the Netherlands. Borgs (in Friesland called stins) date from the fourteenth century. They consisted of a fortified house, a wall and a wet ditch. Many lost their military function in the sixteenth century and were converted into comfortable residential country houses or elegant manors for the gentry.

Borj (or Burj): Arabic term meaning fort. In northern Africa, it usually designated a fortified residence built on top of a hill or in any other place with difficult access. The term still exists in Algeria in topography, for example Borj Menaiel, Borj-Bou-Arreidji and Borj de Chegga.

Borough: Also spelled burg, burgh and burh, a borough (aka a chartered town) was originally a medieval town with various privileges and the right of self-government granted by an official written document called a charter.

Boulder wall: A boulder wall (also boulder-wall or bowlder-wall) is a kind of wall made of round flints and pebbles smoothed by erosion and laid in a strong mortar.

Boulevard: A wide street in a town or city, typically one lined with trees. The boulevard often originated from a dismantled bulwark, an element of fortification intended to house artillery. See Bulwark and Bolwerk.

Box: A 'box' was an all-round fortified defensive position, particularly built by the British in North Africa during the Second World War (e.g. the Gazala Line). Boxes were intended to stop or delay swift tank attacks. Each box included a perimeter with a multitude of foxholes, artillery and infantry combat emplacements, trenches and communication saps, underground kitchen, field infirmaries and dressing stations, dug-outs, shelters and supply dumps in field fortification (q.v.) style. All these were levelled, well camouflaged and difficult to spot. All boxes were surrounded by large anti-tank and anti-personnel minefields, making the terrain a death trap. Gates and narrow patrolling lanes were established in the minefields in order to maintain contact with neighbouring boxes. See Hedgehog, Island and Igel.

Boyau: Either a small gallery in a mine or a branch of a sap (q.v.) linking trenches (q.v.), batteries (q.v.) and parallels (q.v.). For infantry, they were often deep and rather narrow (some 4–5ft), enough for the passage of two men. For artillery use, dimensions were increased in order to move guns into position and for ammunition carts to be towed by horses or oxen.

Bracket/Bracketing: A wooden or masonry projection near the top of a wall, which was used to support a hoarding (q.v.) or a brattice (q.v.). See Console and Corbel.

Braie, Bray or Braye: A sort of bulwark (q.v.), an exterior artillery emplacement of trifling height, made of earth or masonry as a protection at the foot of the main enceinte. The braie was often constructed outside and alongside the wall between two towers. It was generally open and often fitted with embrasures (q.v.). It could also be a continuous outerwork placed inside a dry ditch in order to protect and defend the main enceinte. See *Fausse-braie* and Transitional fortification.

Brattice: A brattice was a small masonry or timber projecting balcony or moucharaby (*q.v*) resting on corbels. The brattice originated from the Middle East and was introduced into Western Europe by Crusaders in the twelfth century. Placed above an entrance, gate or door, its floor was fitted with one or more machicoulis (q.v.), openings permitting defenders to throw missiles down upon assailants. It was a cheap substitute allowing vertical flanking. Its summit was either roofed or open and furnished with one or two crenels.

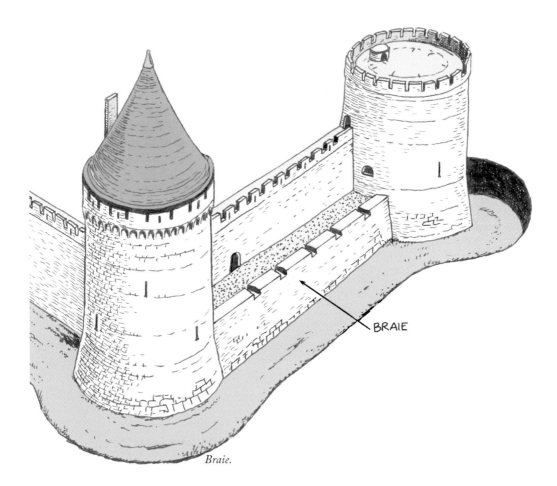

Braie.

Various forms of brattice.

Brattice.
Left: Front view.
Right: Cross-section.

Breach: A gap in a fortification made by besiegers in siege warfare. See Part 2 (Siege Warfare).

Breastwork: The term is usually applied to temporary fortifications, often an earthwork thrown up to breast height to provide protection to defenders firing over it from a standing position. A more permanent structure, normally in stone or masonry holding earth, would be described as a parapet (q.v.) or a battlement (q.v.).

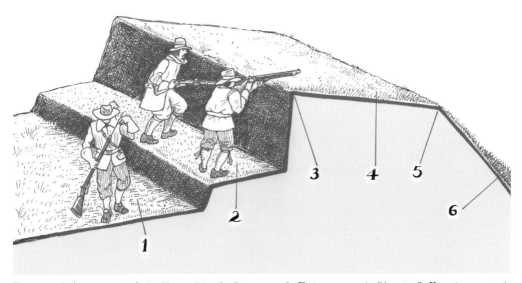

Breastwork (cross-section). 1: *Terre-plein*; 2: *Banquette*; 3: Firing crest; 4: *Plongée*; 5: Exterior crest; 6: Exterior slope.

Bremer wall: A US-made, 3.7m (12ft) high, prefab, modular, T-shaped, steel-reinforced protective concrete blast wall. Used in Iraq and Afghanistan by Coalition forces. Because they proliferated during the administration of former US envoy in Iraq L. Paul Bremer, they became known as 'Bremer walls'.

Brick: A brick is a block of ceramic material used in masonry construction, usually laid using mortar. Employed since Antiquity, brickwork has been used to make both civilian buildings and fortification works.

Bridgehead: A bridgehead was a military fortification that protected the end of a bridge and a riverbank when a town was established on a river. In modern times, the term has been generalized to mean any kind of position secured by a force inside enemy territory. Also called a foothold, it allows an attacker to continue advancing.

Bridgehead. 1: Urban wall; 2: Gatehouse; 3: Fortified bridge; 4: Bridgehead.

Broch: An Iron Age drystone hollow-walled windowless edifice encountered only in Scotland. Brochs varied in shape and size, but the majority had the appearance of a circular tower some 16–50ft in diameter, rising to a height of 40–50ft with walls 10ft thick, often enclosed with an outer stone wall. Brochs presumably combined a number of purposes, such as defensive fortification, refuge, store place and farm building. See Dun and Nuraghe.

Mousa Broch.

Buffington-Crozier mount: A form of disappearing gun carriage designed in 1894 by the American officers Adelbert Buffington and William Crozier. The Buffington-Crozier carriage, using the energy of recoil, was used in US coastal fortifications during the Endicott era (1885–1905). See Disappearing gun and Elswick mounting.

Bullet proof: Anything protecting against small-arms projectiles as well as grenades and small-calibre shell splinters. See Breastwork, Embankment, Sandbags and Armoured plate.

Bulwark: Early English for bastion (q.v.). Originally an earth entrenchment in the transitional fortification (q.v.), the bulwark was either an earth rampart or a masonry wall around the whole Middle Ages enceinte or a simple entrenchment reinforcing a vulnerable point or a platform for artillery. In whatever material, shape, size and dimension, the bulwark presented many advantages. Its dimensions were calculated in order to place, supply and fire artillery. Situated outside the enceinte, the bulwark created an additional line of defence and increased the range of the guns. Its profile was generally low in order to maximize grazing fire. It offered space where the besieged might regroup for withdrawal or a sally (q.v.). It functioned as a shield protecting the scarp of the main enceinte and put the inside of the castle – or the suburb of a city – out of range of enemy artillery. The bulwark was relatively cheap to build when constituted of a rampart (q.v.). Later, the term designated fortification in general, and when urban defences were dismantled in later periods, the bulwark acquired its modern meaning: a boulevard or an avenue, a wide lane often with trees planted alongside.

Here a bulwark has been built outside a portion of curtain wall and two medieval towers in order to create a low advanced artillery platform.

Bunker: A common generic term to designate a concrete permanent fortification of any type and size (for machine guns, artillery, front or flank fire, shelter for personnel and supplies, shelter for submarine, nuclear shelter etc). A bunker is a hardened shelter, often buried partly or fully underground, designed to protect its occupiers. Typical of the twentieth century, bunkers were used extensively in the First and Second World War and the Cold War for weapons facilities, command and control centres and storage facilities (for example, in the event of nuclear war). The concrete nature of bunkers means that they are features of prepared positions. They are often camouflaged in order to conceal their location and to maximize the element of surprise. They may be part of a trench system or form an interlocking line of defence with other bunkers by providing covering fire to each other (defence in depth). They may be placed to guard strategic points, or they can also be giant structures, for example to shelter submarines. In bunkers occupied for prolonged periods, used as combat positions or quarters for a garrison, ventilation or air conditioning were provided. See Blockhouse, Pillbox and Stand.

Burg: An ancient medieval term designating a fortified town or a castle.

Burgward: A form of settlement used for the organization of the north-eastern marches of the kingdom of Germany in the mid-tenth century. Based on earlier organizations within the Frankish Empire and among the Slavs, the burgwards were composed of a central fortification (burg) with a number of smaller, undefended villages (wards),

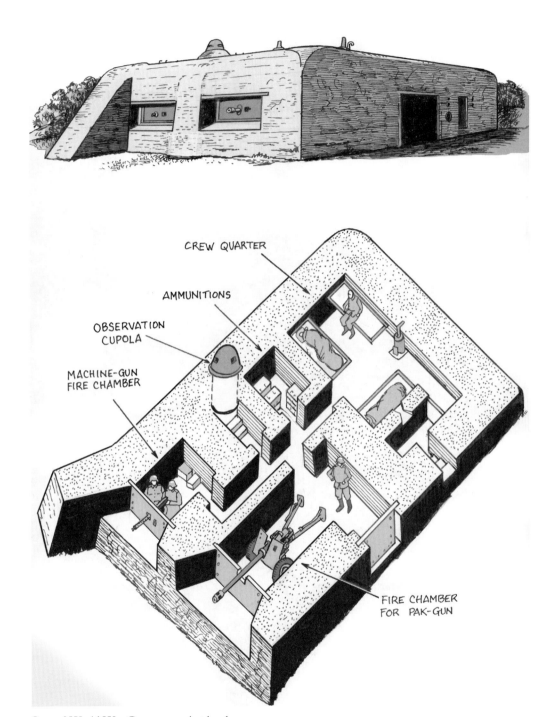

Second World War German combat bunker.

perhaps ten to twenty, depending on it for protection and economic support. The fortified and garrisoned site served as a place of refuge during attack and also as an administrative centre for tax collection, the Church and the court system. The first burgwards (civitates or Burgen) were Merovingian and Carolingian defensive constructions.

Burh: A fortified town in Germany in the tenth century and in England before the Norman Conquest of 1066. When Offa's Dyke (q.v.) and Wat's Dyke (q.v.) were mere boundary marks, burhs (derived from the Latin *burgus*, tower) were fortifications in the true sense of the word. They were made of an earth wall with palisade and ditch, probably a copy or inheritance of earlier Roman practice. In England, the establishment of a system of burhs was started by King Alfred the Great (849–899) and carried on by his successors. They were intended to protect people, goods and trade, and also to provide bases from which cavalry (and on the coast, ships) could operate against rebels, marauders and Viking raiders.

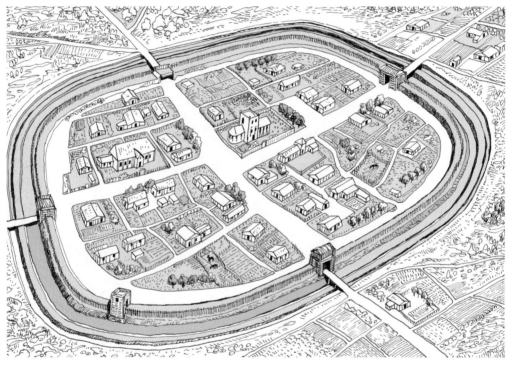

Burh.

Burster course: A 2ft concrete layer placed just below the surface of a thick earth cover. It was designed to detonate projectiles before they penetrated to the principal structure below.

Buttress: A projecting pillar, abutment, pilaster, pier or mass of masonry added to a wall to support or strengthen it against lateral forces arising out of the roof structure.

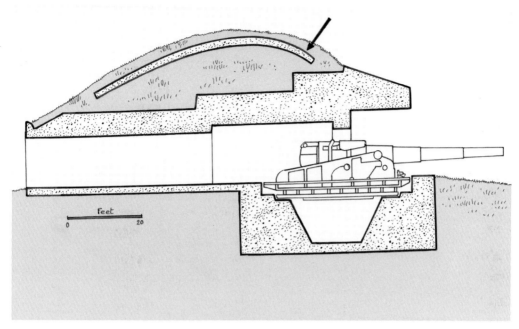

Burster course. Battery Richmond Davis, San Francisco, USA.

Buttress.

C

Caer: A Welsh word for the Roman *castrum* (q.v.). It forms part of the name of several Welsh towns, e.g. Caernarvon, Caerphily or Caerdydd (Cardiff). See Hillfort and Oppidum.

Caltrop: Also known as a crow's foot, this was a small anti-personnel passive weapon comprising four sharp spikes arranged in such a manner that one of them always pointed upward. Placed and concealed on the ground, they were dangerous and efficient to lame pedestrians and wound horses. In modern times, caltrops are still used to impede pneumatic wheeled vehicles. See Fakir's bed.

Caltrop.

Camouflage: Camouflage on a large scale has been used since the First World War, when air reconnaissance was first employed. The exterior aspect of fortification has ever since been very important. All military facilities have to be hidden from sight and concealed from enemy fire according to the 'three S rule' that is designed to avoid and reduce shadow, shine and shape. Camouflage measures should not attract attention, but at the same time they should not obstruct observation, view and a weapon's field of fire. Camouflage demands a great deal of flexibility, ingenuity and initiative in order to adapt to the varying terrain, weather conditions and available weapons and materials. First of all, any natural advantages of the terrain must be utilized to the maximum in order to avoid silhouetting against the sky and contrasting backgrounds. Emerging parts must be covered with fresh-cut local tree branches, brushwood, sod, vines and twigs, and these must be replaced regularly. Camouflage nets and canvas tarpaulins – possibly garnished with foliage – are also used in order to break up the outline, as well as paint (dark yellow, red-brown and various shades of green) in order to blend in with the surroundings.

All signs of work, such as spoil or turned earth, have to be removed and spread around. Camouflage includes the dispersal of fortifications, positions, facilities and vehicles in irregular patterns. It is also a matter of art and theatrical bluff. Bunkers and other military buildings can be painted in *trompe-l'oeil*. This subtle art technique utilizes realistic imagery to create the optical illusion that depicted objects exist in three dimensions. Military buildings might thus resemble civilian houses, disguised by brick exterior walls with fake windows, a tiled roof and sometimes even a landscaped garden, and thus appear from a distance to be peaceful houses or villas, harmless country barns or commonplace civilian buildings.

In addition to visual illusion, deception can also be a measure. Dummy positions, phony bunkers, false airfields with mock-up airplanes, fake supply-stores, mock-up vehicles and fake tracks, fictitious batteries with wooden guns and knee-deep dummy

Camouflaged pillboxes. Top: *Trompe-l'oeil* pile of logs. Bottom: Phoney barn.

trenches can all be installed as decoys. Also part of camouflage is the use of artificial fog. Smoke devices are set up and, in case of attack, the position or the target disappear behind a cloud of synthetic chemical fog.

Camouflet: A subterranean explosive charge used as a countermeasure against tunnelling and mining (q.v.). The camouflet wrecked the enemy's mine, released deadly carbon monoxide gas that poisoned enemy miners and buried them under debris.

Camp retranché:
1) In the eighteenth century, a *camp retranché* (French for entrenched camp) included the addition of exterior lines of field works or semi-permanent fortifications. Redoubts, earth walls flanked by bastions and redans and preceeded by ditches were appended around an existing fortress. These extensions were intended to accommodate whole armies in addition to the fortress garrisons and increase the perimeter of a defensive zone, thereby obliging the besiegers to multiply the approach works. Having numerous troops available enabled the besieged to make sallies and counter-offensives.
2) In the nineteenth century, the term could also designate a city surrounded by a girdle of forts (e.g. Antwerp, Verdun).
3) In the twentieth century, a *camp retranché* consisted of earthworks constructed to fortify a position or place, for instance a *base aéroterrestre* (q.v.). A French *camp retranché* (such as Dien Bien Phu) was divided into several *centres de résistance* (CR, resistance centres), which in turn included several *points d'appui* (PA, support points).

Canadian pipe mine: Later known as the McNaughton Tube after General Andrew McNaughton, this was a prepared demolition device designed in 1940 when Britain was threatened by a German invasion. It was a horizontally bored pipe packed with explosives, and once in place it could be used to instantly ruin a road or destroy a bridge or runway.

Canonnière: French for embrasure (q.v.) in transitional fortification (q.v.) in the late fifteenth century. It was used to fire an arquebus or a small gun. The term also designates a riverine gunboat in the nineteenth century.

Cap-house: A small chamber at the top of a spiral staircase in a tower or turret, leading to the open wall-walk or terraced platform on the roof.

Capital line: The main line of a fortifed work, the imaginary line bisecting the salient angle of a bastion or *demi-lune*, for example.

Caponier:
1) In a transitional fortification (q.v.), the caponier, also called a *moineau* (q.v.), was a small low-profiled flanking work installed across a dry moat. It projected at the foot of a wall or a tower and was concealed by the counterscarp. The caponier usually included only one storey with closed, vaulted casemates (q.v.) fitted with small firing-holes, through which musketry fire could be directed against any enemy advancing in the ditch. The work might continue across the moat up to the counterscarp to form a covered passage. The *moineau* was used in the second half of the fifteenth century (at Bonaguil, Blaye, Toulon, Bayonne and Rhodes, for example).
2) In a bastioned fortification, the caponier was a protected passage made of two parapets installed across the ditch of a fortified place designed to shelter communication with the outer-works – usually a *demi-lune* (q.v.) – which at the same time could also be used as defensive position for flanking the ditch.
3) In a nineteenth century polygonal fortification, the caponier became a large casemated structure projecting from the main body of a place into a ditch in order

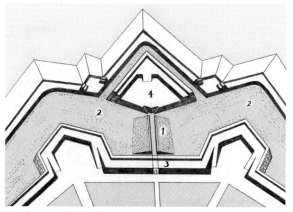

In a bastioned fortification, a caponier was a protected passage (1) across the ditch (2) between a main curtain (3) and a *demi-lune* (4).

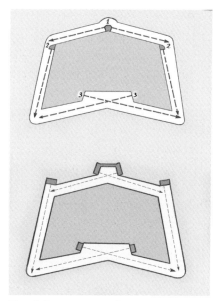

to provide flanking fire. While fortifications were evolving to the simpler polygonal style in the second half of the nineteenth century, the caponier took the form of a low casemate set in the shoulders and front of a fort, providing close-range defence of the ditch. It was often partly sunk into the floor of the ditch, projecting outward into the ditch, with

Top: Schematic view of caponiers in a nineteenth-century polygonal fort. 1: Double front caponier; 2: Single shoulder caponier; 3: Casemate defending the gorge. Bottom: Caponiers were replaced with coffers placed under the counterscarp after 1885.

access from the main fortress via a passage through the curtain wall, or as fortresses became largely underground, via a tunnel from within the fort. The front caponier, which often had the appearance of a small bastion with *orillons*, was called a double

Cross-section showing double caponier in front of Fort Rijnauwen, the Netherlands.

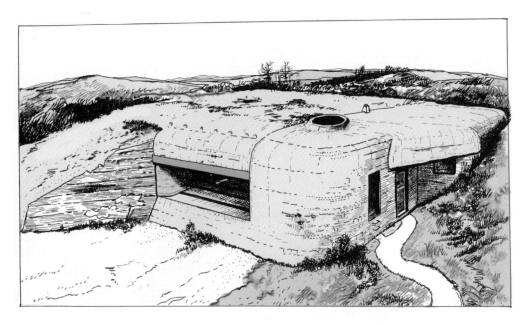

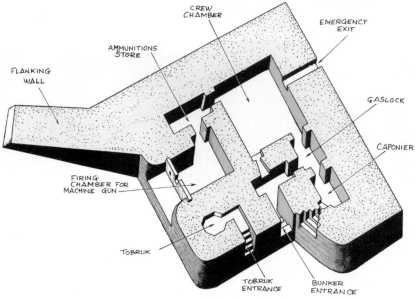

Second World War German flanking machine-gun casemate type 630 with caponier (*Nähkampfraum*, close combat room) defending the access and entrance at the rear of the bunker.

caponier as it flanked both sides of the front ditch. Two simple caponiers, each flanking only one side of the fort's ditch, were placed on the shoulder of the fort. Often a fourth simple caponier was placed in the middle of the gorge to flank the rear ditch and the entrance of the fort. Caponiers were replaced after 1885 with coffers (q.v.) placed in the corners of the counterscarp, giving a similar field of fire but being better protected, and communicating with the fort by means of a tunnel under the ditch.

4) In a twentieth century fortification, a caponier was a small premise jutting out of the rear façade or frontage of a bunker, allowing the occupants to deliver fire on enemies approaching doors and ventilation pipes. Called in German a *Nähkampfraum* (close combat room), it was pierced by a small porthole arranged as a kind of staircase in order to protect against ricochetting splinters and projectiles. Its lateral angle of fire varied from 40–60 degrees. It was closed by a sliding metal shutter.

Cardo: In a Roman town (or camp), the main north–south axis, also known as *Via Superior* (main upperstreet).

Carnot wall: Devised by the Frenchman Lazare Nicolas Carnot (1753–1823), who had been Napoleon's Secretary of War, this was a freestanding stone wall running parallel with the scarp (q.v.). Constructed in the dry ditch surrounding a fort, it was provided with loopholes and niches, which sheltered infantrymen who would defend the ditch in the event of an enemy assault. Although adopted by the British and Germans and used in early nineteenth-century forts, this arrangement proved in due course to be vulnerable, and much less efficient for flanking than the caponier (q.v.) and the counterscarp gallery (q.v.). See Detached scarp.

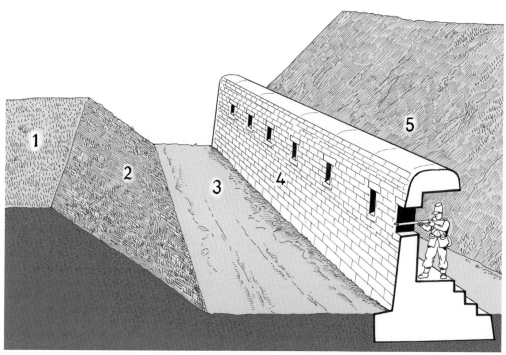

Carnot Wall. 1: Glacis; 2: Non-revetted counterscarp; 3: Ditch; 4: Carnot's Wall; 5: Non-revetted detached scarp.

Casa-torre: Medieval Italian fortified house with a tower.

Casbah:

1) The casbah (or kasbah), meaning citadel (q.v.) in Arabic, is specifically the traditional quarter clustered around a fortified core, the walled citadel of many North African cities and towns. Often the oldest part of the city, the casbah generally appears as a quaint neighbourhood displaying a confusing labyrinth of lanes, small and narrow streets and dead-end alleys flanked by picturesque houses, craftmen's shops and small walled gardens. See Medina.
2) A North African house or palace more or less fortified, built in adobe, serving as a residence to a local person of high status.

Casemate:

1) Vaulted gun chamber usually set within a fort wall or within a rampart. The gun was fired through a protected opening in the wall called a gunport or embrasure (q.v.). Casemates provided good protection for weapons and gunners and allowed a fort's guns to be arranged in multiple levels, but due to the thickness of its wall, the field of fire was considerably reduced and observation extremely limited. The ventilation of a casemate was also a difficult problem to solve, at least until the nineteenth century when efficient mechanical devices were created for the provision of fresh air. In spite of vents, shafts, vertical chimneys and other air channels intended to evacuate smoke, after a few shots the chamber was usually full of choking fumes, making it very difficult for gunners to operate. In peacetime, the casemate was generally an obscure, humid, draughty, malodorous and unhealthy place.

Casemate. Cross-section.

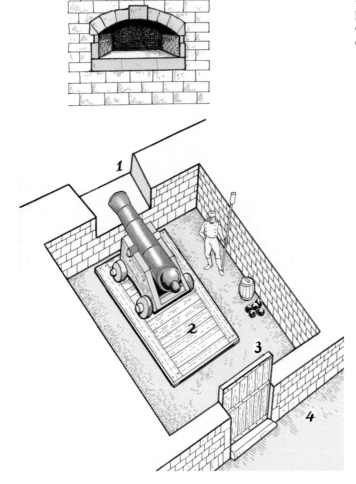

Plan with: 1: Embrasure; 2: Gun platform; 3: Door; 4: Gallery of communication. Top: Front view of embrasure.

2) In modern fortification, a casemate is a synonym for a concrete armed bunker (q.v.), pillbox (q.v.), any concrete shelter or position with weapons embrasures in its walls and designed for independent operations, or for an artillery position under concrete.

Casemate de Bourges: Flanking casemate (q.v.) characterized by a lateral concrete shield protecting the embrasure. The name originated from the French military range at Bourges (Berry, France), where this type of flanking emplacement was experimented with and designed in 1895 by the French engineer-commandant Laurent. This manner of positioning weapons was applied to late nineteenth-century polygonal forts, the German *Festen* (q.v.) constructed before the First World War, the French Maginot Line (q.v.) and the Atlantic Wall (q.v.). See *Traditore* battery.

Casemate type G: A small Dutch machine-gun pillbox designed and built in the late 1930s. It consisted of an armoured steel core inserted inside a concrete base.

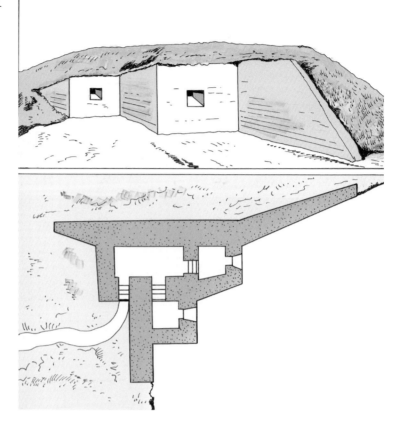

Casemate de Bourges.
Top: Front view.
Bottom: Plan.

Casemate type G (1): Front view.

Casemate type G (2): Cross-section.

Casemated tower: A large multi-storey tower with many firing chambers. See Artillery tower.

Casement: Bomb-proof vaulted accommodation for sheltering troops, supplies or weapons.

Case-pit: In modern artillery bunkers, cases (cylindrical containers filled with propelling charges) stayed in the firing-chamber after shooting. They were hot, smoking, bad smelling and cumbersome, and were therefore automatically ejected into a special concrete case-pit. This was generally 2m deep and placed either outside the bunker, under the embrasure or under the firing-chamber.

Castellum: A Roman temporary camp or a permanent fort, the work of an efficient, highly organized professional army, which built defensive

Casemated tower.

works to a standard pattern wherever they were. A *castellum*, generally rectangular with rounded corners, consisted of a *vallum* (q.v.) with earth wall, palisade and ditch, and wooden turrets. Each of the four main entrances was defended by a *clavicula* (q.v.). A *castellum* enclosed a large space occupied by tents for the troops, possibly barracks when the camp was intended for permanent use, and quarters for officers. In addition there were service buildings and supply stores required by a military community that could total 6,000 men, and much more when several legions were gathered for a campaign.

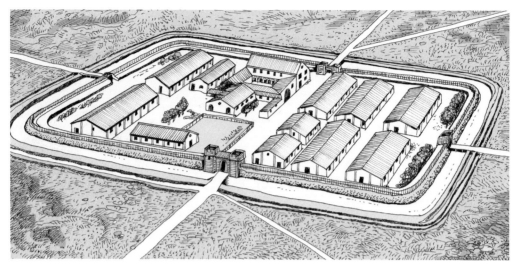

Castellum.

Castelnaux: *Castelnaux* (also called new-castle, *neufchastel*, *châteauneuf* or *castet*) were newly created fortified villages in the vicinity of a previously existing castle. The development of a *castelnau* was generally caused by demographic growth. It was either spontanous or encouraged by the local lord, who granted attractive economical, fiscal and juridical advantages to settlers coming to live and work on his feudal estate. Created between AD 1000 and 1300, they were particularly numerous in medieval southern France. See Bastide and *Sauvetés*.

Castillo: Castle in Spanish, but the term could also designate any type of fort.

Castle: A castle – from the Latin *castellum* (q.v.) – is a defensive structure seen as one of the main symbols of the Middle Ages. The term has a history of scholarly debate surrounding its exact meaning, but it is generally regarded as being distinct from a fort, fortress, fortified place and palace.

A medieval castle was many things at the same time: a fortified residence owned and built by a local feudal lord; a symbol and display of feudal authority and an expresion of the lord's power and prestige; a place of social and cultural life; an administrative and economic centre commanding a specific territory (fief) within a social organization (feudalism) – a successful castle must have two-way relations with its territory; a place of military defence; a base from which operations in enemy territory were launched; and a place of refuge in times of crisis. When the castle became no more than a refuge, this meant that its lord had lost control of the surrounding territory and was probably about to be deposed. However some castles had a wholly or primarily military purpose rather than a residential function. In this case, the term 'fort' may be applied. For example, forts were built to control a mountain pass or dominate rivers, to collect tolls and taxes or to prevent enemies from travelling up a river.

The accepted definition of a medieval castle amongst academics is 'a private fortified residence combining military, residential, administrative and economic functions'. Nevertheless, the word 'castle' is sometimes used to mean a hillfort (q.v.), a citadel (q.v.)

or a detached fort (q.v.) in modern times. The earliest-recorded structures universally acknowledged by historians as 'castles' were motte-and-bailey castles (q.v.) built in the late ninth and tenth centuries. Wood and earth structures were gradually replaced with stone towers and *donjons* in the tenth and eleventh centuries. Castles grew in size, surface, capacity and complexity throughout the Middle Ages, until the introduction of firearms in the fifteenth century limited their effectiveness, rendered them militarily useless in the sixteenth century and led to the rise of bastioned cities and military forts.

However, medieval castles and fortified towns remained significant strategic points in the wars of early modern Europe. From the Renaissance onward, the loosening of military importance allowed for a more aesthetic and comfortable approach to design and construction. Castles were thereafter opened up and expanded into prestigious pleasure dwellings. Their 'castle' designations, relics of the feudal age, often remained attached to the dwelling, resulting in many non-military castles, residential palaces and châteaux. From the late eighteenth century to the early twentieth century, as a manifestation of a romantic interest in the medieval period and as part of the broader Gothic revival in architecture, many so-called 'castles' were built. These castles had no defensive purpose at all, but incorporated high, vertical and stylistic elements of earlier periods, such as crenellation, battlements, arrow slits, machicoulis, keeps, gatehouses, pinnacles, spires, turrets and towers purely as ornament.

Castrametation: Derived from the Latin *castrum* (q.v.) and *metari* (to lay out), castrametation is thus the art of setting out, making or laying out a military camp, and of placing the troops so that the different arms of the service can support each other in the best manner. There are three main operational requirements governing a military camp.

First, it must be secure (protected by outposts, guards, patrols and entrenchments). Second, it has to be so sited that the troops can easily and quickly be marshalled for battle, and it must be close to a line of communication for logistical considerations. And third, it has to be positioned to guarantee maximum freedom of action for its defenders while restricting the options of the enemy.

Castro: In Galicia, Asturias, Cantabria and northern Portugal, a *castro* was a fortified pre-Roman Iron Age Celtic village, usually located on a hill or some naturally easy defensible place. See Hillfort and Oppidum.

Castrum: The Latin *castrum* (plural *castra*) designates a Roman military defensive position. *Castra* varied from simple temporary camps made of earthwork thrown up by armies on the move, known as a *castellum* (q.v.), to elaborate permanent forts and fortified town with defences made of stone. A *castra aestiva* was a summer campaigning camp, while a *castra hiberna* was a winter base. The Castra Praetoria was the fortified barracks of the Praetorian Guard at Rome, established in AD 23 by the emperor Tiberius.

Castrum Arenanum: The barbarian invasions in the fifth century AD marked a significant decrease of urban life in Western Europe. Roman towns were reduced to a small nucleus which could be better defended. New walls were hastily raised by using

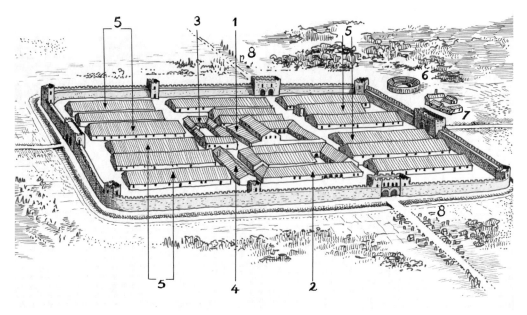

Castrum.
1: *Principia*, administrative headquarters; 2: *Praetorium*, commander's residence; 3: *Valetudiranium*, hospital; 4: *Horrea*, supply store; 5: Barracks; 6: Amphitheatre; 7: Bathhouse; 8: Cemetery.

Castrum arenarum.

stones and construction materials from buildings of abandoned neighbourhoods. In certain cities of southern Europe (Arles, Nîmes or Rome, for example), the huge oval amphitheatre or arena intended originally for circus entertainment was transformed into an urban fort or castle called a *castrum arenarum*.

Cathar castles: Strongholds built before, during and after the crusade against the Cathars or Albigensians in Languedoc (south-eastern France) in the thirteenth century. Cathar castles were generally built on top of 'pogs' (craggy pinnacles of rock or steep rocky ridges) in the vertiginous and rugged spurs of the Pyrenees. Examples of Cathar castles are Roquefixade, Montségur, Puivert, Puilaurens, Peyrepertuse, Quéribus and Lastours.

Cat's ears: A rather infrequent defensive element composed of two small projecting half-circular or angled casemates forming a caponier (q.v.). It was occasionally used in the 1860s, for example at the Kleparz III fort at Krakow or in the front caponier at Fort Pannerden in the Netherlands.

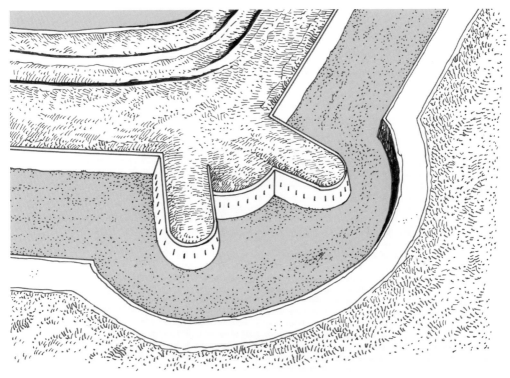

Cat's ear, Kleparz III fort, Cracow, Poland.

Cavalier: An armed defensive interior work raised on the *terre-plein* (q.v.) of a bastion (q.v.) and of similar tracé to the bastion. The cavalier could also be raised in the middle of a curtain (q.v.). In both cases, the purpose was to add firepower and increase height to the weapons so as to command the surrounding ground. The height of the cavalier could also act as a traverse (q.v.) to protect from enemy enfilading fire.

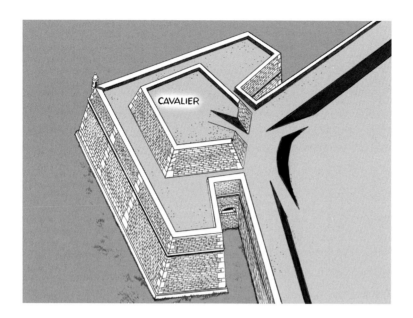

Cavalier de tranchée: Advocated by the French engineer Vauban, this was a temporary raised structure used in seventeenth and eighteenth-century siege warfare. Made of three or four tiers of gabions (q.v.), the trench cavalier's purpose was to dominate and neutralize the enemies defending the covered way (q.v.) and the places of arms (q.v.).

Cavalier fort: In French fortifications built in the late nineteenth century (particularly in the late 1870s), a cavalier fort (*fort à massif central*) was a stronghold with a large,

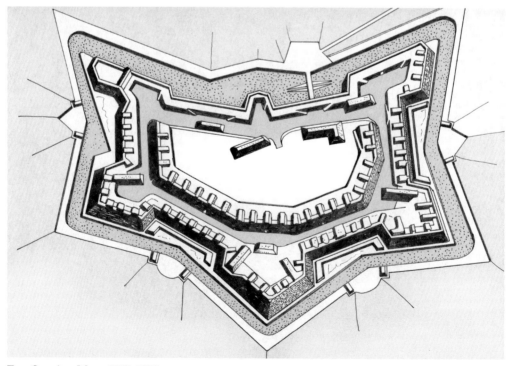

Fort Queuleu, Metz, 1867–1870.

central, dominating, raised structure named a cavalier (q.v.), on top of which artillery was deployed.

Cave: Natural caves, underground chambers and tunnels have been used as refuges and defensive positions by prehistoric men, French peasants during the Hundred Years War, Italian peasants in the wars of the early sixteenth century, during the Vietnam wars (1946–1975) and by Afghan rebels at the end of the twentieth century. Natural caves could be turned into formidable underground complexes that were extremely difficult to overrun. They could be enlarged and improved by the establishment of man-made underground passages, reinforced rooms, secret doorways and disguised entrances, peepholes, booby-trapped twists and turns, dead-end tunnels, concealed weapons caches and escape routes. Any enemy venturing into such a narrow refuge could easily be picked off by the defenders. Attackers would therefore usually remain outside and try to smoke or gas the occupiers out. If there was no secondary exit or air holes, or any form of ventilation, such a cave refuge could quickly become a death trap. See Shelter.

Cervi: A sort of abatis (q.v.) used by the Romans. Sharpened tree branches were often set up on top of the inner side of a ditch in field fortifications. See *Vallum*.

Chain: Chains were used in medieval towns at night to guard or fence the ends of streets and to block the entrance of harbours and the passages of rivers. The mechanism housing the chain and allowing it to be raised and lowered was housed in a defensive tower, often a small fortress in its own right. Chain towers were built at Dartmouth (Devon), East Cowes (Isle of Wight, Hampshire) and Kingston-upon-Hull (Humberside). Such towers can still be seen at the entrance of the harbour of La Rochelle in France.

Chandelier: A wooden frame filled with fascines (q.v.) acting as a traverse (q.v.) or a mantlet (q.v.) in order to protect besiegers during digging or sapping operations.

Château-fort: French medieval castle (q.v.), literally meaning 'strong castle', a generic term for a medieval fortified castle. The stone keep of Langeais, built in AD 994 by the count of Anjou Foulque Nerra (Fulk the Black, who ruled over the lush and fertile valley of the Loire, south-west of Paris), is generally regarded as the first French *château-fort*.

Châtelet: A defensive exterior work (meaning 'small castle' in French) placed in front of a gate or on a bridge. It could also designate a gatehouse (q.v.). In Paris, the Petit Châtelet and Grand Châtelet were imposing castle-like structures defending access to the Île de la Cité. See Bastille, Bartizan, Coverport, Gatehouse and Tambour.

Checkpoint: A small defensive position or post manned by a few soldiers who have a control, observation or surveillance mission. The most famous was Checkpoint Charlie (or Checkpoint C), a Cold War crossing passage in the Berlin Wall (q.v.) between East Berlin and West Berlin located at the junction of Friedrichstraße with Zimmerstraße and Mauerstraße.

Chemin couvert: See Covered way.

Chemin de ronde: The *chemin de ronde* (literally 'round path' or 'patrol path' in French) was a walkway placed on top of a wall protected by a battlement or parapet (q.v.). The *chemin de ronde* was devised as a continuous communication allowing defenders to patrol the top of a rampart or wall. It was also an observation post and a combat emplacement, placing the defender in an advantageous position for shooting or dropping projectiles down on assailants. It was very often an intregral part of the top of the curtain, but could also be a wooden structure resting on horizontal wooden beams secured into the wall by means of putlogs and vertical poles. It could also be covered with a roof that protected guards and soldiers against the elements and small-calibre enemy projectiles. See Wall-walk. The term is also used to designate the path along the berm (q.v.) or *fausse-braie* (q.v.).

Chemise: In medieval castles, the *chemise* (French, meaning 'shirt') was typically a low exterior wall hemming the keep or protecting the base of the main tower. An alternate term, more commonly used in English, is mantle wall. Eventually enlarged, flanked by wall towers and its access defended by a gatehouse, it could become an enceinte (q.v.) or enclosing wall.

Cheval de frise: The *cheval de frise* (plural *chevaux de frise*, literally meaning 'Frisian horse') was an obstacle consisting of a portable frame (sometimes just a simple log) covered with many long iron or wooden spikes or spears. The *cheval de frise* was principally intended as an anti-personnel and anti-cavalry obstacle, as it could be moved quickly to help fill a breach or block a road. The *cheval de frise* is still in use in modern times (often wrapped with barbed wire), but it is generally ineffective as an anti-tank obstacle. See Frizzy horse.

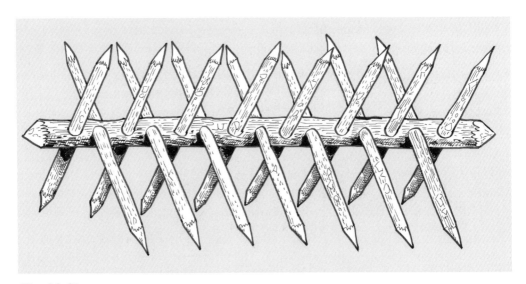

Cheval de frise.

Chèvre: French for 'goat', this term was used in the seventeenth and eighteenth centuries to designate an engineer officer, a group of labourers and a wagon full of spades and pickaxes scouting ahead of a major French force. This party would assess the state of the roads and undertake repairs with rounded-up local peasants as necessary.

Chicane: A defensive structure, which denies direct access. Often a sharp double-bend narrow passage built around the head of a traverse (q.v.) in order to let through friendly troops. Sometimes they were two or more walls covering an entrance or inside a gallery to form a maze. A chicane was a standard method for blocking roads.

Church: In the European Christian world, each castle or fort included a chapel or church. The castle chapel or garrison church was the focus for spiritual life, and soldiers were supposed to attend religious services, observe Christian morality and behave well. The garrison church was often solidly built in a sober style, and the top of the bell tower provided an excellent lookout post. See Fortified church.

Cippe: Roman obstacle formed of sharp poles or sharpened tree branches often placed in a ditch. See *Cervi*.

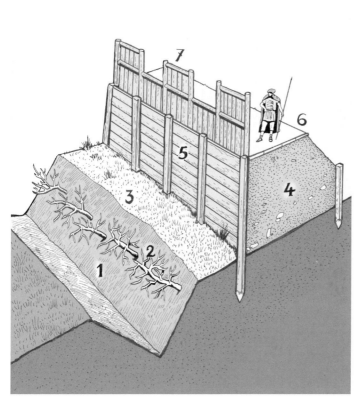

Cippe.
The depicted cross-section of a Roman earth and timber rampart displays the following: 1: *Fossa stigata* (V-shaped ditch); 2: *Cippe*; 3: Berm; 4: *Vallum* (earth rampart); 5: Timber revetment; 6: Wall-walk; and 7: *Lorica* (breastwork in the form of a crenellated wooden palisade).

Circumvallation line: A continuous outer entrenchment dug by besiegers around a besieged place in order to invest it and isolate it from relief. While the countervallation faced the target, the circumvallation was turned in the opposite direction to face any relief force that could come to rescue the besieged. See Investment, Blockade, Countervallation and Part 2 (Siege Warfare).

Citadel: From the sixteenth to the eighteenth centuries, a citadel was a very particular kind of detached work. Like a detached fort, a citadel had a purely military function,

105

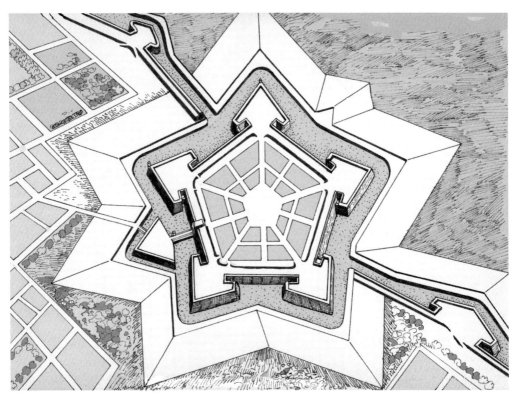
Citadel of Antwerp.

but it was a fortress built within a fortified city. The citadel was placed on a dominating position inside the town or mostly overlapping the urban fortifications, which allowed its access to be independent from city-gates. The citadel was accessible by a main gate turned toward the city and a secondary access leading directly to the countryside. In certain cases, the citadel was an old medieval urban castle which had been modernized or a former work adapted to modern warfare. If the work was entirely new, a geometrical bastioned form was chosen, often a regular pentagon, which fulfilled military demands, reduced dead angles and offered a practical and efficient internal organization. Between the city and the citadel, a wide and bare glacis was established; this space, called the esplanade (q.v.), allowed a wide open field of fire and could be used as a military training ground. The citadel, esplanade and new fortified enceinte (q.v.) cost a lot of money and sometimes required the destruction of individual houses or even larger urban areas. The citadel fulfilled three distinctive roles.

The first function was logistical, as the citadel contained everything needed in order to resist a long siege, such as barracks, food, water and foraging stores, arsenal, powder-house, workshops and so on. It was also a supply point for armies on campaign, provided winter quarters and a military administrative centre.

Secondly, the citadel was a powerful military bulwark. Just like the keep in the medieval castle, it acted as a final fall-back position, a reduit (q.v.), from which to continue the defence even when the town was conquered. Therefore the work was always constructed on a high position in order to both command and protect the city.

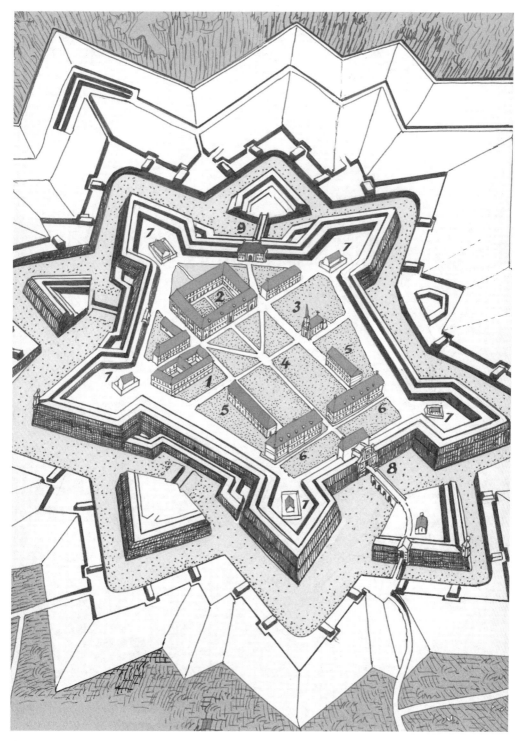

Citadel. 1: Governor's hotel; 2: arsenal; 3: chapel; 4: central place of arms; 5: officers' house; 6: soldiers' barracks; 7: powder-house; 8: main gatehouse; 9: secondary postern.

It was strongly fortified with powerful bastions, ditches with numerous outworks and a covered way. This display of strength was also meant to deter enemies from laying siege and to impress the local population.

The third and often most important role was political. A citadel was intended to subjugate, control and overawe recently conquered populations with questionable loyalty or rebellious propensity. Some of the weapons were directed towards the esplanade and the city to repress insurrections. Its garrison might sally forth to subdue malcontents, dissidents and opposers at any time, and could also discourage by force the inhabitants from surrendering at a premature stage in a siege. The construction of an expensive citadel was often financed by the occupying garrison's pay and by citizens' money. For all these reasons, the citadel represented a threat: it was an unpopular and hated place, an object of terror and dictatorship as well as a financial burden. As soon as relationships between the occupiers and the conquered population improved, urban authorities asked for its dismantlement or at least for the military to take over its financing.

In the nineteenth century, citadels lost a part of their military role because of the creation of outer rings of detached forts. Citadels remained military administrative centres and many were transformed into prisons. See Acropolis, Arx, Fort, Keep and *Réduit*.

City: The City is the oldest part of a town. The City of London, for example, is a small area within Greater London, the historic core of Britain's capital. So is the Île de la Cité in Paris. In German it is called the *Altstadt* ('old city').

City wall: The ancient and medieval urban enceinte (q.v.) served several purposes. First of all it had a defensive military function. It was also an object of pride and prestige, a sign of independence, a source of confidence and self-awareness for the burghers. It contributed to the establishment of peace and security and thus to the development of a safe and fruitful business. The wall was certainly a stimulant to economic growth. The enceinte also constituted a juridical border, defining the urban space – distinct from the surrounding countryside – and indicated the space to be populated. The city wall was very expensive to build, but in the long term it constituted an investment: it allowed the control of entry and exit and facilitated the collection of import and export taxes. In certain cases, it also worked as a dike against the dangerous flooding of a nearby river.

In time of war, the walls and towers were manned by a few professional hired soldiers and by the watch, a municipal militia drawn from traders and craftsmen. The militia was organized in companies, and each unit, headed by a captain, was alloted to man a part of the defences. The watch was also used as a police force, patrolling the city at night during the curfew from dusk to dawn.

The evolution of urban military architecture was directly connected to castle fortification, and most elements used to protect castles were applied in the protection of towns – including ditches, walls, towers, gatehouses and barbicans. Until the introduction of reliable firearms in the Renaissance, the concept of defence focused on two major ideas in order to counteract the main means of attack. Verticality was the key to oppose assault by ladder and allowed the defenders to benefit from manning a high position. Sturdiness and thickness of walls permitted resistance to battering rams and underground mining. The only difference was that a private castle housed a tiny group of combatants and their servants in a small space, while a town embraced a large number of non-combatant inhabitants whose lives and activities were not connected to the military, and who were spread over a relatively large area. The configuration of a fortified town was the result of difficult compromises between the requirements of defence – which demanded inaccessibility – and living, working and business conditions, which tended on the contrary to establish the city near a commercial road, to develop the area and to provide many easy access points.

Civitas: The Latin word *civitas* (plural *civitates*) was the social body of Roman citizens. By extension it meant city, and in the European conquered provinces, the term could cover the land around a hillfort, or an oppidum or a village controlled by a Celtic or Gallic tribe.

Clamping: Clamping or ties involved the vertical or horizontal superimposing of heavy and strong stones, which formed pillars or bands holding the masonry together and increasing the stability of the walls. They were commonly built to reinforce the most vulnerable parts of masonry at the angles of a bastion (salient and shoulders) or a tower.

Clamping. Left: Vertical; Right: Horizontal.

Clavicula: A *clavicula* (plural *claviculae*) was an exterior defensive work raised outside the gates of a Roman camp. Made of earth (possibly with a palisade on top), it often had a semi-circular shape, which obliged those who endeavoured to enter the camp to present their flank to the defenders on the *agger* (q.v.).

Clay kicking: A method for digging mine tunnels designed by the British engineering contractor John Norton Griffiths during the First World War. With this method, the digger did not use a pickaxe but sat on a narrow seat secured to a long wooden plank that was lodged at an angle at the end of an underground gallery. A short timber attachment supported the back, giving the plank a cross-like appearance. Consequently, the method was also known as 'working on the cross'. The 'clay kicker' kept both feet on a modified spade (fitted with projections for both feet), which the digger used to cut out the subsoil face in front of him. The spoil was gathered by his mates and passed back along the gallery. This method of mining was swift and quite silent – an important asset in First World War underground warfare. In good conditions in soft ground, this method could progress by some 4m or more a day. See Mining.

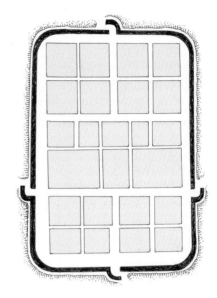

Clavicula.

Cliff castle: A fortified usually coastal settlement situated on a spit of high ground and protected on three sides by sheer cliffs, leaving only one line of approach which, of course, was strongly defended by a rampart and ditch across the narrowest neck of the peninsula. Also known as a promontory fort. Some can also be found further inland on heights above rivers. They were easily constructed and could be defended by only a small force. However, they had one major flaw: if an enemy did manage to break in, it was difficult and sometimes impossible to escape.

Cloche: The cloche (literally 'bell' in French) was a small cast steel observation dome-shaped cupola. It was most often fixed (non-moveable) and built on late nineteenth-century forts and on top of First World War bunkers to provide observation or close-range defence. In the latter case, the cloche was armed with a light machine gun. See Beobachtungsglocke, Cupola, Maginot Line, Cloche Guet-Fusil-Mitrailleur and Periscope.

Cloche Guet-Fusil-Mitrailleur (Cloche GFM): A small armoured cloche (q.v.) – a cupola for observation and active defence armed with a light machine gun. See Maginot Line.

Cloche Pamart: Designed in 1917 during the First World War by the French Commandant Léon Pamart, these armoured machine-gun casemates were built to enhance the firepower of several forts and strengthen their defence. The partly subterranean armoured work included a metal cupola with one or two portholes (q.v.)

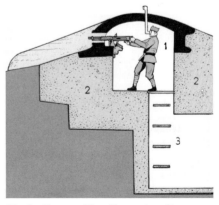

Cloche Pamart. Top: Front view. Bottom: Cross-section. 1: Armoured cupola; 2: Concrete; 3: Access gallery.

protected by concrete screens. The metal casemate was placed into a mass of concrete and accessed via an underground gallery and a vertical pit fitted with rungs. It was armed with one or two machine guns, usually with an arc of fire of 160 degrees, and was fitted with a periscope for observation. A ventilation system ejected toxic gases, ensuring that the air remained breathable inside the casemate. While the Pamart casemate was fixed, it proved more reliable than the eclipsible turret (q.v.), which occasionally could get jammed by rubble when heavily bombarded. Examples of Pamart cloche can still be seen at Fort Souville near Verdun.

Coastal battery: A special type of gun emplacement or anti-shipping naval interdiction fortification used in coastal defence to protect areas such as beaches where a landing could occur, anchorages, harbours and river mouths. Coastal batteries (and forts) were used in restricted waters such as straits or channels, or coastal inland waterways, with the tactical purpose of denying an area to the enemy.

Coastal fort: A fort (q.v.) constructed to defend sensitive naval spots like an island, sea strait, anchorage, entrance to a harbour, navy arsenal or base, or to defend a beach where a landing could occur. Until the end of the nineteenth century, landing techniques and large-scale amphibious operations were at a very elementary stage. The scale of attack to be expected from the sea was usually much smaller than that on a land front. In the seventeenth and eighteenth centuries, a sea fort was usually composed of a low,

A Second World War German *MKB* (*Marine Kust Batterie*, Navy Coastal Battery) in the Atlantic Wall included the following elements: 1: Fire leading post; 2: Bunkers armed with long-range cannons; 3: Ammunition stores; 4: Gunners' shelters; 5: Service and logistical buildings; 6: Barbed wire fence; 7: Mines and beach obstacles; 8: Anti-tank ditch; 9: Trenches and flanking pillboxes.

The Camaret coastal battery, aka Tour Dorée ('Golden Tower') because of the colour of its shining bricks, was built in 1689. It was intended to defend Crozon Point near the harbour of Brest in Brittany, France.

masonry, semi-circular gun-battery with a thick breastwork pierced with embrasures for grazing fire. In those times, one cannon on land (provided it was protected in a fortified emplacement) was estimated to be five to ten times more valuable than one gun embarked on an unsteady ship. A tower was often built in the gorge of the battery. The

Fort Lupin, completed in 1683, was intended to protect access to the military port of Rochefort in south-west France.

various floors were arranged as powder-magazine, food and water storage, lodgement for the garrison and equipped with loopholes for close-range defence. The top of the tower was covered with a roof or arranged as a terrace used as an observation post, armed emplacement and possibly as a lighthouse. On the land front, the fort was often surrounded by a wet ditch, covered way and glacis.

Coastal fortification: Initially, the concept of coastal fortification did not diverge greatly from land fortification. It was only a sub-branch of permanent fortification, which was intended to prevent, resist and repulse enemy landing and protect military harbours and naval installations from attacks from the sea. A coastal fortress was treated as a land stronghold, with bastioned defences (sixteenth to eighteenth centuries) and polygonal forts (nineteenth century). The introduction of heavy ordnance in land-based batteries in the last decades of the nineteenth century, however, induced new elements in coastal fortification, notably the tendency to place heavy batteries in-line along the coasts, firing control posts coupled with long range observatories and target illumination devices (searchlights). In the twentieth century, coastal defences also included aerial reconnaissance, concrete bunkers housing optical range-finder and radar installations and protection against air attack with anti-aircraft guns.

Coffer: After 1885, owing to temendous advances in artillery and explosive shells, the flanking caponier (q.v.) appeared very vulnerable. It was therefore replaced with a flanking casemate called a coffer, placed no longer on the scarp of the fort but on the counterscarp. The coffer was linked to the main body of the fort by an underground passage under the ditch. The coffer, like the caponier, was said to be 'simple' when it flanked only one stretch of the ditch and 'double' when flanking two branches of the ditch. See Caponier, Flanking and Ditch.

Coles Turret: An armoured turret designed by the British Captain Coles (1819–1870) of the Royal Navy. In 1859, Coles filed a patent for a naval revolving turret, allowing good protection to crew, gun and ammunition and enabling a wide arc of fire. The British Admiralty accepted the principle of the turret gun as a useful innovation and incorporated it into other new designs, notably on HMS *Prince Albert*. Coles' turret was a major contribution to naval armament, armoured ship design and fortress armoured artillery.

Command: A fundamental principle of fortification by which the vertical elevation of one work over another, or above the surrounding country, enables it to overlook and dominate an area by virtue of its height. Any work raised higher than another is said to command it. For example, in seventeenth and eighteenth-century bastioned fortifications, the covered way (q.v.), half-moon (q.v.) and ditch (q.v.) were always lower than the scarp in order to be commanded by the main wall.

Command post: A place where an officer and his staff can exercise authority and direction over a force for the accomplishment of a mission or task. This place can be any fortified position or secured building. It can also be a bunker including study-rooms, map-rooms and communication means, as well as various accommodation for crews.

Commandery: A rural settlement, fortified farm or hamlet, estate or small fortified village or manor belonging to an order of religious knights, such as for example the Knights Templar. The commandery was headed by a commander, and the agricultural goods generated by the estate served to finance the religious military order's campaigns. It was also a place where young trainees and novices were housed, and a home for old, disabled, sick or crippled veterans.

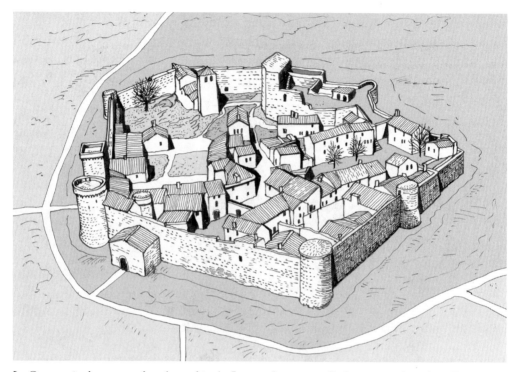

La Couvertoirade commandery, located in the Larzac plateau near Caylar in central southern France, was first a Templar establishment in the twelfth century. After the dissolution of the Templars, the hamlet became a Knights Hospitaller fortified possession.

Commission d'Organisation des Régions Fortifiées (CORF): This commission was created in the late 1920s to set up the fortified areas and prepare the plans and designs of the Maginot Line (q.v.).

Communication trench: See Boyau and Sap.

Compound: A secure open area enclosed by a fence inside a factory, prison or camp.

Concave flank: A flank (q.v.) in a bastion (q.v.) having an inward curving shape.

Concentric castle: A concentric castle (or multiple castle or double *castrum*) was a castle with two circuit walls. The external wall, called a forewall, antemurabilus or the lists (q.v.), created an additional obstacle and worked as a delaying line of defence. Indeed, should the enemy capture the outer defences, they would face another line of defence, which constituted the principle of defence in depth (q.v.). The lists embodied the whole

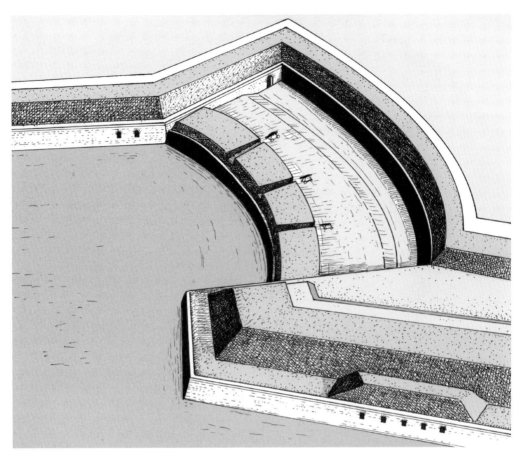

Concave flank, Naarden, the Netherlands.

castle or included only a particularly exposed or weak façade. In some mountainous sites, the lists often formed a succession of fortified points spreading out on the steep access road. In other cases, the walled area was further enlarged so that it came to enclose two or more yards, each defended by a wall. The lists were frequently a stone wall similar to the main enclosure, but flanking wall towers were often open in the gorge. If the external defences were conquered, the attackers became vulnerable to projectiles hurled by the defenders deployed on the main enceinte. According to the principle of command (q.v.), the external wall and towers were lower than the main enclosure, so defenders on the higher walls could fire arrows at the enemy over the lower outer defences. Communication between the main and external enceintes was carried out by means of posterns (q.v.). The space between the main enceinte and the lists had a varying width. When broad enough, this belt of land was used in time of war to place hurling machines and as a camp where local peasants could find a refuge. In peacetime it was used as pasture, a training ground for soldiers, a social place where tournaments and jousts were held or as a fairground or market for traders and merchants.

In the concentrentric castle, the keep lost a part of its significance, being no longer the lord's dwelling place. However, it seemed that the medieval castle-builders could not renounce this symbol of power. In many cases, the keep already existed, the concentric

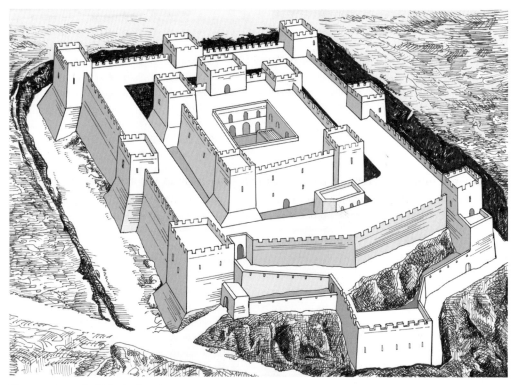

Concentric castle, Belvoir, Israel.

enceinte around it being constructed later. Generally, the keep only played a military role as a *réduit* (q.v.) where resistance could go on even when the rest of the castle had fallen.

Concentric castles originated from the Middle East, and were known and used in Antiquity, for example at Bouhen and Hierakonpolis in Egypt. The concept was introduced into Europe during the Crusades in the thirteenth century. The Krak des Chevaliers in Syria, Beaumaris Castle and Caerphilly Castle in Wales and the urban enceinte of Carcassone in southern France are excellent examples of this type of fortification.

Concertina wire: Concertina wire, or Dannert wire, is a type of barbed wire (q.v.) that is formed in large coils, which can be compressed for storage and transportation and then easily expanded like an accordion in the field.

Concrete: Concrete is a compact and dense construction material composed of cement and other cementitious materials such as fly ash and slag cement, and an aggregate (generally a coarse aggregate made of gravel or crushed rocks such as limestone or granite, plus a fine aggregate such as sand) bound with water. Reinforced concrete, widely used to construct bunkers, casemates and other structures, is concrete in which reinforcement steel rods (or rebars), grids or plates have been incorporated to strengthen it. Concrete offers a good resistance to compression when a metal framework opposes to traction. A combination of concrete and metal rebars forms a solid, compact and monolithic material. See Masonry.

Concrete battleship: A coastal fort having the shape of a ship. The best example is the US Fort Drum in Manila Bay in the Philippines, which was self-contained, decked, compartmented and armed with two armoured turrets, each housing two 14in guns. See Seafort.

Contravallation: See Countervallation.

Corbeil: A basket filled with earth used to protect or reinforce a parapet. See Gabion.

Corbel: A corbel (or console) is a piece of stone, wood or iron jutting out of a wall to carry any superincumbent weight. A piece of timber projecting in the same way was called a 'tassel' or 'bragger'. In medieval architecture, the technique was used to support upper storeys or a parapet projecting forward from the wall plane, often to form machicolation where openings between corbels could be used to drop projectiles onto attackers. This later became a decorative feature, without the openings. Corbelling could also support a projecting corner turret, brattice and *echauguette* (q.v.).

Cordon:
1) A line of military posts or stations to guard an enclosed area from unauthorized passage, e.g. a military or police cordon, and especially a sanitary cordon, a line of posts to prevent communication from or with an area infected with disease.
2) In architecture, a cordon is a semi-circular band of stone masonry projected along the outside of a building. A synonym is cornice, which designates a decorative projection along the top of a wall. In bastioned and nineteenth-century fortifications there were actually two such projecting elements: the tablette built on top of the scarp (q.v.) and the cordon a few feet below. The practical purpose of these elements is rather unclear. Were they intended to throw off rainwater, to reinforce the cohesion of masonry at the top of the wall, to help prevent the climbing of rats from the wet moat or to act as an obstacle to enemy escalade by ladder? These purposes are all plausible. Perhaps both the cordon and tablette were actually solely ornamental – aesthetic concessions in an architecture based on solidity, functionality and efficiency.

Corner tower: See Tower and Wall tower.

Cornichon: Literally 'gherkin', in French bastioned fortification an *ouvrage à corne* – a hornwork (q.v.) with two short wings.

Cornice: Decorative projection along the top of a wall. See Cordon.

Corona muralis: Roman decoration for gallantry in the form of a garland awarded to the first men to climb over the walls during the assault of a besieged place.

Corps de garde: The *corps de garde*, or guardhouse (q.v.), was a post intended to shelter the sentinels checking the entrance of a fortified city, fort, citadel or barrack. It was not a combat emplacement, although it might be lightly fortified, but it was a useful building for day-to-day police and control purposes. It generally included an administrative office, a rest-room for the guards and a porch.

Corps de logis: Architectural term which refers to the principal block of a large, usually classical, castle, mansion or palace. It contains the principal rooms, hall, state apartments and an entrance, generally arranged in a wing of the castle. See Hall.

Corral: See Wagon fort.

Cortina: In Italian, the main wall of a bastioned work, most generally the part between two bastions. See Curtain.

Counter-approach: Any temporary work, often improvised, built by the besieged and intended to hinder the progress of a besieging force. See Approach.

Counter-battery fire: A task assigned to an artillery unit, which consists of locating, firing at and silencing enemy artillery.

Counterfort: Solid internal pillars of masonry (also called buttresses) built within the body of the revetment (q.v.). Counterforts were very often built to strengthen churches and cathedrals, as well as the scarp and counterscarp in bastioned works and masonry forts in order to support the enormous weight of the rampart fill.

Counterguard: In the seventeenth and eighteenth-century bastioned fortification, the counterguard was an outwork placed in front of a bastion or *demi-lune*. The purpose was to protect the salient point and both faces. The counterguard was an active combat emplacement fitted with a breastwork and an infantry *banquette*, as well as a wide wall-walk suitable for artillery, ascents/ramps and staircases. If this was not the case, when the width of the wall-walk was only suitable for infantry fire, then the narrow outwork was called a *couvre-face* (face cover). In order to multiply the number of obstacles opposing the progress of besiegers, counterguards could be divided into secondary works. Two autonomous parts were called tenaillons, which only gave protection to the faces;

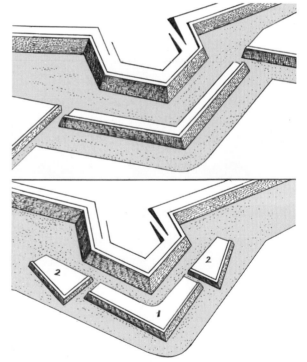

Top: Counterguard.
Bottom: Counterguard divided into sub-elements.
1: Bonnet; 2: Lunettes.

according to local adaptation, one of these could be ommited: the work was then called a half-counterguard. The counterguard could also be divided into three loose parts: a bonnet ahead of the salient and two lunettes protecting the faces.

Countermine: Countermining was an operation carried out by the besieged when enemy mining (q.v.) activity was detected. From the counterscarp gallery (q.v.), a countermine tunnel was dug in the direction of the enemy's mine with the objective of blowing it up. This was often anticipated, and many fortresses were provided with a prepared countermine network, built in a regular and symmetrical pattern at the same time as the fortress was constructed. This network would consist of a maze of permanent countermine tunnels and underground listening-posts – aka *ecoutes* (q.v.) – that would have their entrances on the counterscarp under the covered way or under a *demi-lune* and would spread under the glacis. From the main galleries, secondary branches could be dug when enemy activity had been detected and located. Gunpowder was then placed and ignited with the purpose of blasting enemy galleries, killing attacking miners and exploding defence works taken by the besiegers. The attacking mine and defending countermine could also strike into each other, either inadvertently or on purpose. Attackers and defenders then fought a terrifying hand-to-hand battle in subterranean darkness. This subterranean, dangerous and gruesome kind of warfare was still used for attacking and defending entrenched positions during the First World War.

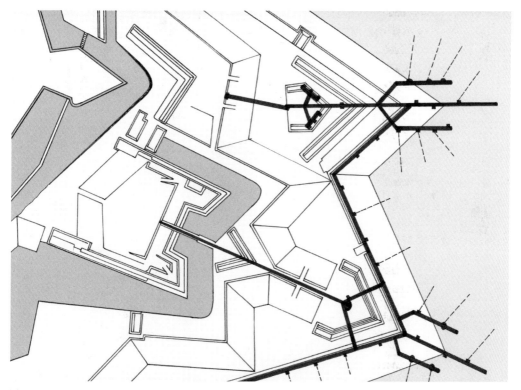

The black lines indicate permanent masonry tunnels under the glacis, from which secondary countermine galleries could be dug.

Countermure: Also known as a contramure, a wall raised behind another to fill a gap in the event of a breach. See Retirade.

Counterscarp: The vertical, nearly vertical or sloping outer wall of the ditch or the exterior bank of a wet moat nearest the besiegers, below the covered way (q.v.) and opposite the scarp (q.v.). The term, however, sometimes included the outer wall of the ditch, covered way and glacis. The counterscarp was generally faced or revetted, reinforced by buttresses and decorated with cordons and tablettes (q.v.). In some cases it could be fitted with a counterscarp gallery (q.v.). In nineteenth-century fortification, it could be non-revetted, gently sloping or fitted with a grille, a grating or a screen of metal bars.

Counterscarp gallery:

1) A passage or a series of firing chambers inside the counterscarp wall. Fitted with loopholes and casemated, it allowed reverse fire (q.v.) to be brought to bear into the ditch. It could also act as a base line or store place for digging countermine (q.v.) tunnels beneath the glacis (q.v.).
2) A large roundish screen made of masonry filled with earth intended to protect a Dutch *torenfort* (q.v.).

Countervallation: A line of fortification composed of an earthwall with parapet, redans, redoubts and ditch, established by a besieging force to secure themselves against the sallies of the besieged garrison. The countervallation also served to isolate the besieged and to starve them until they surrendered. See Circumvallation, Blockade and Part 2 (Siege Warfare).

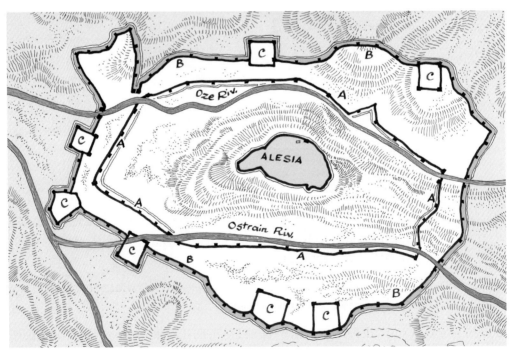

During the siege of the Gallic fortified oppidum of Alesia in 52bc, Julius Caesar ordered his soldiers to build two fortified lines in order to blockade the Gauls. The first line, called a countervallation (A), faced the besieged and was intended to repulse any sally. Another line, known as the circumvallation (B), was established to encircle the whole perimeter of the town and prevent any attack by a relief force. The latter was approximately 11 Roman miles (16.7km) long and included redoubts and camps (C).

Coupure: This word, which comes from the French verb *couper* ('to cut'), has two main meanings.

1) A ditch, earthwork or wooden palisade built behind a breach (q.v.) in the walls of a fortress or city, hastily made by the defenders. Its purpose was to slow down, frustrate and repulse an assault made by the besiegers. See Retirade.
2) A way of allowing communication through a fortified structure, for example a passage leading to a glacis to create a sally port so that the defenders could launch a sortie against the attackers.

Courtine: A curtain or section of wall between two towers or bastions. See City wall, Curtain, Rampart and Wall.

Courtine brisée: French, meaning 'broken curtain'. A section of wall having the particularity of being not straight but presenting a protruding shape for better flanking. See Reinforced order.

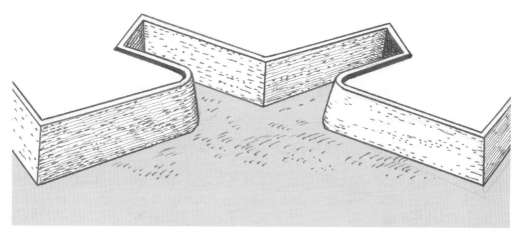

Courtine brisée.

Courtyard: A walled enclosure in a castle.

Courtyard castle: Type of castle consisting of a stone curtain wall that surrounded a central courtyard, with domestic buildings constructed inside the courtyard, normally against the curtain wall. See Rectangular castle.

Couvre-face: A counterguard (q.v.) with a narrow wall-walk, not wide enough to receive artillery and thus only suited for infantry musketry fire.

Couvre-porte: A small defensive work designed to defend a gate or door. See Cover-port.

Covered way: A continuous broad walkway or lane running all around a fortress along the top of the counterscarp and following the outline of the ditch. It was protected from enemy view and fire by a parapet (q.v.) and traverses (q.v.), and this embankment formed the outer slope of the glacis (q.v.). The idea of establishing this protecting outer

Covered way (plan).

Covered way (view).

lane beyond the ditch was said to have been invented by Italian military engineer Nicolo Tartaglia. Together with the places of arms (q.v.), the covered way was an essential element of the bastioned fortification. They were actually the defenders' eyes and ears. The covered way served as a protected walkway for patrol and placing sentries, an assembly area for the defending infantry, and it allowed troops to be posted as a first line of defence at the periphery of the fortress. Covered ways and places of arms were practically always fitted with traverses (q.v.), and could be reinforced by fences, palisades (q.v.), fraises (q.v.) or thorn hedges acting as primitive barbed wire in order to oppose scaling and prevent it being overcome by a sudden enemy rush. Covered ways and places of arms also allowed the besieged not to resign themselves to a passive attitude. On the contrary, they contributed to action, aggression and the offensive. It was practically impossible to regroup troops from out of the main enceinte – particularly if the ditch was wet. It was thus from the covered way and from the places of arms (and from the dry ditch) that a sally (q.v.) could be launched. For this purpose, re-entering places of arms included sorties, which were passages opened in the breastworks which, when not in use, were closed by a barrier or a strong gate and guarded by a sentry. According to the fundamental principle of command (q.v.), covered ways and places of arms were always lower than outworks but slightly higher than the glacis.

Cover-port: A defensive work placed in front of a gate. See Advanced work, Bastille, Bartizan, Chatelet and Tambour.

Crannog: An artificial island built in lakes, rivers, estuarine waters, swamps and other wetlands, and most often used as an island settlement or dwelling place. Dating from prehistoric times, the oldest crannogs were reported in use as early as 4500 BC (and

Crannog.

were sometimes still occupied until early medieval times). This kind of settlement was most common in Ireland, where at least 2,000 examples are known. They are also very common in Scotland, with at least 600 sites known, and in Switzerland, where they are known as *cités lacustres* (lake villages). Archeaological excavations suggest that crannogs typically appeared as raised platforms with wooden dwellings, surrounded or defined at the edges by timber post and plank palisades. They communicated to the shore either by means of a causeway built up with stones, a wooden gangway built on raised piles or by boat. It is unclear whether these sites were originally of any military significance, but they may have been constructed and used at times of danger, as the surrounding water acted as a deterrent and efficient defence.

Cratering: A large pit, a hollow bowl-shaped cavity in the ground, typically caused by an explosion. See Anti-tank ditch.

Cremaillère: A tracé (q.v.), possibly created by the Italian artist Antonio di Pietro Averlino, alias Filarete (1400–1469). The tracé *en crémaillère* featured receding or serrated steps enabling a greater development of flanking fire in a line (q.v.) or in the parapet of a work, and sometimes given to a covered way (q.v.). In plan it appeared 'saw-toothed'.

Créneau de pied: A form of machicoulis (q.v.) built in nineteenth and twentieth-century French forts. It consisted of narrow voids or vertical pipes placed in the scarp for close-range defence by firing vertically with a rifle or by dropping hand grenades on attackers in the ditch. See *Goulotte à Grenade*.

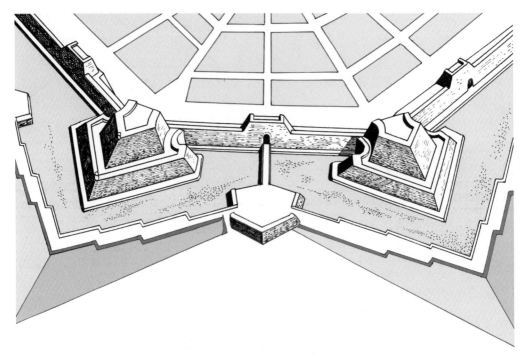

Bastioned front with covered way *en crémaillère* designed by Daniel Specklin in 1589.

Créneau de pied.
Left: front view.
Right: cross-section.

Crenel: A void in the parapet (q.v.) between two solid merlons (q.v.), in other words an opening through which defenders could fire their weapons. The crenel could be fitted with a wooden hinged shutter, called a huchette or mantlet (q.v.), for extra protection.

Crenel (Assur, Iraq).

Crenels were very important defensive elements, but they also had a decorative function and their shapes and ornamentation styles were extremely varied. See Breastwork, Crenel shutter and Shutter.

Crenellate: To fit a work with battlements, loopholes, crenels or embrasures. The so-called medieval 'right to crenellate' was a licence granted by a king or lord to his barons allowing them permission to build strongholds, castles and other fortified residences. See Adulterine castle.

Crenel shutter: A wooden hinged protection which covered a crenel, enabling the defender to open the shutter to fire at the enemy while gaining protection from the shutter in the closed position. See Huchette and Shutter.

Crest: The top of a breastwork (q.v.).

Crochet: A hooked passage or chicane (q.v.) – a sharp double bend built around the head of a traverse (q.v.) in order to let friendly troops through. Also a particular hooked tracé given to a sap (q.v.).

Crossfire: Also known as interlocking fire, crossfire is a term for the siting of weapons (often automatic weapons such as assault rifles or sub-machine guns) in two or more different locations directed at a target crossing the same general zone.

Crosslet: A crosslet slit (or loop) was a narrow vertical cruciform opening (having the shape of a cross) in the wall of a medieval castle for firing a bow or crossbow. See Arrow loop.

 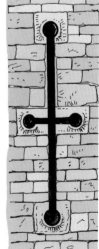

Crosslet.

Cross-wall: Internal dividing wall in a castle. This could be erected so that the lord's quarters (including kitchen and food stores) constituted a separate unit within the castle, being accessible only to his personal servants. The separation of the lord's quarter is assumed to have been due to the uncertain temper of mercenary retainers when they were not paid. It is also likely that extra internal fortification might have been to increase defence in depth (q.v.) and also to keep out non-resident refugees if they felt that the lord and his entourage were getting more than their fair share of available rations during a siege.

Crownwork: In the classical bastioned fortification, a projecting advanced work (q.v.) composed of two attached hornworks – in fact two bastioned fronts (q.v.). The crownwork was linked to the main body by two wings (q.v.), while it always had its own ditch and ravelins could be built at its front and back. Crownworks and hornworks were frequently combined to create large defensive areas.

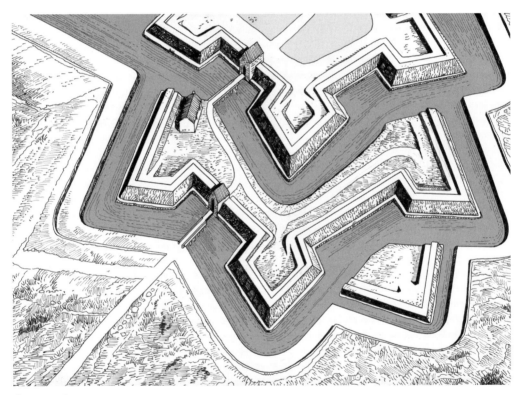

Crownwork.

Crow's foot: See Caltrop.

Crusaders' castle: After the initial success and enthusiasm of the First Crusade in 1099, and the establishment of the Latin kingdom of Outremer, there was a continuous shortage of fighting manpower, so fortifications were vital to hold the new Christian realm in the Holy Land. The earlier crusaders' castles were simple structures rather similar to the European stone keep (q.v.). After Saladin's successes in 1187, the situation of the

Latin kingdom was drastically changed. In order to resist new siege techniques, existing strongholds were improved and reinforced, while newly built castles tended to become elaborate and sometimes giant structures, often featuring a system of concentric walls with towers at intervals – e.g. Krak des Chevaliers and Belvoir Castle. See Concentric castle and Krak.

Cunette: A narrow excavation or furrow dug in the middle of a dry ditch, intended to drain rainwater and also obstruct the enemy. In a wet ditch, the cunette was generally still excavated and formed a deeper ditch of running water that took longer to freeze in winter. See Ditch and Moat.

Cupola: A general term for a small domed armoured cloche (q.v.) or armoured turret (q.v.). The cupola could be used to mount a machine gun or a searchlight, or as an observation post. The term also describes a rotating or fixed turret that carries no weapons but instead sighting devices, as in the case of tank commanders and in a bunker.

Curtain: The curtain (aka *courtine* or *cortina*) is the part of wall (q.v.) or rampart (q.v.) between two towers (q.v.) or bastions (q.v.). Its length depended on the range of the weapons used by the defenders and on the nature of the ground. In medieval fortification, the curtain was generally lower than the towers. The top of the curtain practically always

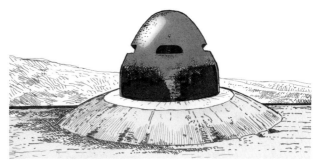

German Second World War concrete bunker.
Top: cross-section of observation cupola.
Bottom: armoured observation cupola.

featured a wall-walk (q.v.). The inside of a thick curtain might also be fitted with a corridor, occasionally called a gaine (q.v.). In a bastioned fortification, curtains and bastions were at the same level, usually 8–10m, to thwart scaling ladders. The width of the curtain varied according to the thickness of the breastwork and the importance of the wall-walk. Its shape in plan was mostly straight, but it was sometimes furnished with two small recessed casemated walls to increase the capacity of flanking. This feature, called the reinforced order, was created by the Italian engineer Zanchi in 1554. See City wall, Enceinte, wall and Wall-walk.

A medieval curtain (here seen from the inside) included a wall-walk (1), protected by merlons (2) and crenels (3). It could be covered by a roof (4) protecting soldiers and guards against ennemy projectiles and elements. The wall-walk could rest on arches (5).

Cut: A short excavation made across a *terre-plein* to prevent an enemy, having made a breach, from being able to penetrate further. See Retirade and Coupure.

Czech hedgehog: The Czech hedgehog (in German *Tschechenigel*) was designed as an anti-tank obstacle by the Czechs before the Second World War. Reportedly it could stop a 12-ton tank. The obstacle was composed of three steel bars (or three rails) which

Czech hedgehog.

were bonded together, but makeshift hedgehogs were made out of anything that could withstand a head-on collision with a tank. The height of the hedgehog was generally 1.80m and its weight was about 150kg depending on what it was made from. The obstacle was effective in keeping tanks and landing craft at bay when it became stuck underneath them. It maintained its function when tipped over by an explosion, and did not offer much cover to advancing infantrymen. After the annexion of Czechoslovakia by Germany in 1938, hundreds of hedgehogs were captured and later reused in the Atlantic Wall (q.v.). To reinforce its stability and solidity, the *Tschechenigel* was commonly anchored into concrete footbases. To avoid sinking in loose sand, the device often rested on a mattress made of brushwood. Hedgehogs could be linked to each other in as many as three belts. Jutting-out bars were often provided with notches for attaching barbed wire.

D

Dacoit fence: A fence used in late nineteenth-century British forts. Built in combination with the Twydall profile (q.v.), the spiked fence was about 8ft high and made from strong steel angle iron or simple thick railings 5ft 6in high. The fence was usually anchored in a concrete base for extra strength.

Datum: The singular form of 'data'. In geodesy, datum (or plane of construction) refers to a standard position or level that measurements are taken from. In fortification, datum designates the natural level of the site, from which command (q.v.) is calculated.

Davit: A small jib crane used in fortification to hoist ammunition up to a higher level, for example from an ammunition store to a firing chamber, or to lift and load a heavy shell to the muzzle or breech of a gun.

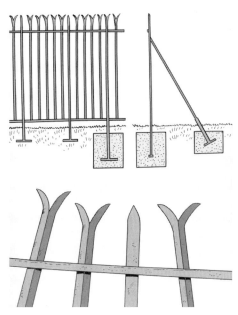

Dacoit fence.

Dead angle: The angle below and beyond which the ground cannot be seen, and shot at from a parapet or from an embrasure. Dead angles, also called blind ground or blind spots (q.v.), could be reduced by the use of hoarding (q.v.), flanking towers or some other flanking defences. See Blind spot and Flanking.

Déblai/remblai: The *déblai* – the excavated earth from a ditch – was used to make a *remblai* in the form of a wall or breastwork or by filling up the revetment of a rampart.

Decauville: A narrow-gauge railway system named after French inventor Paul Decauville (1846–1922). A Decauville railway is composed of ready-made sections of light, 60cm

Decauville railway.

narrow-gauge tracks fastened to steel sleepers. The track was portable and could be assembled and disassembled very easily by unskilled labourers and soldiers. Used in civilian industry and mining sites, the Decauville system was also widely adopted by the military as an essential part of logistics, notably for the construction and supplying of fortifications.

Decumanus: In a Roman town or military camp, the main east–west axis.

Defended industrial site: Since the introduction of long-range bomber aircraft in the 1930s, industrial sites (mines, food storage areas, dumps for raw materials and finished goods, data storage, manufacturers, power plants, fuel refineries and other essential production sites, and economic and administrative centres) have become primary targets and must be defended. Typical Second World War industrial defences against aerial bombardment included detection means (radar, searchlights), the use of interceptor fighters, anti-aircraft artillery and balloons, and also camouflage. The same applied to railroad infrastructure such as bridges, tunnels, stations and marshalling yards.

Defence in depth: A basic military tactic, sometimes referred to as elastic defence or deep defence. Its purpose is to delay rather than prevent the advance of an attacker, buying time and causing additional casualties by slowly yielding space and retreating in full order. In fortification, defence in depth requires the deployment of defensive works in several lines. When attackers breach one line, they continue to meet resistance as they advance, and one captured work or line does not mean the collapse of the whole defensive system. See Concentric castle, Advanced works, Box, Igel, Island, Outworks and Trench warfare.

Defilade: Any work (such as a shield, traverse, parados, wall or cavalier) placed across or close to another in order to screen from enemy view and protect from enfilading fire.

Defilade wall: See Flanking wall.

Dehors: French term designating outworks (q.v.).

Demi-bastion: A bastion (q.v.) with only one face and one flank. See Half-bastion.

Demi-lune: The *demi-lune* (French for half-moon, *mezzaluna* in Italian) was an outwork originally semi-circular in shape like a barbican (q.v.) or a roundel (q.v.). An extremely important sixteenth-century Italian development, also called a ravelin. It was the most indispensable outwork in the bastioned fortification. It was often placed in the ditch, in front of the curtain between two bastions. The *demi-lune*/ravelin was systematically placed in front of a gate and also built in the gorge or ahead of crownworks and hornworks (q.v.). The *demi-lune* thus shielded a curtain or the entrance to a fort, citadel or city. It also covered the flank of a bastion and formed an additional obstacle before the main work. It was very often triangular, composed of two faces protuding towards the enemy, but it could also be given two short flanks and thus have a pentagonal shape. Its gorge was always open. Its dimensions were carefully defined. According to the fundamental principle of command (q.v.), its profile was always lower than the main enceinte but higher than the covered way (q.v.). The outline of its gorge was built so as not to hinder crossfire from the flanks of adjacent bastions. In its gorge, one or two staircases were arranged for accessing the *terre-plein* from the bottom of the ditch. The *demi-lune* could be fitted with a traverse (q.v.) – a thick wall built on its capital line. The *demi-lune* could also be fitted with a reduit; it was then divided into two parts by an inner ditch and called an entrenched *demi-lune*.

Demi-lune.

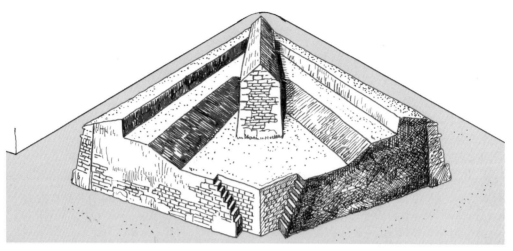

Demi-lune (with traverse placed along the capital line).

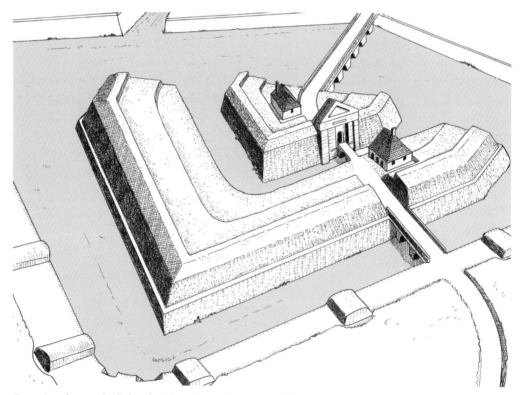

Demi-lune (entrenched, fitted with an inner ditch and reduit).

Detached scarp: In nineteenth-century fortification, a detached scarp designated a retaining wall, which also formed an obstacle and a defensive position in a dry ditch at the foot of the scarp. A semi-detached scarp, as the name implies, included a wall partly attached to the scarp. See Carnot's Wall.

Detached scarp.

Detached work: An independant self-defensive work designed to occupy a strategically important position. While outworks and advanced works were always related to the main enceinte, and therefore were always provided with open gorges, detached works were isolated fortified positions. When a fortified town included a civilian population, detached works were exclusively military. Because they could be attacked from all sides, they needed to be given a complete enclosure and full autonomy. They were employed in important strategic places such as crossroads, waterways, dominating hills, passages, mountains and valleys. They were also widely used as coastal defences in observation and combat roles. Detached works could be permanently built as parts of an organized defensive system or temporarily constructed during the time of a campaign or a siege. Their dimension, shape and strength depended on the importance of the objectives to be defended. There were various types of detached works, from small to large: post (q.v.), lunette (q.v.), battery (q.v.), redoubt (q.v.) and fort (q.v.).

Dike: Also spelt dyke; a causeway, long wall or embankment built to prevent flooding from a river or the sea. Also a low wall or earthwork serving as defence, or used to mark a boundary, like Offa's Dyke (q.v.) in Britain. See Reave and Wall.

Directorate of Fortifications and Works: See FW3.

Disappearing gun: A type of heavy (mainly coastal) artillery where the gun retracted or recoiled down into a protected pit or wall after firing. The system was invented in the 1860s by Captain Alexander Moncrieff. The American generals William Crozier and Adelbert Buffington further refined the concept in the late 1880s by incorporating hydropneumatic recoil control to assist the counterweight action. The advantages of the system included protection of the gun crew, concealment and cover from enemy fire, especially during reloading. Disappearing guns were highly popular for a while in the British Empire, the United States and other countries, and often employed in coastal artillery. The concept fell out of use in the early twentieth century due to its disadvantages: the high cost involved, technical complexity, limited rate of fire and

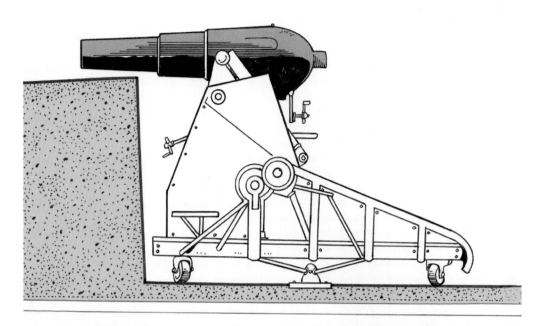
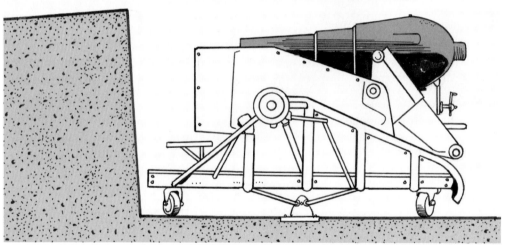

Disappearing gun.
Top: Firing position.
Bottom: Loading and rest position.

vulnerability to air attack when bombers, dive-bombers and ground attack aircraft were introduced and developed in the 1930s. See Elswick mounting, Buffington-Crozier mount and Eclipsing turret.

Disappearing turret: See Eclipsing turret.

Dismantlement: Breaking down and deconstructing a fortified place on purpose. This costly demolition was carried out when a fortification was no longer needed or no longer efficient.

Ditch: From prehistory until today, the ditch (also called a fossé or moat) has always been a fundamental element of fortification, forming a passive and extremely effective obstacle. It is from this excavation that earth for parapets, breastworks and ramparts is obtained. It was discovered that when the earth to construct an entrenchment was taken from immediately in front of a wall, the resulting ditch formed a further obstacle to the approach of the enemy. The ditch was limited by the scarp (q.v.) on the inside and the counterscarp (q.v.) on the outside. Ditches could be dry or wet depending on the availability of a water supply.

The plan shows a wet ditch (aka moat).

A dry ditch was mostly deep and relatively narrow, forming a continuous obstacle around the whole fortress. It had to be wide enough to hold a sizeable raiding party and make bridging and filling difficult, but not so wide as to allow the besieger to breach the base of the scarp with artillery fire. The dry ditch could be used in peacetime as a training ground. In wartime, it could be used as a refuge for the fleeing inhabitants of the countryside, for cattle, as a communication or as an assembly place for a party getting ready to make a sortie. Access to the dry ditch was by a postern (q.v.) or a sally-port (q.v.). A dry ditch was often furnished with a cunette (q.v.). Where water was available, the dry ditch could be flooded through sluices from a nearby river to produce a sudden torrent of water that was able to wash away any attackers during their attempt to cross the moat.

A wet ditch (also called a moat) was permanently filled with water. It formed a serious and very efficient obstacle protecting against a surprise attack and made mining (q.v.) impossible. Wet ditches came in two kinds. Firstly, those filled with still water, which represented a health hazard in the days of primitive sanitation and poor disease prevention. Before the end of the nineteenth century, disease was always a greater killer in warfare than weapons. In winter, still water could freeze, rendering the wet ditch useless as it provided the enemy with a platform of approach. In a wet ditch with still

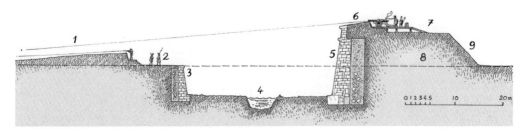

Cross-section of a ditch in bastioned fortification.
1: Glacis; 2: Covered way; 3: Counterscarp; 4: Ditch with cunette; 5: Revetted scarp; 6: Breastwork; 7: Wall-walk; 8: Rampart; 9: Internal slope.

water, the cunette was also dug: the purpose was to keep a deep running current of water which took longer to freeze. In very frosty weather, the garrison had to break up the ice. The second kind of wet ditch, one that held running water, came with the danger of erosion and flooding during intemperate seasons of the year, but they could provide the garrison with fresh fish. Both types of wet ditch also hindered sorties to some extent. Water supply in both still and moving wet ditches was regulated and controlled by hydrological elements such as batardeaus, sluices and water-gates. See Anti-tank ditch, Batardeau, Déblai Remblai, *Fossé Diamant*, Moat and Watergate.

Dom bunker: Also known as a Cathedral bunker, a large and high concrete Second World War German shelter intended to protect a submarine or a heavy gun mounted on a railway.

Dom bunker.

Domus Magna: In medieval Italy, a large house or manor inhabited by an aristocratic or wealthy family. See Tower house.

Donjon: French term for keep (q.v.). The *donjon* was the *tour maitresse* (master tower), the main tower, the chief retreat of the defenders of a castle. It could be the residence of the lord or simply an expression of his power, wealth and authority. The *donjon* was often separated from the rest of the castle either by a motte (q.v.), a ditch (q.v.) or a *chemise* (q.v.).

Dos d'âne: Knife-edge profile (an obtuse ridge formed at the apex of two inclined planes) often given to a batardeau (q.v.).

Chambois (*donjon*), Normandy France.

Rechteren (*donjon*), Overijssel, the Netherlands.

Double hornwork.

Double hornwork: An advanced work (q.v.) constituted by two hornworks (q.v.) placed in a row, forming a strong fortified unit.

Double tenaille: An infrequent form of outwork in the form of two coupled *tenaille*. See *Tenaille* and Advanced works.

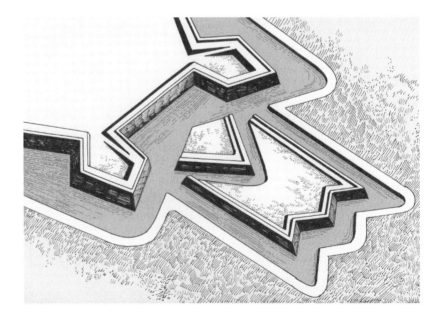

Double *tenaille*.

Dover quad pillbox: Built only around high ground commanding the port of Dover in 1940, these were square structures measuring 4m by 4m (13ft by 13ft). Each wall was fitted with two large embrasures suitable for rifles and light machine guns, and the pillbox's roof was covered with a thick overhanging concrete slab.

Dover quad pillbox.

Dragon's teeth: Anti-tank obstacles used by several nations before and during the Second World War, comprising several tiers of reinforced concrete blocks usually given a square truncated pyramidal shape. The distance between and the height of the blocks were calculated so as to make crossing impossible for any tanks. The idea was to slow down and channel tanks into 'killing zones' where they could easily be fired at by anti-tank weapons. In practice, however, the use of combat engineers with explosives and specialist clearance vehicles enabled the Dragon's teeth to be disposed of, and they proved far less of an obstacle than many had expected. When threatened with invasion by Germany in 1940, the British established concrete Dragon's teeth barriers called pimples (q.v.) along the coast. The Germans made extensive use of them in the Siegfried Line and the Atlantic Wall – under the designation of *Höckerhindernisse* (q.v.). Typically, each tooth was 90–120cm (about 3–4ft) tall, depending on the precise model. Mines were often laid between the individual blocks, and further obstacles employed along the blocks – such as barbed wire to impede infantry or diagonally placed steel beams to further hinder tanks.

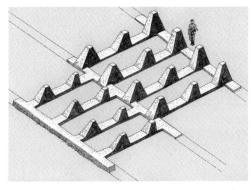

German model 1938 with heavy movable metal beams that allowed passage through the obstacles.

German model 1942.

Drawbridge: A movable hinged bridge at a castle's gates providing entry across a defensive moat. Raising the drawbridge to a vertical position kept intruders at bay and formed an additional barrier to entry. In prehistory and early medieval motte castles, the bridge was often a thick movable plank or a primitive and semi-permanent structure designed to be destroyed or removed in the event of an attack, but as time went by sophisticated models were designed. When the ditch was wide, there was a non-movable section made of wood resting on stone-piles – eventually composed of masonry arches. Some 4.5m from the gate, this permanent part was interrupted by a drawbridge, which could be quickly raised in moments of crisis. Removable bridges existed in many variations. A typical arrangement had the drawbridge immediately outside a gatehouse, consisting of a wooden deck with one edge hinged, pivoting at the gatehouse threshold, so that in the raised position the bridge would be flush against the gate, forming an additional portal to the entry.

Saint Honoré Gate, Paris, France.

Drawbridge operated with ropes.

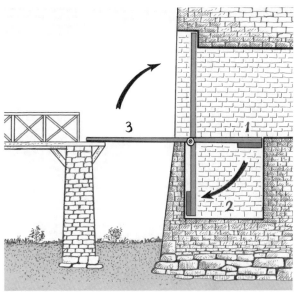
Cross-section of a swing-back drawbridge. By swinging the counterweight (1) set on the beams, the rear part of the mobile bridge came down into a pit (2) arranged on both sides of the passage, while the fore part moved into a vertical position (3).

The bridge was raised or lowered using ropes or chains attached to a windlass placed in a chamber in the gatehouse above the passage. A variation included counterweight beams that dropped into slots in the floor. The raising chains could themselves be attached to counterweights. By the fourteenth century, a bascule arrangement was provided by gaffs (lifting arms) above and parallel to the bridge deck whose ends were linked by chains to the lifting end of the bridge; in the raised position, the gaffs would fit into slots (called rainures) in the gatehouse wall. Inside the castle, the gaffs were extended to bear counterweights, or might form the side-timbers of a stout gate, which would be against the roof of the gate-passage when the drawbridge was down, but would close against the gate-arch as the bridge was raised. This sytem was criticized for the vulnerability of the beams, chains and grooves. Eventually, other sytems appeared. One of them consisted of counterweights fixed at the rear of the bridge, which was closed by swinging back the counterweights, which were lodged into two pits arranged sidewise behind the doorway. See Gaff.

Drum-tower: A large circular tower, usually thick, low and squat, and often adapted for the use of artillery.

Dry stone wall: A wall that is constructed from stones without any mortar to bind them together. As with other dry stone structures,

Dry stone wall.

the wall is held up by the weight and interlocking of the stones. From about 4000 BC, such walls were used in building construction, field boundaries and fortifications.

Dugout: A temporary or permanent shelter (q.v.) or reinforced position (very often excavated) constructed as an aid to a specific task or mission. A dugout may also, due to the potential for concealment, serve as a hiding place for an ambush. See Blockhouse, Bunker, Casemate, Shelter and Zemlyanska.

Dun: A generic term designating a Celtic roundhouse or a fortified village made of a circular or oval wall associated with the first-century AD Iron Age culture. Early duns had a near vertical wall made of stone laced with timber. Duns continued to be used in some cases into the medieval period. Duns, as roundhouses, shared many characteristics with brochs (q.v.), often including galleries and stairs, but were lower.

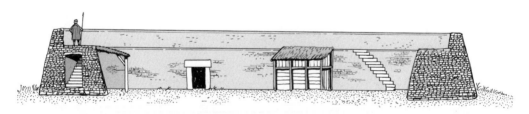

View and cross-section of a Celtic dun.

Dungeon:

1) Archaic term for *donjon*. See keep.
2) A room or cell in which prisoners were kept, especially underground. Dungeons are generally linked with medieval castles, though their association with prisoners left to rot is greatly exaggerated, as underground cellars were used more as cisterns or grain stores than prisons. See *Oubliette*.

Dunum: A small exterior work made of piled stones or earth, placed ahead of the entrance to a Celtic oppidum (q.v.) for the purpose of observation or advanced defence.

Dutch Water Line: The Dutch Water Line (in Dutch, *Hollandsche Waterlinie*) was a military system of defences originally designed in the early seventeenth century. Combining inundation (q.v.) and fortifications, the *Waterlinie* was successfully used during the Eighty Years War of Independence against Spain (1568–1648). Eventually the system was improved and became an essential element of Dutch national defence. Sluices were constructed in dikes, and forts, batteries and fortified posts were created at strategic points along the line, covering the dikes that crossed the line. In times of war, the water level in the flooded areas was carefully maintained to a level deep enough to make an advance on foot difficult or impossible, and shallow enough to prevent the use of boats (other than the flat-bottomed gun barges used by the Dutch defenders). The Dutch Water Line proved its value during the Franco-Dutch War in 1672 when it halted the armies of Louis XIV, but it failed to stop the French Revolutionary armies in the winter of 1794/1795 due to heavy frost. After the fall of Napoleon in 1815, the United Kingdom of the Netherlands was formed and King William I decided to modernize the defence. The Water Line was partly shifted east of Utrecht. In the nineteenth century, the main Dutch defence line, now called the New Water Line, was further extended and constantly modernised. It became a many-tentacled military defensive system with *torenforten* (q.v.) – forts with large round artillery towers and sophisticated inundation systems, including dikes, sluices and polders that could be flooded at the threat of war.

The Water Line, which showed remarkable cohesion as a strategic landscape structure, was put in a state of readiness but not attacked during the Franco-Prussian War in 1870, and also during the First World War. Between the First and Second World Wars, the vulnerable earth and brick fortifications in the Water Line were reinforced or replaced with concrete pillboxes, bunkers and *rivierkazematen* (q.v.). At the same time, the Dutch extended their defences by creating new fortified lines intended to repulse any Nazi German attack. However, during the attack on the Netherlands in May 1940, modern German warfare tactics – including airborne troops, 'lightning' tank assaults supported by dive bombers and a devastating aerial bombing of Rotterdam – forced the Dutch to capitulate. After the Second World War, against the background of the Cold War, the Dutch government redesigned and modernized the waterline to counter a possible Soviet invasion. This third version of the waterline was never tested, and was dismantled in the 1960s. Today, many of the forts and bunkers are still intact, some being open to the public, and there is a renewed interest in the waterline for its technical prowess, now inserted within peaceful landscapes and natural beauty.

E

Ear: A roundish or square protruding screen built on the shoulder of a bastion in order to protect the flank batteries. Ears (aka *orillons*) were typical of early bastioned systems based on Italian design in the sixteenth century. In the following centuries, ears had the tendency to be discarded as they limited the arc of fire. See Bastion, Flank, Flanking and *Orillon*.

Eared pillbox: The British concrete eared pillbox, designed in 1940, had the plan of an irregular hexagon. It was designed to house two Vickers machine guns firing through two wide and narrow loopholes facing forwards. The two embrasures were at 90 degrees to each other, allowing for an arc of fire of 180 degrees. The wall bulged out beneath the loopholes to allow space for water-cooling cans for the Vickers machine guns. It was a particularly poorly designed contraption, as its walls were rather thin, it was not fitted with rifle loopholes for close-range defence and the two forward-facing entrances were badly exposed to enemy fire, leaving very little possibility of exiting once under attack. See FW3.

Ears (bastion).

Earthworks: Earthworks are military engineering works created through the moving of massive quantities of soil or unformed rock. In military engineering, earthworks are more specifically types of fortification constructed from soil comprising earth mounds, banks and ditches. Although soil is not very strong, it is cheap and huge quantities can be used to make resilient structures. Examples of earthwork fortifications are numerous, including for example hillforts (q.v.), dykes (q.v.), Roman and Saxon walls, motte-and-bailey castles (q.v.), ramparts (q.v.), breastworks (q.v.), trenches (q.v.) and anti-tank walls and ditches.

Echauguette: A sentry box or bartizan (occasionally called guérite, garite or garetta), generally corbelled out from an angle of a medieval wall or from the salient angle of a bastion or rampart. The purpose was to have an observation post to watch over the ditch. The jutting-out turret sheltered a single standing guard from wind and rain. The sentry box was fitted with small and narrow loopholes for observation and firing, should the need arise. Access was by means of a

Echauguette.

narrow corridor in the thickness of the breastwork. In ground-plan, the *echauguette* was circular or polygonal, and its roof was covered by an adorned domed cupola. *Echauguettes* also had a decorative function due to their elegant shapes, gracious silhouettes and their coupling with cordons (q.v.) and tablets (q.v.). Some were elaborately embellished with heraldic devices and other ornementation. More prosaically, the floor (overlooking the ditch) could be fitted with an opening and used as a latrine.

Eclipsing turret: An armoured turret with one or two short-barrelled guns. Such retractable turrets were developed by the end of the nineteenth century, and further in the interwar period (1918–1939), some being incorporated into the Maginot Line (q.v.) for example. The 'disappearing' armoured turret was retractable. It was raised by counterweights for firing and lowered for reloading or when not in operation. As a result, the crews and guns were perfectly protected; the only visible feature from a distance was a grassy mount, with the metallic turret roof flush with the concrete surface. The main drawback was that due to their high cost, forts saw their firepower vastly reduced. Moreover, armoured eclipsing turrets could be armed with only comparatively light guns, which could engage just one target at a time. Disappearing turrets employed counterweight and hydraulic systems to move up and down, and these mechanisms – as a result of the enormous weights involved – appear to have often been temperamental and prone to jamming, even without the hazard of enemy shellfire. The use of retractable eclipsing turrets was thus restricted to relatively light guns of about 75mm. Retractable searchlight and eclipsing machine-gun turrets were also fitted to some forts. These might remain retracted until an assault on the fort was attempted and were then unmasked. See Armoured fort, Disappearing gun and *Tourelle Galopin*.

Ecoute: A listening-post, a prepared underground chamber as part of a countermine network installed under the glacis, from which observers could detect enemy mining activity and engage countermining operations.

Edwardian castles: The castles constructed by King Edward I of England (1272–1307) to control his newly acquired territories in Wales. These castles (such as Flint, Rhuddlan, Hope, Conwy, Harlech, Caernarvon and Beaumaris) are amongst the finest examples of fortifications of the period.

Eingangsverteidigung: In First and Second World War German bunkers, the *Eingangsverteidigung* (entrance defence) was a small firing-hole (closed by a sliding metal shutter) placed in the prolongation of the corridor, allowing enfilading fire on enemies trying to penetrate inside.

Elastic defence: See Defence in depth.

Element Cointet: Also called Element C. See Belgian Gate and Rollbock.

Elswick mounting: A system of disappearing gun (q.v.) constructed by Armstrong's Tyneside works. The Elswick mounting (named after a ward of the city of Newcastle upon Tyne) used the energy generated by the recoil of a gun to move from the upper firing position into the lower loading position. The movement of the weapon was used

Edwardian castle, Harlech, Wales.

to compress air by means of a pneumatic piston. After reloading, the same energy was used to raise the gun back into its upper position for firing. This method was used in the 1880s and 1890s for coastal artillery. However, the system was extremely complex and expensive, and also had the disadvantage of a low rate of fire. Disappearing guns were thus replaced with the more conventional *barbette* (q.v.) mount, which offered less protection but permitted a quicker rate of fire for less expense and lower maintenance costs. See Buffington-Crozier mount and Eclipsing turret.

Embrasure: A void in a parapet or an opening in a casemate allowing artillery to fire through. It offers protection to weapons and their crew, but although one or both sides of the embrasure can be splayed or slanted outward, it also reduces the angle of fire.

Embuscade: French term for 'ambush', but in fortification it designated a concealed place where combatants could hide themselves to attack enemies by surprise.

Emplacement: A specially designed position, structure or platform (offering both protection and a large arc of fire) from which a weapon can be operated, loaded, fired and recoiled. See Casemate.

Emplecton: In ancient Greek fortification, the filling made of rubble and stones held by masonry revetments constituting the rampart (q.v.).

Empty bastion: A bastion (q.v.) whose *terre-plein* is lower than the wall-walk (q.v.). See Bastion and Solid bastion.

Embrasure, Front view.

Embrasure. Plan
1: Narrow inner part of the opening (throat); 2: wider outer part (splay); 3: the bottom (sole); 4: side of the embrasure (cheek); 5: *banquette* or fire-step for infantry; 6: merlon, a thick screening mass between two embrasures.

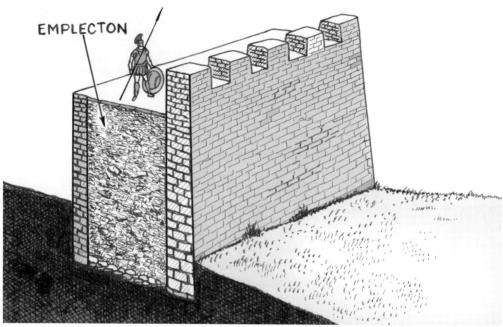

Emplecton.

En Barbette: See *Barbette* and Breastwork.

En bec: Expression generally applied to a tower having a beaked projection pointing outwards. See Apron.

Enceinte: The continuous line of inner fortification enclosing a fortified perimeter or a wall hemming a castle, town or fort; the outline of the main rampart but excluding all outworks. In plan it coincides with the scarp. In a medieval castle, the area delineated by the enceinte was known as the bailey (q.v.) or courtyard.

Enceinte castle: A type of castle developed in the thirteenth century in which the keep (q.v.) was completely discarded, the castle becoming a fortified enclosure. The defence focused on the gatehouse, corner and wall towers and curtain walls. This arrangement was a great improvement for the daily life and organization of the community living in the castle. The bailey (sometimes covering several acres) offered more space and easier communication between combat emplacements, service buildings and living quarters.

Endicott-Taft: A coastal defence programme for defending the harbours of the United States, based on a 1886 report and amended in 1906.

Enfilading fire: Fire directed from one location from the flank of a line, for example raking the entire length of an enemy position. Enfilade fire is effective because more of the position is exposed to gunfire and can inflict greater casualties or damage. For instance, a trench is enfiladed if the opponent can fire down along its whole length. A column of cavalry, vehicles or marching troops are enfiladed if fired on from the front or rear in such a way that projectiles travel the length of the column. See Traverse.

Entrée: French for 'entrance'. In the Maginot Line (q.v.), a distinction was made between: *Entrée Hommes* (EH), the entrance for troops or the men's entrance; *Entrée Mixte* or *Entrée Hommes et Munitions* (EHM), a single entrance of a work used for both troops and munitions; and *Entrée Munitions* (EM), the entrance for munitions. The latter was a larger entrance, designed to take trucks or narrow-gauge railcars.

Entrenched bastion: A bastion making up part of an urban enceinte (q.v.), often situated opposite the citadel (q.v.), which could be used as a reduit (q.v.) or a secondary citadel. The bastion was made a self-contained and defensible fort by the addition of an enclosing wall, a rear moat and a drawbridge in its gorge. Examples in France can be seen at Gravelines, Besançon (Fort Griffon) and Lille (Fort Saint-Sauveur).

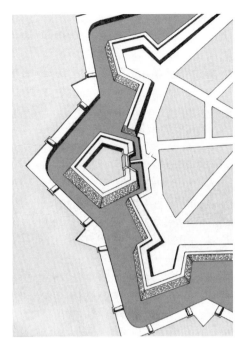
Entrenched bastion.

Entrenched camp: See *Camp retranché*.

Entrenchment:
1) A position fortified by trenches or any other fieldworks (q.v.).
2) Any work, permanent or improvised, made to increase the defensive strength of a place within existing fortifications, so as to multiply obstacles in the path of the besieging force. Often a synonym of bank or embankment. See Breastwork.

Entrenching tool: An entrenching tool, or E-tool, is a small spade (often collapsible and portable) used by military forces for a variety of purposes, notably digging field fortifications. The use of this important tool of war goes back at least to the times of the Roman legions.

Envelop: *Demi-lunes* (q.v.), counterguards and any secondary outworks (q.v.) could be linked together in order to form a continuous envelop. This succession of connected elements allowed rapid communication all around the fortress and constituted an additional external line of defence.

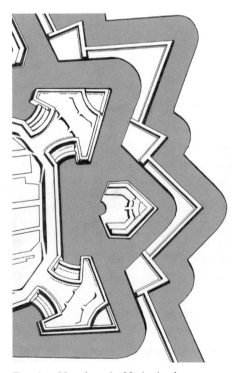
Envelop, Naarden, the Netherlands.

Epaule: Meeting point where the flank and face of a work or bastion join. See Shoulder.

E-Plan: Outline given to a tower house (q.v.) with a main block and at least two wings at right angles (in plan evoking the letter 'E'), dating from the sixteenth and seventeenth centuries, typically in Scotland.

Escalade: The climbing, scaling and assaulting of a fortification wall using a ladder or hooked grab.

Escarp: The outward slope of a rampart, on the inner side of the ditch. See Scarp and Counterscarp.

Escarp gallery: A series of chambers or a vaulted passage built inside the scarp to provide communication around the work and to enable defence of the ditch through loopholes in its walls. See Scarp.

Escutcheon: A decorative shield carved in stone, generally placed above a gate, bearing ornaments, coats-of-arms and other heraldic emblems.

Esplanade:
1) A cleared space, a kind of glacis (q.v.) between a town and its citadel (q.v.). It was a large, open and level area straight outside a fortress or city walls to provide clear fields of fire for the defenders' guns.
2) A large open space, also called a parade ground (q.v.), placed in the middle of a fort, camp or citadel, where muster, drills, inspections, ceremonies and meetings are held.

Expense magazine: A small made-up powder or ammunition store placed near a gun, containing enough ammunition for immediate use.

Exterior slope: The side of a parapet facing the enemy. It continued as the scarp into the ditch.

F

Face: The two protruding parts of the bastion (q.v.), between the flank and the projecting point that form the salient angle.

Faggot: A bundle of sticks of wood or twigs bound together, generally shorter than a fascine (q.v.). It was used as revetment, to fill a ditch or as fuel for lighting a fire.

Fahrpanzer: See *Panzerlafette*.

Fakir's bed: A heavy plank fitted with sharp and strong nails placed across a street or a road to control, channel or forbid the traffic of tyre-wheeled vehicles, often set at a checkpoint (q.v.) or at a control post.

Fangrost: A reinforced concrete structure composed of two rows of concrete beams (each 2m high and 1.5m wide) placed on top of German Second World War submarine

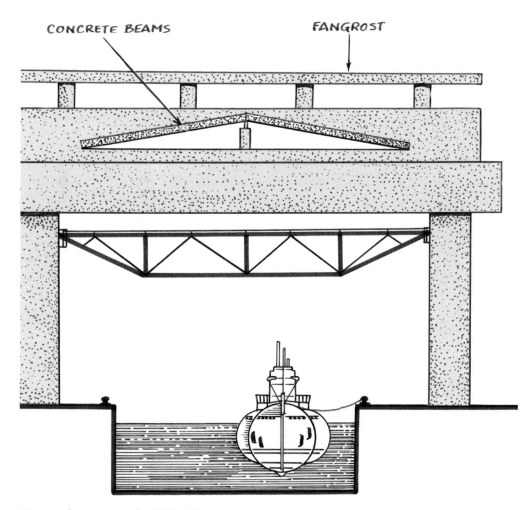

Fangrost. Cross-section, La Pallice, France.

bunkers. The *Fangrost* was intended to explode bombs before they hit the actual roof. The total structure of the roof might include a thickness of 7 metres. At Saint-Nazaire in western France, the submarine base built during the Second World War by the German Navy (Kriegsmarine) still displays a part of its *Fangrost*.

Fascine: A rough cylindrical bundle of brushwood used by the military from ancient times until today, employed as fuel but also to fill a ditch, to cover and reinforce an earthwork (e.g. the sides of a trench or a siege battery) or to make, level or strengthen a path across uneven ground, quagmires and wet terrain.

Fausse-braie: Deriving from the late medieval *braie* (q.v.), the *fausse-braie* (literally 'false bray') was a low continous parapet placed in front of the ditch, on the berm (q.v.) at the foot of the main rampart. It formed a communication and combat emplacement enabling grazing fire at intruders in the ditch. Communication between the *fausse-braie* and main enceinte was by a postern (q.v.) connecting under the rampart. Widely and successfully used under the designation of *onderwal* in the Old Dutch Fortification

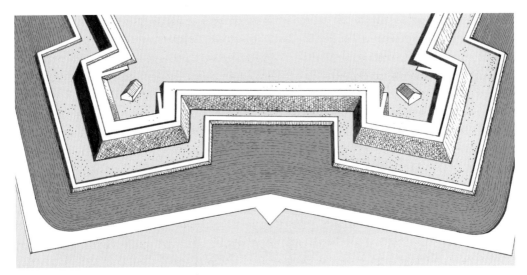

Fausse-braie. (Old Dutch Fortification).

system (q.v.) where ditches were very broad and always wet, the *fausse-braie* nevertheless presented serious disadvantages in fortifications with (comparatively) narrow and dry ditches. Indeed, if the enemy had taken possession of the counterscarp (q.v.), then he dominated the defenders deployed in the *fausse-braie* and could fire at them because the *fausse-braie* was lower than the counterscarp. Moreover, the defenders of the *fausse-braie* were dangerously exposed to splinters and possible collapse of the main wall behind and above them when this was submitted to heavy breaching-fire. For these reasons the use of the obsolete *fausse-braie* was discontinued by the late 1690s, being replaced with *tenailles* (q.v.) and counterguards (q.v.)

Fence: A barrier, railing or other vertical structure, typically of wood, spiked iron bars or barbed wire (q.v.), enclosing an area of ground to prevent or control access or escape. See Dacoit fence.

Fer à cheval: Expression used to designate any work whose shape in plan appears as a 'D' or horseshoe.

Feste:
1) General German term for fortress.
2) In particular, the term designates modern fortifications built by the Germans in the annexed French province of Lorraine after their victory in the war of 1870. A *Feste*, also named *Panzergruppe* (armoured group), was a large fort consisting of a number of fortified positions, well protected and defended, operating as one large unit under a single command. Design, dimensions, groundplan and shape were completely adapted to the local situation. All elements of the *Fest* were widely dispersed, so the outer face could vary from 100–200 hectares and even larger (Feste Keiser Wilhem II, built in Molsheim in 1890, was 2km^2). The *Feste* concept was based on dispersion, concrete and armour protection and self-sufficiency of individual positions. The close-range defences included *Infanterie Stützpunkte* (infantry positions) consisting

of trenches, fortlets and strongholds protected by a ditch, mortar emplacements and enfilading machine-gun concrete casemates. These elements were scattered all over the perimeter in order to defend the long-range artillery batteries. Guns were placed inside armoured rotating turrets, which were installed on top of partly underground concrete structures. Artillery included cannons and mortars, and fire was directed by special armoured observatories and fire control stations. Troop barracks, ammunitions stores and service facilities were buried deep underground. An important innovation was the ability of each unit to be individually defended and self-sufficient. They were fitted with electricity provided by their own powerplant equipped with diesel engines, heating and telephone, defended by ditches and pillboxes and linked together by underground passages. All equipment and most weapons were kept on a rather simple level so that only a small cadre of technical specialists would maintain a *Feste*; the bulk of the garrison were regular infantry and artillerymen. The *Festen* were camouflaged, enclosed with a wide ditch protected with concrete caponiers, and the glacis were covered with barbed wire entanglements. They were supplied by means of special military communications, roads and narrow-gauge railways.

The most modern *Festen* were constructed between 1899 and 1918 around Metz and Thionville in France. They were not tested during the First World War as they were simply bypassed. After the German defeat in 1918, the provinces of Alsace and Lorraine were returned to France. The former German *Festen* were incorporated into the French defence system and renamed *Groupes Fortifiés* (fortified groups). The formidable *Festen* largely inspired the Maginot Line designers and became direct ancestors to the German fortified systems of the Siegfried Line (q.v.) and Atlantic Wall (q.v.). The Metz *Festen* finally played a military role during the Second World War and proved hard nuts to crack when their garrisons resisted against Allied progression in October 1944.

Festung:

1) General German term for fortified place, stronghold, fortress or castle.
2) Fortresses created on Hitler's order in January 1944 in the Atlantic Wall (q.v.). *Festungen* (known to the Allies as Atlantic Pockets) had total priority in men, arms and defence. In theory, *Festungen* were intended to deny enemy occupation of areas of decisive operational importance. The fortresses would allow themselves to be surrounded, thereby holding down the largest possible number of enemy forces and establishing conditions favourable for successful counter-attacks. Hitler had ordered his commanders to hold fast rather than make a timely tactical withdrawal that might save their forces. Each commander had to personally swear affidavits to the Führer to hold and resist until the last man and the last round. However, these unfortunate officers had no absolute powers inside their fortresses because local naval and air force commanders also had a say in the matter. Hitler had a passion for fortifications; the very term *Festung* was more evocative than *Verteidigungsbereich* (defensive zone), and had a reassuring effect upon him. Much time, materiel and labour were devoted to the establishment and reinforcement of these fortresses. A *Festung* was supposed to have a garrison of at least two divisions, with ammunition, food and supply stocks to support all of its positions for three months.

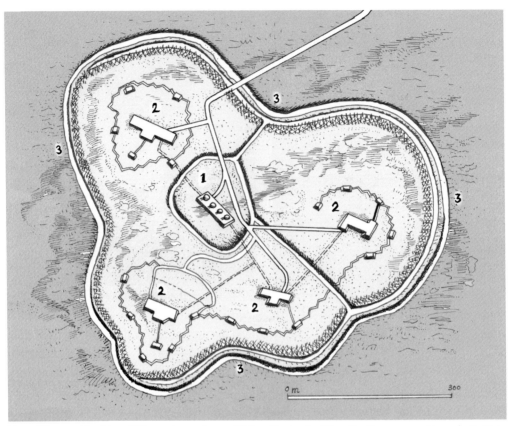

Feste Illingen (aka Fort d'Illange located near Thionville in the Moselle département, France). Built in 1900, the *Feste* included: 1: Central core with gun battery in armoured turrets placed on top of a concrete building; 2: Infantry position featuring trenches, resistance nests and bombproof barracks; 3: Enclosure featuring a dry ditch and barbed wire. Note that artillery batteries, infantry positions and barracks were linked by roads and underground passages.

Field fortification: Field fortifications are temporary defensive works thrown up at short notice in wartime to defend previously neglected sites, to secure territory captured from the enemy or to give temporary protection to troops on the battlefield. The basic components are a ditch that serves as an obstacle and supplies the soil for an enbankment or breastwork high enough to protect troops. The ditch can also become a trench with a parapet. Although field fortifications had been used as early as Roman times, and were widely used in siege warfare between the sixteenth and nineteenth centuries, the final impetus to their universal adoption came with the introduction of the rifled shoulder arm and the machine gun at the end of the nineteenth century. Field fortifications, whenever possible, adhered to the basic tenet of permanent fortification, being built with an eye to flanking, to safe alignment to prevent enfilade fire and to all the other factors governing fortress design. Far from being performed in a hasty or careless manner, their construction was as precisely defined as any other warlike activity. As a rule each infantryman was issued an entrenching tool and a handbook describing various types of field fortifications. The most basic of them was a simple one-man shallow pit known as a foxhole, which could be dug deep enough to stand in. There was also a standardized

Cross-section of Roman field fortifications built by order of Julius Caesar in 52 BC during the siege of the oppidum of Alesia in Gaul (France). The fieldwork included a *lorica* (1, palisade) made of poles with *pinna* (2, crenel) and merlon (3). The palisade served as a breastwork, and was placed on top of a *vallum* or *agger* (4), an earth wall. *Cervi* (5) were installed in the upper part of the *fossa* (6, ditch). *Turris* (7, watchtowers) were placed at intervals as observation and combat posts. A second ditch (8) was defended by a row of *cippe* (9, sharp poles), while the outer vicinity of the line featured various obstacles like *lilium* (10, pits with sharp stakes) and *stimulus* (11, iron hooks).

two-man version, and several of these, when linked together, could constitute an embryonic trench. Similar but larger positions were designed for three or more soldiers serving a machine gun, mortar or light anti-tank gun. The soil from the excavation was thrown on the enemy's side to form a protective screen known as breastwork or parapet. More complex positions of semi-permanent nature – resembling hunters' blinds – could be made with logs, beams, wooden planks, corrugated plates, sandbags, thick layers of earth and other available materials for the purpose of building combat positions, observatories, command posts, shelters, field infirmaries, supply stores, kitchen and so on. Observation posts could also be built on top of a tree.

Already used in First World War trench warfare, there was a more elaborate form of field fortification known as reinforced field fortification, made of masonry and concrete, with various degrees of protection according to concrete thickess. These could be used as semi-permanent units for reinforcing fixed concrete fortifications. The Crimean War (1853–56), American Civil War (1861–65), Russo-Turkish War (1877–78) and more particularly the First World War showed that improvised fieldworks and reinforced semi-permanent fortifications could be as difficult to storm as any purpose-built permanent fortification.

Field of fire: The field of fire of a weapon (or group of weapons) is the area around it that it can easily and effectively reach. The term is mostly used in reference to firearms.

The field of view (also field of vision) is the angular extent of the observable zone that can be seen from a position. See Arc of fire and Blind spots.

Fieldwork: A general descriptive term for non-permanent field fortifications. See Field fortification.

Fire control station: Artillery emplacement or post equipped with modern and sophisticated optical instruments (binocular, telescope, range finder, radar) and including observatory and plotting rooms, allowing the preparing and directing of artillery fire. Its highly specialized crew receive information from observatories and orders from a command post. They calculate the angle of fire and distance to the target, and issue orders to battery gunners (e.g. the ammunition to employ and the moment to fire). After firing, the crew observe the results and indicate corrections. Fire control stations can be of many shapes, e.g. a concrete tower, mounted on an open steel frame or a bunker partly sunk into the ground.

German Second World War fire control concrete bunker. This impressive type S487 (nicknamed 'Barbara') control bunker was located near Bayonne in southern France.

US World War Two fire control station at San Juan in Puerto Rico.

Firing crest: The upper part of a breastwork (q.v.) over which soldiers can fire.

Fire-step: A narrow flat surface placed behind a parapet or breastwork (q.v.) allowing the protection of combatants. See *Banquette*.

Fire-step. Cross-section of a trench with: 1: Breastwork; 2: Revetment; 3: Fire-step.

Flak: Anti-aircraft fire. The term comes from the German abbreviation of *Fliegerabwehrkanone*, literally 'aircraft-defence gun'.

Flakturm: A Flak tower (plural *Flaktürme*) was a large, thick concrete bunker built above the ground, used by the Luftwaffe to defend against Allied air raids on certain important Third Reich cities (notably in Berlin, Hamburg and Vienna) during the Second World War. The tower included a top terrace fitted with gun pits for heavy and light anti-aircraft artillery, as well as searchlight, radar and command post to coordinate air defence. Inside the tower, the various floors were arranged as ammunition stores and gunners' quarters. A *Flakturm* was always connected to another tower similar in design, this radar-tower housing detection equipment, fire-control and gun-laying installations. Both towers were connected to Luftwaffe radar

Flakturm. Vienna, Austria.

stations and command posts, which coordinated and conducted regional anti-aircraft fire. In many cases the towers were not exclusively military. Some had large rooms left for use by civilians as refuge. They would also house rescue teams, doctors and medical personnel, police squads, firemen, bomb clearance squads etc. They could also be used to store important or precious items like museum artworks and priceless archives. The towers were thus often both active and passive defence objects, and were an extension of the German air raid shelter programme. See Maunsell forts and *Luftschutzraum*.

Flank:

1) The lateral extremes of any military position.
2) In bastioned fortification, the flank was the part of the bastion (q.v.) that joined the face to the rampart (q.v.). The line of fire from a flank would run parallel to the wall that it abutted and defended. Bastion flanks came in two main forms. First, a single flank which was connected to the curtain by a straight plain portion of wall, generally referred to as the right flank. Second, a flank with *orillon* which increased the defenders' safety: the *orillon* (q.v.) or ear (q.v.) was a protruding screen built on the shoulder protecting the defenders in the flank from oblique enemy bombardments but allowing them to enfilade the ditch. The protective *orillon* was round or square, shapes which gave bastions their characteristic arrowhead or ace-of-spades form in plan.

Flank, Bastion.

Flanking: Flanking is one of the basic and fundamental rules of fortification. It is the disposition of two parts of a defensive work emplaced in such a way that enemies attacking one part are exposed to fire coming from the other. There are two main forms of flanking: vertical flanking (from an upper position downwards, from a machicoulis

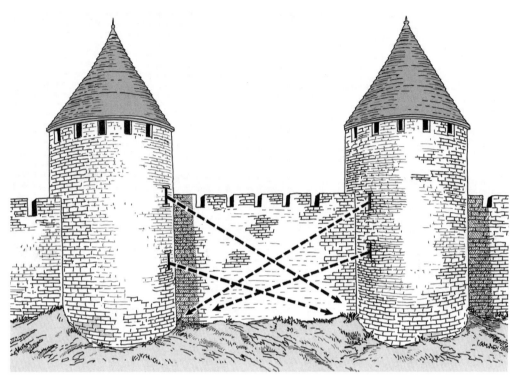

Medieval.

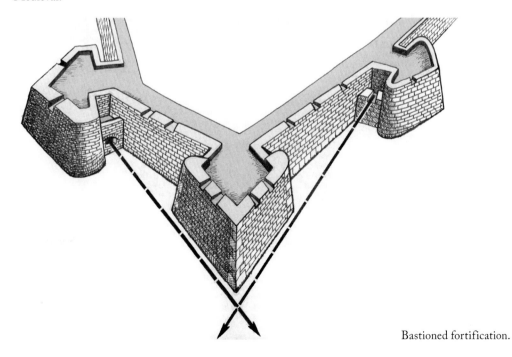

Bastioned fortification.

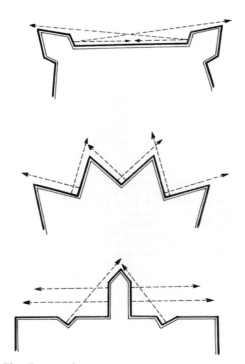

Top: Bastioned system;
Middle: *Tenaille* system;
Bottom: Perpendicular system.

Schematic view of flanking. It takes only two armed concrete flanking casemates to defend a whole stretch of beach against a landing force.

for example) and horizontal flanking. Horizontal flanking is an enfilade fire nearly parallel to the wall and ditch coming from a perpendicular salient allowing the defender to fire at the side or flank of the target. This method was very convenient and allowed a great economy of personnel. Indeed, it only took a few armed soldiers placed in a projecting tower or protuding bastion to defend a whole length of wall. In modern times, it takes only one or two armed casemates to defend a whole stretch of ground or to enfilade a beach.

Flanking casemate: A casemate (q.v.) especially designed to give flanking or enfilading fire sideways to where enemies were expected, thus perpendicular to the way it was supposed to come from. Flanking casemates often had their embrasures protected by a thick screen (ear or sloping concrete wall). This disposition efficiently protected the embrasure but considerably reduced the arc of fire. See *Casemate de Bourges*, Ear, Flanking wall and *Traditore* battery.

Flanking gallery: A passage or chambers with embrasures for firing along the length of a ditch or wall. See Caponier and Coffer.

Flanking wall: A sloping screen protecting the embrasure of a flanking casemate (q.v.).

Flat bastion: A bastion (q.v.) in which the two faces formed together an unprotuberant angle with little or no salient at all.

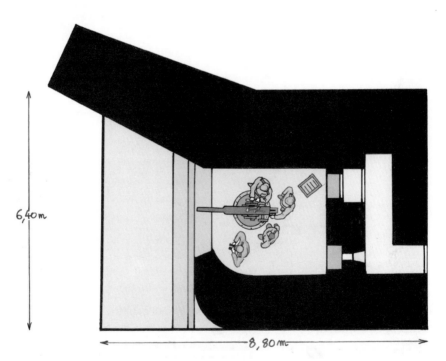

Flanking casemate. Front view and plan of German Second World War flanking casemate type 667.

Flèche: A small arrow-shaped outwork or redan (q.v.) generally placed in the glacis just ahead of the salient of a re-entering place of arms (q.v.). Connected to the covered way by a narrow passageway, it enabled troops to be posted in an advanced combat emplacement.

Floating battery: A type of military boat often fitted with heavy armament. The floating battery was frequently a cumbersome, slow and poorly manoeuvrable ship, so it was often posted for river and coastal waterway control in conjunction with sea forts (q.v.) or coastal fortification (q.v.). Offensively, a floating battery could be used to bombard coastal defences.

Flooding: Flooding (or inundation), the creation of an artificial extent of water, was the voluntary and controlled submersion of zones of varying breadth that otherwise would remain dry in order to create inaccessibility in moments of crisis. Military flooding presented many advantages. Employed on a large scale it was very profitable because fortifications and defensive troops were thus only necessary on high and dry ground. When used on a small scale, it made impossible the establishment and digging of entrenched approaches to lay siege to a place. It also made it difficult or impossible to use underground mines. To be effective, flooding had to be high enough to make impossible the progress of infantry, horsemen, artillery trains and supply waggons, but low enough to prevent navigation. The military use of tactical inundation required great technical knowledge and hydrological installations in order to dominate and control such a dangerous element as water. For example, one had to calculate the surface to be flooded, supply enough water, take into account ground-absorption and evaporation, estimate erosion, and build and maintain water-gates, dams, sluices, batardeaus and supply-canals. Low-lying grounds had to be quickly flooded in moments of crisis, but left totally dry for more productive use in peacetime. To these huge civilian engineering works were added military considerations such as surveillance opposing sabotage or counter-employ and dispositions to facilitate combat conditions.

Inundation also presented serious disadvantages. Obviously it could be used only on low or marshy lands. While it could delay or even stop enemy progress, it also made a friendly counter-offensive equally difficult. It was slow to organize and to effect, especially on a large scale. Furthermore, as we have seen regarding wet ditches, when it froze, flooding lost much or all of its value. Flooding was also extremely unpopular. For the local peasantry, it could mean the destruction of homes, the loss of a harvest, the death of cattle and long-lasting degradation or even infertility of the inundated fields and meadows, especially when corrosive sea water was used.

Throughout the history of warfare, flooding has played a major role, especially in the Low Countries. This strategy was the basis of Dutch defence from the sixteenth century until the 1960s. Dutch Protestant independentists and Spanish troops used it in sieges, for example at Den Briel in 1572, Alkmaar in 1573, Leiden in 1574 and Den Bosch in 1629. Large-scale inundations around Amsterdam stopped Louis XIV's French army and saved the Dutch Republic in 1672. See Dutch Water Line.

Flying bridge: A small and often narrow footbridge built as communication between different parts of a fortification, for example between a motte and a bailey, between a tower and a wall or between a ravelin and a curtain. Flying bridges were invariably made of wood because they would be dismantled, demolished or set on fire when the defenders were obliged to withdraw in a hurry.

Flying sap: A sap (q.v.) or breastwork (q.v.) made of soil-filled gabions (q.v.), quickly built and often under cover of darkness.

Forebuilding: In a Norman keep in Britain, an external structure, lower than the main tower and containing the defended entrance. Some forebuildings contained chambers, chapels and stairs.

Fort: A fort was quite different from a traditional private medieval castle (q.v.). It was a stronghold built by the state to defend a strategic point (a passage, border, valley, pass or stretch of coast) and manned only by a professional permanent military garrison. It was also distinct from a redoubt (q.v.) due to its larger dimensions, superior capacity and greater firepower. It was a strong permanent self-sufficient stronghold, often a major artillery position with a garrison. The great age of the fort was the nineteenth century. See Armoured fort, Arresting fort, Bastioned system, Coastal fort, *Fort d'arrêt* and Polygonal fort.

Fort à cavalier: See Cavalier fort.

Fort à massif central: See Cavalier fort.

Fort d'arrêt: In French fortification as designed by Général Raymond Séré de Rivières (1815–95) during the period 1874–1914, an isolated, detached, advanced and self-contained polygonal fort (q.v.) defending an important passage. See *Barrière de Fer*.

Fort palmé: A kind of fortress designed by Frenchman Colonel Tricaut in 1923. Based on the German *Feste* (q.v.) concept, it was a vast irregular perimeter enclosed with infantry assault-proof barbed wire, rows of metal fencing and anti-tank ditches. It comprised underground entrances, subterranean facilities, barracks and store placed at the rear, connected by tunnels and corridors to advanced observation posts and surface combat blocks (machine-gun casemates and artillery bunkers). The *fort palmé* design was widely used in the Maginot Line (q.v.).

Fortaleza: Spanish for castle, fort or fortress.

Fortificazione alla moderna: 'Modern fortification', created and designed in Italy in the late fifteenth century, which developed into a style known as *Fronte Bastionato all'Italiana*, or Italian Bastioned Front. See Bastioned system, Old Italian system, New Italian system and Venitian bastioned system.

Fortified abbey: Convents, abbeys and other religious establishments were often located in the countryside during the Middle Ages. While these places were holy in theory, the monks' wealth was a tempting target for marauders. Religious establishments were therefore practically always fitted with fortifications.

Fortified bridge: Throughout history, crossing a river has always been of vital importance. Fords were therefore defended, with bridges over wide rivers often fortified. Good examples of fortified bridges can still be seen at Cahors (France), Verona (Italy), Toledo and Besalu (Spain). In the nineteenth century, with the development of railway networks, many rail bridges were fortified too. See *Rivierkazemat*.

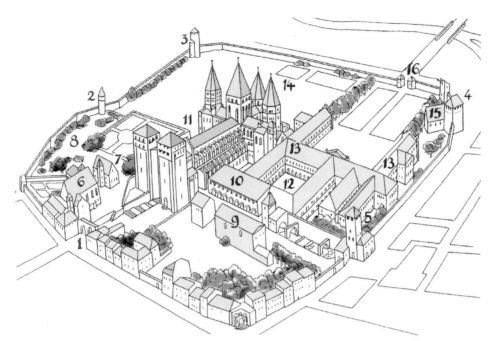

The sketch shows the abbey of Cluny in Burgundy, France, before the destruction of the period 1790–1810. The abbey featured an arched entrance (1) and was surrounded by a wall punctuated with flanking towers, including a Fabry tower (2), Round tower (3), Mill tower (4) and Cheese tower (5). In times of trouble, these fortifications were manned by a militia provided by the inhabitants of the town of Cluny. Inside that protected area were the following buildings: Palace of Abbot Jean de Bourbon (6); Palace of Abbot Jacques d'Amboise (7); Abbatial garden (8); Saint Hugues' medieval stables (9); Pope Gélase's Palace (10); huge abbatial church (11); eighteenth-century cloister (12); eighteenth-century conventual buildings (13); eighteenth-century garden (14); medieval mill and grain store (15); and eighteenth-century entrance (16).

Ponte Scaligero at Verona, Italy. The 120m-long fortified bridge over the Adige River was built between c. 1354 and 1356 and gives access to the Castelvecchio (Old Castle).

Fortified bridge, Nashville, Tennessee, built in 1864 on the Cumberland River.

Fortified church: Constructed in great number in the Middle Ages, fortified churches were a common feature all over Europe. The village church could easily be converted into a defensive structure with just a few adaptations: for example by narrowing the windows into loopholes, crenelating the top of the walls, reinforcing the door and using the bell-tower as an observatory and refuge. Medieval country churches were often surrounded by the village cemetery; if the cemetery wall was well maintained and adapted to defence, it could be used as an external line of combat. Consequently, with determination, a good deal of luck and many prayers, frightened villagers were often capable of resisting a gang of bandits, looters or raiders. Examples of fortified religious buildings are numerous in Europe: Sé Vilha (old cathedral) in Coïmbra and Lisbon in Portugal, the church of Signy-le-Petit and Liart in the French Thiérache, the church of

Moissac Abbey, France.

Saintes-Maries-de-la-Mer in Camargue, the cathedral Saint-Etienne in Agde and the cathedral of Albi in France, or the Sankt-Michaelis Kirche at Hildesheim in Germany.

Fortified group: A large military defensive structure composed of combat elements including infantry and artillery positions, batteries, stores, barracks and shelters, with all components dispersed, sunk in the ground and camouflaged. See *Feste*, *Fort palmé* and Maginot line.

Fortified house: Medieval cities were very insecure owing to the weakness of the watch (defensive militia also tasked with police duties). Furthermore, relationships between rich and poor were always tense, and riots and rebellions could consequently occur. Rich merchants and wealthy bourgeois, patrician families and noblemen therefore resided in private fortified stone houses. A stone house had the advantage of being much less vulnerable to fire than wooden and thatched housing. An urban private fortified residence often consisted of a sort of small keep (q.v.), generally square or rectangular, with defensive elements such as a crenellated roof terrace, defended access and combat emplacements such as loopholes. It could also include more buildings enclosing an inner courtyard or a small garden surrounded by a high stone wall. Private urban fortifications could not resist a siege by an organized army, but they could hold at bay rioters, brigands and robbers. In the countryside, a fortified private house could be termed a manor (q.v.). Farms, mills, wells and other important logistic and economic infrastructures were also often fortified.

Fortified monastery: The medieval Roman Catholic Church was preoccupied to protect its personnel and properties. Clergy residences and monasteries – within or right outside the city walls – were places of culture, learning and spirituality, but the Church was also a wealthy feudal landowner, which meant that its establishments were significant centres of economic and temporal power. Monasteries and priories were therefore fortified with walls, towers and gatehouse. The defensive enceinte also marked the boundary between the profane outside world and the religious establishment.

Fortin: French for fortlet.

Fortlet: A generic term for a small stronghold. See *Castellum*, Redoubt, Sconce and Watchtower.

Fortress: Generic term designating a fortified place. It is typically a term that admits several definitions, depending largely on the context or the personal inclinations of the person doing the defining. It can be a castle, stronghold, fortified city, place of security, fortified region or 'a military position, sited and equipped so as to provide a point of resistance in case of attack, and act as a rallying point for the troops who may be compelled to fall back from more exposed positions' (*Harmsworth's Encyclopedia*). The notable British military author Ian V. Hogg (1926–2002) defines a fortress as 'A series of defensive works for the protection of a specific area or point and under a single command.'

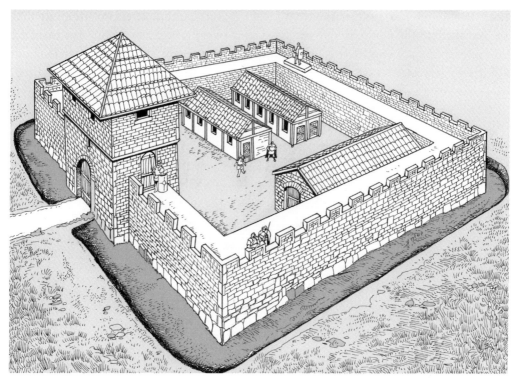

Fortlet (Roman).

Fortress carriage: The fortress carriage or garrison mount was quite similar to the navy mount. It consisted of a simple, robust wooden truck fitted with four small wheels; this had two cheeks of several thick planks, strongly jogged or mortised together. The small wheels gave only limited mobility, but that was not an issue on a ship's deck or on a rampart.

Fortress carriage.

167

Fortress mount: During the nineteenth century, more elaborate fortress mounts than the previous simple navy carriage were designed in order to improve the aiming of the gun and speed up the rate of fire. The traversing platform was a refinement that included a ship's gun carriage without wheels, which was simply placed on a strong wooden track that could turn owing to rear wheels running in a section of curved rail fixed in the gun platform. See *Barbette*, Montcrief mount and Disappearing gun.

Fortress mount.

Fossa: A ditch, moat, canal or pit which was used to impede the advance of an enemy force. Also the ditch or set of ditches which surrounded a Roman fortification, the excavated soil generally used to construct the *vallum* (q.v.) or rampart. See Ditch and Moat.

Fossa fastigata: A type of Roman 'V'-shaped ditch. See *Cippe*.

Fossa punica: A type of Roman ditch with a steep outer scarp. See *Fossa*.

Fossatum Africae: A Roman boundary lime (q.v.) constructed in northern Africa, comprising an earth wall typically 2.5m (8ft) high with a ditch 4–6m (13–20ft) wide and 2.3–3.4m (7½–ft) deep.

Fossé: French for ditch (q.v.) and moat (q.v.).

Fossé Diamant: Literally a 'diamond ditch'. In posterns, casemates and defended entrances in nineteenth-century forts and in the Maginot Line (q.v.), the *fossé Diamant* was a typical ditch made of concrete placed at the base of the façade. The purpose was to deny enemy access to embrasures, gates and doors, and also to collect debris and rubble in case of heavy bombardment. The ditch was generally 2–3m wide and 3–5m deep.

Fougasse: A cylindrical excavation facing the enemy dug in an access, a dangerously vulnerable spot or in the glacis. The fougasse was filled with gunpowder, pebbles, stones and rocks. It was detonated when the enemy reached its vicinity, and can be regarded as the ancestor of the landmine.

Foothold: See Bridgehead.

Foxhole: Used in field fortification (q.v.), a foxhole is a vertical excavation that allows a soldier to stand and fight with only head and shoulders exposed. The foxhole can sometimes widen at the bottom to allow a soldier to crouch down while under intense artillery fire or tank attack. Foxholes can be enlarged to provide two-man fighting positions, as well as emplacements for crew-served weapons. See Rifle pit and Trench.

Fraise: Sharp poles, stakes or palisades (q.v.) placed in a horizontal or inclined position in a ditch, earth wall or berm to form an obstacle against escalade by assaulting infantry. See Stormpole.

Freccia: See Arrow and *Flèche*.

Frizzy Horse: The so-called Frizzy Horse was employed as early as the sixteenth century (probably employed for the first time in 1594 at the siege of Groningen in Friesland, whence its name). The Frizzy Horse – in German *Spanischen Reiter*, in American 'knife stand' and in French *Cheval de Frise* (q.v.) – was a mobile obstacle composed of a baulk of timber about 4m (13ft) long, with pointed stakes protruding from the side. The stakes acted as legs while the remainder formed an effective obstacle against infantry and cavalry. A modern twentieth-century version consisted of a wooden frame resting on cross bars. Dimensions varied, and the obstacle could be wrapped in barbed wire with carrying handles on each side. It was mobile and was thus used to block a road, passage or gap in a barbed wire network. See Roadblock.

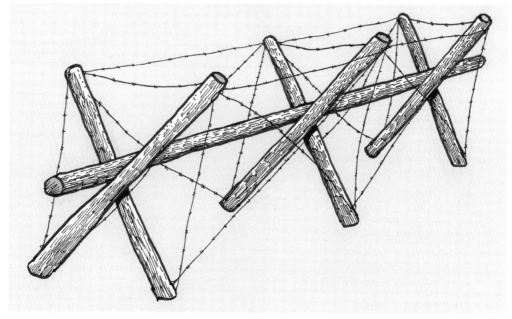

Frizzy Horse (knife stand).

Front:

1) Battle line, combat area, zone of military operations.
2) The part of a fortification facing the enemy.

Front Todt: A large concrete often semi-circular corbelling canopy built above the embrasure of certain types of German heavy naval artillery bunkers in the Atlantic Wall (q.v.). Also used in some American coastal batteries (e.g. Fort Fulton near San Francisco).

Front Todt.

Führer's Headquarters: German Führer Adolf Hitler (1889–1945) was concerned about his own safety to an insane degree. Wherever he went, he first of all issued orders for building bunkers for his personal protection. His historic meeting with French marshal Philippe Pétain in October 1940 – at a time when Allied air activity was extremely limited – took place in the small village of Montoire for one sole reason: there was a convenient tunnel in the vicinity where the Führer's train could shelter in case of a hypothetical British air-strike. Hitler also had several underground concrete command bunkers called Führer's Headquarters (FHQu) constructed at Rastensburg, Berlin, Rodert, Bruly, Obersalzberg, Munich, Salzburg and Bad Nauheim, plus others in Silesia and Thuringia. Each complex, halfway between a fort and a concentration camp, was heavily guarded, fenced and camouflaged. Each command bunker included accommodation for Hitler, guests, escort troops and staff, and featured a communication system, often an airstrip and whenever possible access to a railway line. Many of these costly command bunkers were never used or only briefly visited, and only a few were actually occupied for their intended purpose. See Hitler's Berlin bunker.

Full bastion: A full or solid bastion was a bastion (q.v.) in which the interior area was level with the *terre-plein* of the rampart.

FW3: In May 1940, the Directorate of Fortifications and Works (coded FW3) was set up at the British War Office. Placed under the leadership of Major-General G.B. Taylor, FW3's task was to provide a number of basic pillbox designs, which could be built by soldiers and local labour at appropriate defensive locations. In June and July 1940, FW3 issued six basic designs for rifle and light machine-gun pillboxes, designated Types 22 to 27. In addition, there were designs for artillery emplacements suitable for either the Ordnance QF 2-pdr or Hotchkiss 6-pdr gun (designated Type 28) and a design for a hardened medium machine-gun emplacement. There were also designs for pillbox-like structures for various purposes, including light anti-aircraft positions, observation posts and searchlight positions to illuminate the shoreline, and a number of pillboxes particularly designed to protect airfields from airborne enemy attack.

G

Gabion: Also called a corbeil, a gabion is an open-ended, cylindrical wicker basket made of woven brushwood (sometimes of interlaced iron bands or wire netting). When filled with earth, the basket forms strong protection against small-arms projectiles. The term comes from the Italian *gabbionne*, meaning big cage. Gabions were used from the Renaissance until the end of the nineteenth century as protection and revetment, support or reinforcment for the sides of excavations, trenches, fieldworks, earthworks and field batteries. Gabions were discarded in the twentieth century, but have more recently reappeared in the form of hollow wire boxes filled with rocks and dirt to construct dikes or foundations. Similar items are used by the military to protect against explosive, fragmentary and indirect fire, such as from mortars or light artillery. See HESCO barrier and Sandbags.

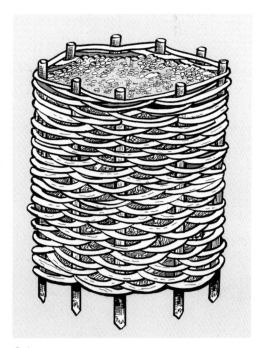

Gabion.

Gaffs: A pair of lifting arms placed above and parallel to the bridge deck, linked by chains, used to operate the common type of bascule drawbridge (q.v.). In the raised position, the gaffs fit into slots in the gatehouse wall (called rainures).

Cross-section of medieval drawbridge with counterweight and gaffs. By pulling down the chain (1), the mobile counterweighted inner part of the gaffs pivoted down (2), lifting the mobile bridge roadway (3). The outer part of the gaffs pivoted up (4) and fitted into rainures or grooves (5) installed for this purpose in the façade of the gatehouse.

Left: Open.
Right: Closed.

Gaine: A kind of vaulted gallery or passage pierced into the thickness of a curtain (q.v.) allowing garrison troops to move rapidly and under safe cover from one place to another. It was not only an easily protected route of communication but also a combat emplacement as it could be furnished with arrow-slits.

Gallery:

1) A long, narrow passage or room, often overlooking a great hall or garden.
2) A vaulted passage, generally within a defensive wall. The gallery could sometimes be fitted with loopholes through which defenders could observe or shoot. See Counterscarp gallery, Hoarding, Gaine and Mining.

Galopin turret: An eclipsing armoured turret (q.v.) designed in the 1890s by the French senior officer Alfred Galopin. Using huge counterweights for rapid movement, it was 5.5m in diameter, its roof was 30cm thick and the side walls 45cm of hard steel. The retractable Modèle 1907 turret could house single or twin 75mm or 155mm Bange guns served by six artillerymen. Galopin turrets included ventilation systems and a lift to bring up ammunition. While they were advanced pieces of engineering, their costs were exorbitant. Only a few were ever installed in concrete blocking forts in the regions of Toul and Verdun and in the Charmes Gap in north-eastern France.

Garderobe: French term designating a small storeroom to keep dresses. It has come to mean a primitive toilet in a castle or other medieval building. Just like the euphemistic term 'bathroom', a *garderobe* is prosaically a privy, toilet or 'loo'. In a medieval castle it was usually a simple

Gaine.

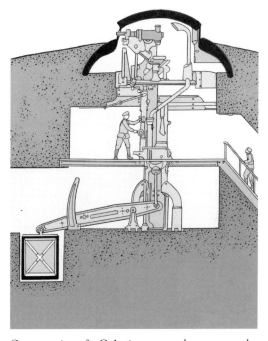

Cross-section of a Galopin armoured turret armed with twin 75mm guns.

hole set over a stone shaft working as a drain discharging to the outside. A *garderobe* tower was a tower specifically constructed to house such privies, usually projecting from the outer wall of a castle. See Cesspit, Latrine.

Garrison mount: Gun carriage especially designed to meet the requirement of a fortress. A typical seventeenth- and eighteenth-century garrison mount was the naval carriage (aka truck) with four small wheels. See Fortress mount.

Gate: A point of entry to a space enclosed by walls, or an access in a fence. Gates, often fitted with a gatehouse (q.v.) and a guardhouse (q.v.), allow control of entry or exit to a camp, fort, castle, base, fortified city or barracks.

Hattousa Gate, located in Anatolia, Turkey, was the capital of the Hittite Empire in the Bronze Age.

Grave Gate is located in the province of North Brabant in the Netherlands. The gate was designed in 1688 by the Dutch engineer Menno van Coehorn.

Gatehouse: A building enclosing or accompanying a gate in a castle, manor house, fort, citadel, camp, base or any other similar military building of importance. The gates form weak points in a fortified perimeter, since they are by definition points of access. Gatehouses made their first appearance in the Ancient World and eventually in the Middle Ages when they became necessary to protect the main entrance. Over time, they evolved into very complicated structures with several lines of defence in depth. The gatehouse included a wide arched portal – large enough to let a cart through. The portal included heavy stout wooden folding doors reinforced with nails and metal parts, and often fitted with a wicket (q.v.). The portal was arranged either into a rectangular building or a mural tower through which the entryway passed, or deeply recessed between a

Oosterpoort 'East Gate' at Groningen in the Netherlands, built in 1517.

Roman, at Chester in north-west England.

pair of strong flanking towers. This large, complex fortified gatehouse would normally include a drawbridge (q.v.), one or more portcullises (q.v.), machicolations (q.v.), arrow loops (q.v.) and possibly brattice (q.v.) and murder holes (q.v.). Later, embrasures and loopholes were added for rifles and machine guns. In Antiquity and the Middle Ages, there was sometimes one or more outworks defending the access, as well as a small and narrow courtyard arranged behind the gatehouse in order to hold up an assault in a confined space where the defenders could deal at short range with assailants who had penetrated thus far.

Beside military defensive elements, the medieval city gatehouse also included a customs office where taxes and tolls were levied on all persons and goods coming into or going out of the city. The gate taxes were one of the major forms of income for medieval cities. In certain cases, the gatehouse could include an arsenal for weapons and ammunitions, an apartment for the porter (q.v.), lodgings for civil servants and tax collectors and quarters for the garrison, and may be used as a prison. The gatehouse also always played a prestigious and symbolic role. It was often adorned with decorative finery as an expression of greatness, power and splendour. Its imposing defences and decorations displayed the strength and power of the castle lord or the pride and independence of the burghers. Its front side could look like a triumphal arch (q.v.) with lavish architectural ornaments ostentatiously showing to visitors and travellers the pride of a king, as well as the wealth and importance of the citizens.

Throughout the history of fortification, the gatehouse has always been a highly guarded point. For security reasons, access was as limited as possible, resulting on many occasions in annoying traffic-jams, particularly on market days in the case of fortified cities; therefore, secondary accesses – called posterns (q.v.) – were arranged and opened in peacetime. From dusk to dawn, medieval gates and posterns were closed. See *Châtelet*.

Gaztelu: Fortification works constructed during the Iron Age in the Basque country. Generally built on hills at the foot of the western Pyrenees, these were markets, trading places and permanent dwellings. They could be quite large, and like the British hillforts (q.v.) and Celtic oppida (q.v.) included ditches, earth walls and palisades.

Génie: The French Army Engineering Corps.

Genoese tower: A model of coastal watchtower (q.v.) built between 1530 and 1620 by the Republic of Genoa in its possessions in the Mediterranean (on the islands of Corsica and Elba and at Tabarka). Manned with a few *torregiani* (guards), they were intended to warn of and delay attacks by North African pirates. Generally round and made of stone, they were between 12m and 17m in height and 8–10m in diameter. They included quarters for the small garrison, storeplaces and an open crenellated surveillance platform on top. See Martello tower.

Geschützstand: Gun emplacement in German.

Ghibelline merlon: A merlon (q.v.) fitted with a notched or V-shaped apex, common in medieval Italy. The name comes from the Ghibellines ('imperial party'), a political faction that supported the Holy German Emperor and was opposed to the Guelphs ('church party') who supported the Pope from the twelfth to the fifteenth centuries.

Glacis: A wide and totally bare sloping or flat zone, usually turfed, entirely surrounding a fortified place. Gently inclining from the covered way (q.v.) towards the surrounding country, its object was to expose assailants to a conspicuous killing zone deprived of cover as they approached. Its gentle declivity was smoothed on the general profile of all the other works and intended to conceal from view and therefore from the enemy's fire all walls of the fortress. The glacis could be reinforced by an exterior ditch and sometimes by an outer covered way and a second glacis. The glacis was always established in bastioned and modern fortifications. It existed more or less in the medieval period, a very enticing area to citizens just outside the town. In peacetime, it was often used by the citizens as fields, allotments, kitchen-gardens or meadows. In spite of municipal interdictions, even a new suburb could spread out, but the non-defended settlement was certain to be looted or destroyed when a siege occured. See Bastioned system and Esplanade.

Ghibelline merlon.

Globe of compression: A type of mine (q.v.) developed in the late eighteenth century, also known as a supercharged mine, and named after the globe formed by particles of earth when acted upon by an explosion, which marshalled the destructive potential of mining (q.v.) even further.

Gorge: The space at the back, neck or interior side of a fortified work.

Goulotte à Grenade: In the Maginot Line, an adaptation of the *créneau de pied* (q.v.), a vertical pipe or 45-degrees oblique duct placed in the thickness of a concrete wall allowing defenders to drop hand grenades upon intruders. See Machicolation.

Graffe: Old-fashioned English term for ditch (q.v.) derived from the German *Grabe*.

Grazing fire: Firing which sweeps close to the surface it defends, with an elevation of less than 20 degrees. Also called direct fire, as the aimer often sees his target.

Great Wall of China: Beginning in the seventh century BC, a series of massive defensive fortifications were constructed along China's northern border. Built to protect China from northern attacks, the walls stretched for thousands of kilometres, many of them joined together to become the Great Wall of China. Over several centuries, the wall and thousands of supporting structures were built across mountains, deserts and rivers, eventually stretching more than 20,000km in length. Sections of the wall near large cities are still well-maintained, but many in remote areas are slowly being reclaimed by nature.

Grille Belge: See Belgian Gate.

Groupe fortifié: See *Feste* and Fortified group.

Gruson turret: An armoured turret designed by the German Gruson Company from Magdeburg-Buckau – a branch of the Krupp industrial firm. Gruson turrets were used in concrete forts from the end of the nineteenth century. See Mougin turret and Armoured turret.

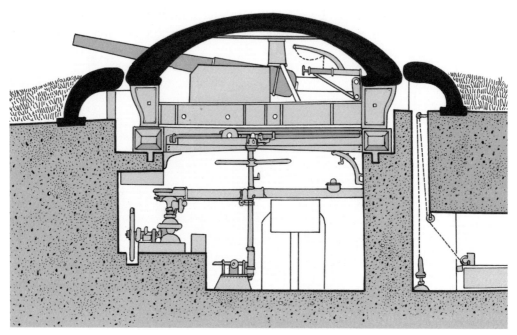

Gruson turret. Cross-section (Fort Pampus, near Amsterdam, the Netherlands).

Guardhouse: A post intended to shelter the soldiers checking the entrance of a fortified city, fort or citadel, camp or base. In the case of a fortified town, the personnel controlling access included guards and soldiers, but also custom officers who levied taxes and tolls on all persons and all goods coming into or going out of the town. Access to a fortress was usually restricted to those having legitimate business within, particularly in time of war. The guardhouse could be a chamber integrated into the gatehouse or an independent detached building constructed on a *demi-lune*. The guardhouse was not a combat emplacement but a useful building for day-to-day policing and control purposes. It could include a chamber with bunks for the sentries, a room/office heated by a fireplace for the officer, and an exterior gallery or porch roof resting on wooden beams or stone arches.

Guardiola: Italian for *echauguette* (q.v.), *guérite* (q.v.) or sentrybox (q.v.).

Guérite: A one-man stone or timber sentry box (q.v.) or a small lookout watchtower. See Bartizan and *Echauguette*.

Guichet: A small opening in the gate of a fortification. See Wicket.

Gun house: An armoured shield with roof, front and sides covering a gun on a barbette (q.v.) mount. The enclosed gun house gives the appearance of an enclosed turret (q.v.) but it is slightly different as its rear is always open.

Gun pit: Open firing emplacements, generally circular or square and constructed at the same level as the surrounding ground. This artillery platform is fitted with a parapet but without the cover of a protective roof. It therefore only gives lateral protection, and is vulnerable to curved mortar fire and to bombs dropped by aircraft. The gun pit enables a full 360-degree arc of fire, and is cheap and rapidly built. It is often a non-permanent artillery position used in field fortification, and is also used for anti-aircraft fire.

Gun platform: An emplacement specially built for cannons in a fortification. A gun platform generally includes a breastwork but no roof. Until efficient ventilation was introduced, the gun platform was a much better solution to artillery emplacement than a casemate (q.v.) because the noise and fumes of gunfire in that enclosed space made it very uncomfortable and unhealthy.

Gun port: Also called gun loop, an opening or embrasure (q.v.) for a gun in a wall or casemate.

Gunport. Bottom left: Medieval arrow slit adapted to firearms by addition of a hole; Bottom right: Gun slit; Top: Gun port or embrasure.

Gun turret: A gun turret is a fully enclosed device that protects both crew and weapon. It is often armoured, fully rotating and mounted on an armoured fighting vehicle, warship or military aircraft. Turrets have greatly varying size according to armament, ranging from one or more machine guns to automatic cannons, flame-thrower, large-calibre guns and missile launchers. In some cases they may be remotely controlled. A small turret is often called a cupola (q.v.). Gun turrets have also been placed in static land fortifications, for example in concrete forts, or on a fortified building or structure such as a coastal battery.

Guthrie rolling bridge: A retractable bridge used in British eighteenth- and nineteenth-century forts providing access across a defensive moat. Unhinged, the movable Guthrie bridge remained horizontal when retracted within the gates of the fort, operating in a similar way to a modern thrust bridge. Guthrie bridges can still be seen in forts of the Portsdown Hill line at Portsmouth, e.g. at Fort Nelson, as well as at Cambridge Battery and Rinella Battery in Malta.

H

Habicht turret: The Habicht turret was designed by Oberst Dipl. Ing. General-Major Franz Rollomann Habicht, of the German Second World War naval engineering corps. It was a special kind of rotating turret made of concrete instead of steel in order to spare metal. Habicht and his team, working in the navy Pionierpark (engineer experimental centre) at Gennevilliers near Paris, made scale-models for 38cm and 40.6cm guns. Field Marshal Rommel, in charge of strengthening the Atlantic Wall, visited the centre on 1 April 1944 and showed great enthusiasm for the project. One Habicht concrete revolving turret was actually built at MKB Waldam, north east of Calais in north-east France. The concrete turret was armed with one 15cm C/28 gun with a range of 37km. It weighed no less than 750 metric tonnes, and was operated by the rotating mechanism salvaged from the captured French warship *Provence*. It was placed on top of a bunker which included two ammunition stores. For unknown reason (probably high cost), Habicht's proposition was not further developed by the German high command.

Hadrian's Wall: Hadrian's Wall (*Vallum Hadriani*) was a line of fortification built by the Romans across the width of what is now northern England. Begun in AD 122, during the rule of Emperor Hadrian (AD 76–138), it was the first of two lines built across Britain, the second being the Antonine Wall further north in Scotland. Hadrian's Wall was 117km (73½ miles) long. Completed in *c.* AD 128, it included a stone wall and ditch, with evenly spaced intermediate square towers, forts and fortlets (mile-castles), and a military road parallel to the wall. It was constructed primarily to prevent attack by small bands of Pict raiders from the north. It was also a symbol of Roman power. Significant sections of Hadrian's Wall have been preserved and today form a popular historic tourist attraction.

Hairspin: British socket roadblock designed in 1940. The hairspin was made of railway lines or rolled steel joists (q.v.) bent or welded at around a 60-degree angle. Like the rolled steel joists, the hairspin was placed in prepared square sockets about 6in (15.2cm) wide inserted in the road, closed by covers when not in use, allowing traffic to pass normally. See Anti-tank obstacles.

Half-bastion: A bastion (q.v.) having one of its faces directly connected to the curtain without a flank. Half-bastions were notably built in sconces (q.v.) as well as in hornworks and crownworks (q.v.).

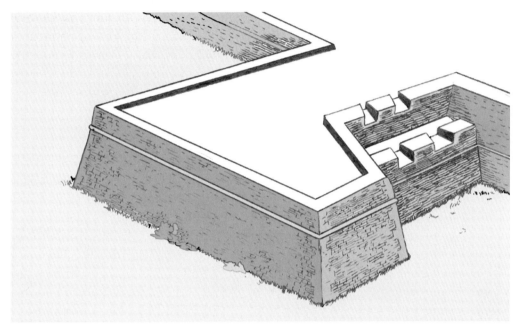

Half-bastion.

Half-counterguard: See Counterguard.

Hall: The Hall or Great Hall was the main room in a medieval castle, often of great dimensions, in which all parts of the household of the castle community would eat and live. It was a large room of relative comfort and status, which usually included a fireplace (with additional braziers and charcoal pans in winter) and decorative woodwork, trophies, tapestries and wall hangings. The Hall was used as a place of social life for entertainment, banquet, feast and celebration, but also as a room to gather a meeting, a council or a court of justice. At night it could be used as a dormitory for servants. In the early Middle Ages it was a large room in the keep (q.v.), but increasingly it was a separate building, a hall-house placed in the bailey (q.v.). Privacy in the Middle Ages was a luxury enjoyed only by persons of status: kings, dukes, counts, lords and ladies who could retire when they wished to their personal rooms (called a camera or solar).

Haxo casemate: A casemate (q.v.) designed by the French military engineer François Haxo (1774–1838). This type of casemate, laid inside the rampart of permanent fortifications, was made of vaulted masonry and shielded from hostile artillery and small-arms fire by a thick layer of earth, which would absorb the shock of shot and shell impacts and prevent the masonry from damage and collapse. It was fitted with a porthole, but its originality was that it was open at the rear, allowing light inside and smoke and other toxic fumes to escape. The Haxo casemate was widely used in nineteenth-century fortifications.

Haxo casemate, (seen from the rear).

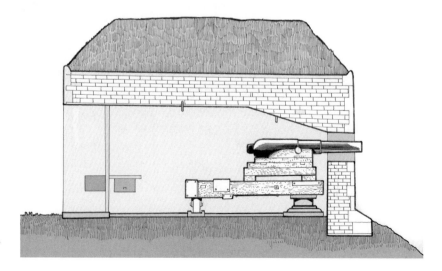

Haxo casemate, (cross-section).

Hedgehog: A hedgehog defence was a military tactic for defending against attack. The defenders deployed in depth in heavily fortified positions suitable for all-around defence. The attackers could penetrate between them, but each position could fight on even when surrounded. This kept large numbers of assaulting troops tied up attacking the well-defended strongpoints, while allowing the defenders to successfully counter-attack the units that bypassed them with their own armoured reserves, cutting off the attackers from their supporting elements. See Box, Island, Igel.

Hedgerow: Typical of Normandy in north-west France, hedgerows created sturdy field and meadow enclosures, called *bocages*, comprising a core of piled rocks made by generations of peasants, topped with earth, vegetation and small trees with dense roots. During the Battle of Normandy in the summer of 1944, the mazes of narrow sunken lanes and thick *bocages* were used by the Germans as clusters of field fortification, proving themselves formidable defensive positions and anti-tank and anti-personnel obstacles. As a counter-measure, the Allies fitted some of their tanks with sharp cutting devices or 'tusks' (prongs) placed at the front of the vehicles. These Rhinoceros tanks worked like bulldozers to create gaps through the *bocage*.

Hemmbalk: A German Second World War beach obstacle consisting of a tree-trunk (about 8–10m long) or a concrete beam resting on supports. The beam made a 30–40 degree angle with the ground. *Hemmbalken* were placed in alternate rows on the beach

Hemmbalk.

and were intended to strand landing craft. The destructive potentiality was increased by placing sharp blades (*Stahlmesser*) and anti-tank mines (*Tellermine*) which would explode and rip boat hulls like can-openers.

Henrician fortification: A typical style of coastal forts built in England during the reign of Henry VIII (b. 1491, reign from 1509–47). Also called Device Forts or Tudor fortification, as Henry was the second monarch of the Tudor dynasty, Henrician fortification was most spectacular along the southern coast of England from Kent to Cornwall, where Henry VIII strengthened defences by the establishment of coastal forts (e.g. at Deal, Sandown, Walmer and Calshot). See Transitional fortification.

Henrician Fortification (Deal Castle).

Heraldry: The system of coats of arms used to identify noble families. Heraldic decorations were often carved in stone and placed above doors and gates in castles and other fortified noble residences.

HESCO barrier: The HESCO barrier is a modern version of the traditional gabion (q.v.) used for flood control and military fortification. It is made of a collapsible wire mesh container and heavy-duty fabric liner, and used as a temporary or semi-permanent dike or barrier against blast or small-arms fire. It has been employed in United States military bases in Iraq as well as in NATO bases in Afghanistan. Named after the British company that developed it, the HESCO gabion is rectangular and comes in a variety of sizes. Most of the barriers can also be stacked, and they are shipped collapsed in compact sets. Typical dimensions 4ft 6in x 3ft 6i x 32ft (1.4m x 1.1m x 9.8m).

Hexamilion Wall: The Hexamilion (6-mile) Wall was built between AD 408 and 450 during the reign of the Byzantine emperor Theodosius II. Stretching across the entire isthmus of Corinth in central Greece, it was designed to protect the Peloponnese from barbarian invasions. The defensive line included a fortress at Isthmia, a wall constructed with a rubble and mortar core faced with squared stones and about 150 wall towers. After the Ottoman conquest of the Peloponnese in 1460, the wall was abandoned. Today, elements of the wall are preserved south of the Corinth Canal and at Isthmia.

Hillfort: A hillfort is a type of fortified refuge or defended settlement, generally located on a hilltop, promontory, ridge or cliff edge, combining natural and man-made obstacles. They are typically European and of the Bronze and Iron Ages. The defensive

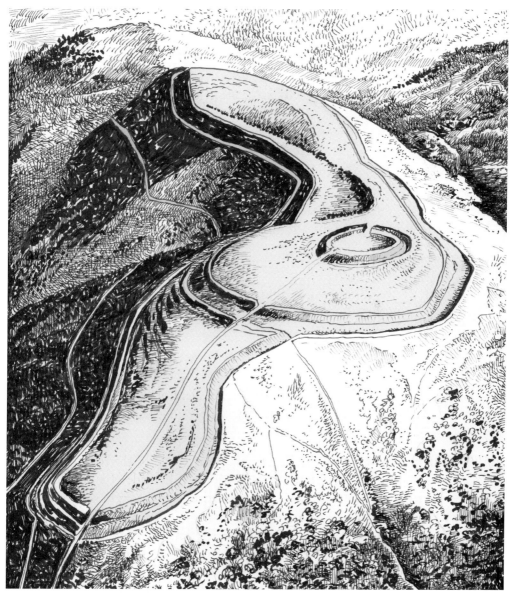

Hillfort at Herefordshire Beacon in the Malvern Hills, England.

enclosure usually followed the contours of the hill, consisting of one or more lines of earthworks, with stockades or defensive walls and external dry ditches. Some European hillforts originated in the late Neolithic period, but they are most common during the later Bronze Age and Iron Age. Their size varied from 1 hectare to 20 hectares. Some were permanent settlements, while others were only occupied seasonally or in times of strife. They could be found in many Celtic areas of Central and Western Europe until the Roman conquest. Julius Caesar described the large late Iron Age hillforts he encountered during his campaigns in Gaul as *oppida*. By this time the larger ones had become more like walled cities than fortresses, and many were assimilated as Roman towns. See *Oppidum* and Promontory fort.

Hindenburg Line: A strongly built line of fortification built by the Germans in northeast France between late 1916 and 1918 during the latter stages of the First World War. To the Germans it was known as the *Siegfried Stellung*. It was not only a network of trenches but a concentration of strong defensive fall-back positions, 3–4 miles deep, stretching from Lille to Soissons. The *Stellung* included several systems named Hindenburg, Wotan, Siegfried, Alberich, Hunding, Braunhild, Hermann and Hagen. The German fortified *Stellung* was composed of four defensive rows, using all possible natural obstacles (hills, ridges, marshes, rivers and forests), field fortifications (trenches and barbed wire) and concrete bunkers (shelters, observatories, outposts, machine-gun pillboxes, mortar posts, command stations, artillery emplacements, gas-proof and bomb-proof troop shelters and subterrean barracks linked by tunnels).

There were always several belts of trenches and obstacles, so arranged that the front-line troops could fall back, allowing artillery to decimate the temporarily successful enemy, after which a counter-attack could be launched. Nothing was straight in traverse to prevent enfilading fire. The *Stellung* was widely regarded as impregnable, but it was sometimes broken easily, at other times with great difficulty, by a novel and innovative use of combined arms and artillery, aeroplanes also being used as artillery spotters. The first Allied attacks on the lines took place at the end of 1917 in an attempt to end the defensive deadlock, but were unsuccessful. By mid-1918, after the failed German Spring Offensive, the Allies finally succeeded in breaking through the *Stellung*. By then the German Army was low in morale and greatly reduced in number. See Trench warfare.

Hitler's Berlin bunker: A heavily fortified concrete shelter in Berlin where Adolf Hitler resided at the end of his regime. It was probably the safest place in whole of Nazi Germany. Originally an air raid shelter, the *Führerbunker* was a subterranean concrete structure located some 15 metres (50ft) below the Chancellery in Berlin.

The bunker's concrete roof was more than 5 metres (16.4ft) thick, reinforced with grids of steel bars, then topped with 10 metres (32.8ft) of earth. The bunker was accessed from the Chancellery by a stairway from the butler's pantry. These stairs led to a narrow tunnel enclosed by three airtight, watertight and thick armoured bulkheads. The first one closed the passage to the pantry, called the *Kannenberggang* (named after Hitler's butler, Arthur Kannenberg). The second bulkhead gave way to an outer stair with access to the garden of the Foreign Office. The third – placed in the middle of the passage – led down to the bunker.

The bunker comprised two levels. The upper level included a central corridor (used as a general dining place) with twelve small rooms, six on each side, for lumber and storage and servants' quarters, including the *Diätküche* (kitchen), where Hitler's vegetarian meals were prepared by his cook, Fräulein Constance Manziarly. At the end of the central passage, a curved stairs led downwards to a still deeper and larger bunker. That was the Führer's bunker proper. This lower level included eighteen small, cramped and uncomfortable rooms, and a central passage divided into two spaces by a partition. The first part of the passage was used as a general sitting room and gave access to utilitarian offices, lavatories and bathroom, a guardroom, an emergency telephone exchange and the powerplant. The second part of the passage was arranged as a conference room. A door on the left gave access to a suite of six rooms reserved for Hitler and his girlfriend (later wife), Eva Braun. She had a private bed/sitting room, a bathroom and a dressingroom. Hitler had a personal bedroom and a study. In addition there were several guest rooms, an anteroom, a small map/conference room and a narrow room known as the *Hundebunker* (Dog's Bunker) used as a rest room for the Führerbegleitkommando (SS escort and bodyguards). At the end of the guard room was a ladder leading to an unfinished concrete observation tower above the ground. At the end of the passage, a door gave access to a small anteroom used as a cloakroom. This led to an emergency exit and a stair leading up into the Chancellery garden. It was in this bunker that Hitler committed suicide on 30 April 1945. See Führer's Headquarters.

Hoarding: A hoarding (sometimes called propugnaclum) was a temporary wooden shed-like construction placed on the exterior of the ramparts and towers of a medieval castle or a town threatened by a siege. The purpose of a hoarding was to allow the defenders to improve their field of fire along the length of wall and towers, particularly, directly downwards to the wall base without the need to expose themselves to danger. In peacetime, hoardings were stored as prefabricated elements. The installation of a hoarding was facilitated by putlog holes (q.v.) in the masonry of castle walls. These wooden overhanging walkways were, however, vulnerable to fire. Later, permanent structures with similar functions known as machicolation (q.v.) were built in stone. See Brattice, Machicolation and Moucharaby.

Hoarding, (cross-section).

Hoarding. Left: Front view; Right: Cross-section.

Hochleitstand: A German Second World War concrete bunker (q.v.) built upward, usually in the form of a high tower intended to serve as an observatory, fire leading station or air raid shelter. Spectacular extant towers are still to be seen, for example at Riva Bella (Normandy, France) and in the Channel Islands. See *Leitstand*, *Luftschutzraum*, Fire control station and Observation tower.

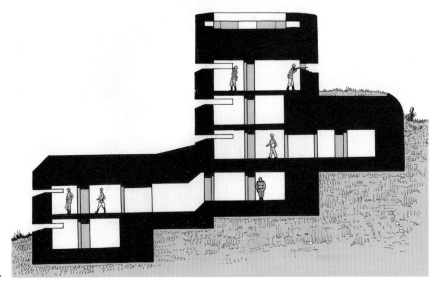

Hochleitstand.

Höckerhindernisse: German for anti-tank dragon's teeth (q.v.). Used in the Siegfried Line (q.v.) and Atlantic Wal (q.v.), the German 1938-type *Höckerhindernisse* had four rows, but in 1939 it was improved by a new model featuring a fifth row.

Hohenburg: A German medieval castle built on a naturally strong site, usually a craggy cliff or a steep hill, with all its defences facing the lines of approach and the entrances. See *Schildmauer*.

Hollandsche Waterlinie: See Dutch Water Line.

Hollow bastion: A bastion (q.v.) that is empty or void, meaning that it was terraced only along its revetment.

Hollow charge: A shaped or hollow charge is a concave metal hemisphere or cone (known as a liner) backed by a high explosive, all in a steel or aluminum casing. When the high explosive is detonated, the metal liner is compressed and squeezed forward, forming a jet whose tip may travel as fast as 10km per second. The shaped charge was introduced into warfare as an anti-tank device in the Second World War, but it was also used to destroy concrete bunkers and armoured doors.

Hollow traverse: Traverse (q.v.) fitted with a passage.

Hooch: Informal US word for an improvised shelter, usually with some protection from enemy fire.

Hornwork: An advanced work (q.v.) formed of a bastioned front (a curtain and two half-bastions) and two long parallel wings connecting back to the covered way. It often featured a ravelin at both the front and in the gorge. Hornworks, as well as crownworks (q.v.), were projecting combat positions designed to force the besiegers to begin a siege from a greater distance and to occupy and cover parts of the ground not easily seen from the main wall. Hornworks and crownworks could be coupled to form a strong fortified unit.

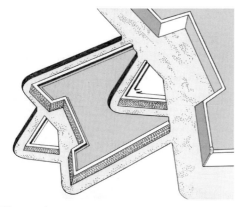

Hornwork.

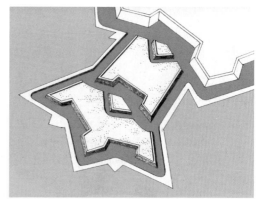

Hornwork reinforced with a crownwork – in French *corne couronnée* ('crowned horn').

Howitzer bunker: A combat concrete casemate (q.v.) specially adapted for the curved firing of a howitzer, thus with a wide embrasure allowing a high elevation field of fire. A howitzer is a type of gun, introduced in the eighteenth century, halfway between conventional gun and mortar, firing with a curved angle of elevation in the middle register (between 10 and 45 degrees). See Mortar.

Howitzer bunker.

Huchette: A small mantlet (q.v.) or wooden shutter placed in the crenel (q.v.) in times of war in order to protect the defenders. It could be raised at the defenders' discretion by means of an axle turning in two iron collars set in the upper angles of the merlons (q.v.). See Crenel shutter.

Hurdle: A moveable section of light fence. Traditionally they were made from wattle (woven split branches) or planks, and intended as revetment for a palisade (q.v.) or to strenghten the side of a trench.

I

Ideal bastioned city: Among Italian engineers of the Renaissance arose the desire to create ideal cities, not focused on a cathedral or appended to a castle but offering an environment for civic life protected by bastioned fortifications. Hypothetical designs were proposed and only a few in fact were implemented. The bastioned walls of Nicosia on Cyprus (built between 1567 and 1570 by order of the Republic of Venice) as well as Palmanova, Italy, display unique examples with perfect circular shapes in outline and a radial or grid street layout.

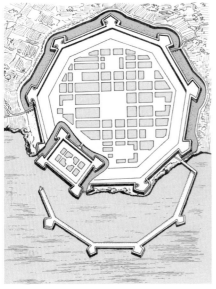
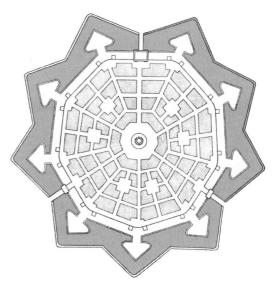

Ideal city. Designed by Girolamo Cataneo in c.1564 with citadel and harbour.

Palmanova, Italy.

Igel: German for hedgehog (q.v.). Defence system favoured by the German Army from the time of the West Wall (q.v.) and also in defensive operations during the Second World War. It consisted of a series of mutually supporting strongpoints capable of all-round defence, designed so as to continue to resist even if surrounded. They were also intended for an immediate sweeping counter-attack. See Box, Island, *Stutzpunkt* and *Widerstandsnest*.

Infantry shield: A small portable screen made of a thick metal plate pierced with a firing hole used by infantrymen, notably in First World War trench warfare (q.v.). See Mantlet and Pavis.

Infantry work: One or more positions of a *Feste* (q.v.) or placed in the interval between *Festen* to defend against enemy infantry attack. Named *Infanterie-Werk* in German and *Ouvrage d'infanterie* in French, it included a glacis (q.v.), a 20–30m belt of spike fences interlaced with barbed wire (q.v.), a ditch (q.v.), covered way (q.v.), flanking concrete casemates (q.v.), concrete infantry parapets (q.v.) and trenches (q.v.) with shelters, and partly sunken concrete barracks (q.v.), typically with two floors and a basement. Elements were linked by underground passages and tunnels, dispersed and conforming to the nature of the local terrain.

Infirmary: The places where wounded are treated during or after a battle, which can be an improvised tent camp (indicated by a large red cross on a white background). As a rule, each fortress had an infirmary or a prepared dressing station for sick and wounded soldiers. The facility was especially adapted for primary medical attention, with wide entrances, corridors, chambers and wards allowing the circulation of stretchers. Casualties unable to walk were carried from the battlefield by stretcher-bearers, while those still capable of walking were directed to an aid station, located as close to the front line as was practicable. The stretcher cases (severely wounded) were sent to the dressing station, where the (often overwhelmed) surgical personnel sorted them out, performed amputations, applied dressings and splints, checked hemorrhages, gave blood transfusions and administered drugs, sedatives and injections. After first treatment, casualties were evacuated further rearward to a military hospital by horse-drawn or automobile ambulance, by train or (in more recent times) by Medevac airplane or helicopter.

During a battle or a siege, the infirmary was always a place of bustling activity, busy confusion and great suffering. For example, during the siege of Dien Bien Phu in North Vietnam (13 March–8 May 1954) the French Antenne Chirurgicale Mobile 29 (ACM, Mobile Surgical Team) headed by Major Dr Paul Grauwin had a total of 424 beds. Only forty were bunks in the protected underground hospital, the rest being spaces set aside for about 150 stretcher-cots and in various HQ shelters, sixty at the Isabelle stronghold and the rest scattered between the various battalion sub-aid posts. Within a week of combat starting, the French field hospitals were crammed with wounded. By the end of the battle, casualties (who could no longer be evacuated by air) amounted to more than 4,000 wounded men surviving in appalling conditions.

Interior slope: The inner sloping talus of a rampart (q.v.).

Interlocking arcs of fire: A defensive position sited in such a way that the arcs of fire of each weapon, position or sub-unit overlap with those of its neighbours.

Interval: In nineteenth-century fortification, the distance between two forts, and in the twentieth century, the distance between two bunkers or groups of bunkers. The dimensions of the interval were obviously determined by the range of the weapons.

Interval casemate: In the 1930s French Maginot Line (q.v.), a *casemate d'intervalle* was a stand-alone, self-contained armed bunker intended to defend a gap or a line of anti-tank obstacles and barbed wire entanglements between blocs and *ouvrages* (q.v.).

Intervallum: In Roman fortification, the open space between the rear of the rampart and the built-up area.

Interval work: A small fortified position, generally placed in a gap between two main strongholds.

Inundation: The voluntary and controlled submersion of an area in order to cut off access. See flooding.

Investment: A military operation (blockade) consisting of surrounding an enemy location to prevent all communication, reinforcement and supplies between the besieged and the outer world. See Siege, Countervallation, Circumvallation and Part 2 (Siege Warfare).

Iron Curtain: The term was coined by the German politician Lutz Graf Schwerin von Krosigk, and made popular by Winston Churchill, who first used it in a public speech in March 1946. The term was initially used to refer to the actual barrier that cut the European continent in two, but soon also became a reference to the ideological barrier.

The Iron Curtain was a physical barrier that stretched for thousands of kilometres, separating Eastern communist and Western democratic countries. It was especially strong in Germany, where the Berlin Wall (q.v.) became an unmistakable symbol of the Cold War. In certain regions, the Iron Curtain was nothing more than a plain restricted and guarded fence. In other places it was a heavily defended area with high barbed wire fences, anti-tank obstacles, anti-personnel minefields, ditches, patrol paths/roads and observation towers. Only people carrying special government permission could approach the border zone. The fall of the communist regime in the Soviet Union and its satellites in 1989–91 marked the end of the Cold War, which was followed by the dismantling of the Iron Curtain.

Island: An all-round, static, enclosed, self-contained and fortified position developed in Britain as an anti-invasion preparation in 1940, particularly designed to counter a tank attack. The islands were co-ordinated strongpoints forming an 'archipelago' for defence-in-depth (q.v.) covering a whole area. The island tactics included the conversion of houses into strongholds; the construction of combat emplacements and dugouts, all connected by trenches or tunnels; and the blocking of roads by anti-tank and anti-personnel mines, barricades and obstacles. Island tactics were thus distinct from those of the line (q.v.). See *Igel*.

Italian machicolation: A machicolation (q.v.) which was corbelled out on a long brick projection, forming ribs around the upper sections of towers and curtains, joined at the top by semi-circular arches. See Ghibelline.

Italian System: Another term for Bastioned system (q.v.). In the 1530s and 1540s, the new style of bastioned fortification began to spread out of Italy into the rest of Europe, particularly to France, the Netherlands and Spain. Italian engineers were in enormous demand throughout Europe, and in the early sixteenth century there was something like an Italian monopoly in bastioned fortification.

Examples include the castle of Civita Castellana from 1497 and fortifications around the Papal Castle Sant'Angelo in Rome which were designed in 1494 by Antonio da San Gallo the Elder. The fortress of Ostia near Rome was designed in 1486 by Guiliano da San Gallo, while Fort Sarzanello near Carrare in Tuscany was designed in 1502 by Francesco Giambetti. The urban enceinte of Civita Vecchia was designed in 1515 by Antonio da San Gallo the Younger, who also designed the citadel of Florence in 1532 and fortifications enclosing the Vatican in Rome between 1537 and 1548. Venetian engineer Michel San Michele designed a fort at Heraklion in Crete in 1538. The fortifications of the German city of Nuremberg were modernized by Antonio Fazzuni between 1538 and 1545. The newly created city of Vitry-le-François (and its citadel) in north eastern France was fortified after a design by Girolamo Marini and Aurelio Pasini in 1544. Fort Mont-Alban near Nice in southern France was designed in 1557 by Domenico Ponsello. The bastioned walls around the city of Lucca in Tuscany were designed by Francesco Paciotto between 1554 and 1568. The citadel of Spandau in Berlin was designed by Rocco Guerinni in 1560. The urban fortifications of Berwick-upon-Tweed in northern England were improved by Giovanni Portinari and Jacopo Aconcio in 1564. The capital

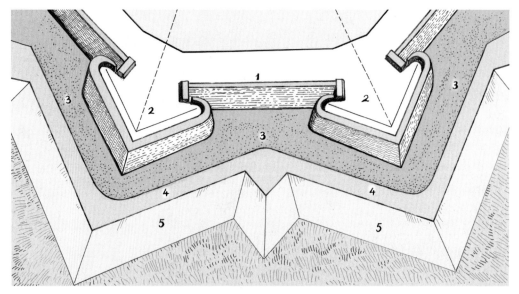

Italian System. 1: Curtain; 2: Bastion; 3: Ditch; 4: Covered way; 5: Glacis.

of Malta, Valetta, was created and fortified in 1566 by Francesco Laparelli. In Flanders, Donato Boni designed the urban fortifications of Antwerp in 1567 and fort Rammekens in 1547. As for the citadel of Antwerp, it was built by Francesco Pacciotto in 1567. The brothers Guilio and Ottavio Baldigara designed the fortress of Nove Zemsky near Budapest in Hungary. The ideal city of Palmanova near Venice was designed and created by Vicenzo Scamotti and Guilio Savorgnano in 1593, while La Rochelle in France was modernized by Scipione Vergnano between 1596 and 1602.

Fagaras Castle, located in Brassov county in Romania, was originally built in the twelfth century, but was enlarged with Italian bastions in the seventeenth century.

K

Kampfstand: An active bunker in German, thus a combat emplacement armed with one or more weapons. The armament (emplaced in the *Kampfraum* – combat or firing chamber) could include machine guns, mortars, grenade-launchers, anti-tank guns, Flak guns, fortress guns, field artillery and cannons originally designed to arm an armoured vehicle or warship.

Kampfstand (German type 677 bunker).

Keep:

1) Originally the residential and strongest part of a medieval castle. Often in the form of a large and high central tower, the keep was the main habitation place and therefore the best defended area of a castle. Functioning as a redoubt in times of trouble, it could also be used as a secure storage area, containing an armoury, food and the main water well, which would ensure survival during a siege. Although there is no such thing as a standard medieval castle, most, even from the earliest times, followed certain standards of design and construction. In plan, the keep had various forms: square, rectangular, round, oval, almond-shaped or quatrefoil (constituted of four interpenetrating round towers). The keep was composed of a number of storeys, including a blind-vaulted ground level used as a storeroom. The entrance was placed on the first floor and was accessible by a ladder or wooden staircase. Other rooms were vertically arranged. The aula or hall (q.v.) was a multi-purpose living room, and the camera was a sleeping room. A special room was arranged as a chapel. The top level of the tower offered accommodation for a few guards. The summit

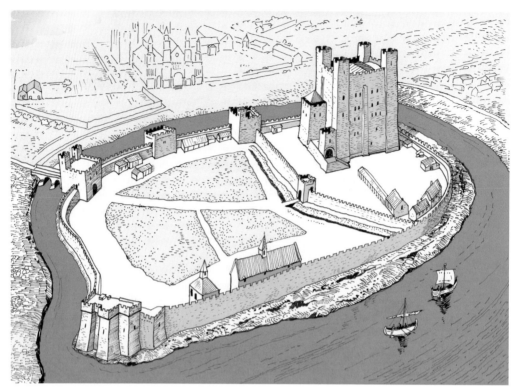

Rochester Castle, Kent, UK.

of the building was fitted with a roof and a crenellated parapet, allowing observation over the surrounding countryside and active defence.

The keep was the central feature of the castle. It was contained within the walls or attached to the walls. The area delineated by the walls was known as the bailey or *basse cour*, and the enclosure was called the enceinte. An earlier form of keep was the motte-and-bailey castle (q.v.). In some cases the keep gradually lost its pre-eminence and became merely the last refuge of the garrison, a strong tower forming part of the enceinte, and sometimes it simply disappeared. In France, the keep was called a *donjon*. In Germany, this type of structure is commonly referred to as a *Bergfried*, and in Spain as a *torre del homenaje*.

Coburg Castle, Germany.

Fort Brockhurst, Portsmouth, UK.

2) By extension, a keep was also an independent self-defensible structure within a nineteenth-century fort, serving to act as a last defence. See *Réduit*, Redoubt and *Kernwerk*.

Keep-gatehouse: A fortified structure combining residence and combat quarters in the gatehouse. Coucy in France or Harlech in Britain are good examples of castles with a keep-gatehouse.

Kelheim-style: See *Pfostenschlitzmauer*.

Kernwerk:

1) A *Kernwerk* was a *réduit* (q.v.) or redoubt (q.v.), a small fort within a German nineteenth-century fort having the same function as the keep in a medieval castle. It formed the last entrenched nucleus, the ultimate place of resistance where combat could still be continued, even when the rest of the fort was taken.
2) In the Atlantic Wall (q.v.), it was a centrally located cluster of defence in the middle of a *Festung* (q.v.). Such clusters consisted of very stout bunkers for heavy artillery and machine guns, with underground barracks, munitions and other storage, generators, hospitals, etc.

Kettle emplacement: A flat and shallow dish-shaped open gun position. See *Bettung* and Gun pit.

Keyhole gun port: A gun port (q.v.) shaped like an inverted keyhole, with a round hole for the gun at its base, and above it a slit used for sighting and as a vent for expelling the gases produced from firing.

Killing ground: An area surrounding all or part of a fortification, which was deliberately kept clear and bare to deprive attackers of any cover, thus exposing them to the maximum amount of fire. See Glacis, No-man's-land and *Zone de servitude*.

Kleinschartenstand: A small, cheap but well-armed casemate (q.v.) built by the Germans in early 1944, in the late phase of construction of the Atlantic Wall (q.v.).

Kochbunker: Also known as a *K-Rohrenstand*, a small German Second World War prefabricated concrete combat/observation circular pit for only one man. Designed by the German Army in the last months of 1944, it was a simplified variant of the Tobruk or *Ringstand* (q.v.). The pit could be open, but could also be covered with a concrete dome about 140cm in diameter. The pit with cover was some 2.4m high. The circular concrete wall was about 20cm thick, and there was an access hatch measuring about 60x75cm. *Kochbunkers* were often part of a trench system and thus partly underground. They could be coupled, and each one could house a single sentry or armed soldier. *Kochbunkers* were hastily constructed in Silesia (Poland), the Netherlands (in Doetinchem, Assen and Arnhem) and probably in the Atlantic Wall (q.v.). Whether this small bunker was named after Nazi gauleiter Erich Koch (1896–1986) remains unclear.

Krak: The word comes from the Syriac *karak*, meaning fortress. The most famous is without doubt the *Krak des Chevaliers*, an imposing Crusader fortress and headquarters of the Knights Hospitaller, located east of Tripoli, Lebanon, in the Homs Gap atop a 650m-high hill along the only route from Antioch to Beirut and the Mediterranean Sea.

Krak des Chevaliers, Crusader castle in Syria, one of the most important preserved medieval castles in the world.

Kremlin: Russian word for fortress, citadel or castle, referring to any major fortified central complex found in historic Russian cities. The word is often used to designate the best-known example, the Moscow Kremlin, and the former Soviet government. See Citadel.

Ksar: A term describing a Berber village consisting of generally attached houses, often having collective granaries and other structures (mosque, bath, oven, shops), widespread among the oasis population of the Maghreb (northern Africa). Ksars are sometimes situated in mountain locations to make defence easier. They are often entirely enclosed within a single, continuous wall. The building material of the structure is normally adobe, or cut stone and adobe. The Spanish term *Alcazar* and Portuguese *Alcacer* are derived from this Arabic word, and appear in place names and buildings originating as fortresses.

Küstenvorfeldsperren: German for coastal beach obstacles (*K-Sperre* in short, but also called *Vorstrandhindernissen*). See Beach obstacles.

L

L-plan castle: An L-plan castle, as the name implies, was a keep (q.v.), castle (q.v.) or towerhouse whose groundplan had the shape of a letter 'L'. The design was quite frequently seen in Scotland, but was also found in England, Ireland, Romania and

L-plan castle: Auldham, Scotland. Located about 3 miles east of North Berwick in East Lothian, Auldham Castle was erected in the sixteenth century.

Sardinia. Typically built from the thirteenth to seventeenth centuries, the evolution of the L-plan design was an expansion of the simple square keep from the early Middle Ages. The design had the advantage of providing a larger and more convenient living space but also the ability to defend the entrance door by enabling flanking fire from the adjacent wing.

Laboratory: A room in a nineteenth-century fort where gunpowder was mixed or made into charges before being stored in a magazine. Shells and grenades were also filled in the laboratory.

Landfront: Battleline or combat area facing the countryside. In a fortification placed along the sea, the landfront covered the sides and the rear of the seafront (q.v.). In modern fortification, it was intended to respond to attacks launched from the rear by paratroopers or offensives launched by troops having come ashore elsewhere.

Land mine: Explosive devices concealed under the ground. A mine is generally composed of a main charge in a container, a detonator which sets off the main charge and a firing mechanism which sets off the detonator. The firing mechanism prevents the mine being set off by interference and guarantees immediate detonation. During the Second World War, mines were activated by pressure, by trip wire or by radio. Mines were (and still are today) a deadly factor in defensive warfare. They could rapidly be put into action, made up for lack of personnel, could funnel the attackers into a killing ground where they would fall victim to machine guns or anti-tank guns, and made all enemy movement difficult and costly. They are relatively cheap but are very insidious and dangerous because their presence is only revealed by fatal explosion. Huge zones can therefore be transformed into impracticable and deadly areas. In several places around the world, there are still large zones full of highly dangerous hidden mines remaining long after the end of the wars that have produced them. See Mine and Booby Trap.

Latrine: A toilet for soldiers. In a medieval castle, the latrine or privy was a small room arranged in the thickness of the wall, with shoots leading to the foot of the wall or corbelled out. For a high-ranking person, the alternative term *garderobe* (q.v.) was used, translated into English as wardrobe or cloakroom, which led to the euphemism bathroom still in use today.

Legionary fortress: The name given to a Roman permanent fortified camp. These camps were often the origin of later cities. Examples in Britain are Lincoln, York, Chester and Gloucester. See *Castrum* and Playing card plan.

Leitstand: German for Fire Control Station (q.v.), often installed in a strong concrete bunker.

Lice: Originally a palisade (q.v.), later the area between the inner and outer city walls, used for a variety of purposes including tilting. A spectacular example is still to be seen at Carcassonne in southern France. See List and Concentric castle.

Licence to crenellate: Authorization given by a lord to a feudal subject to fortify his house by adding walls with crenels, moats, towers, gatehouse, and other defensive structures. See Adulterine castle.

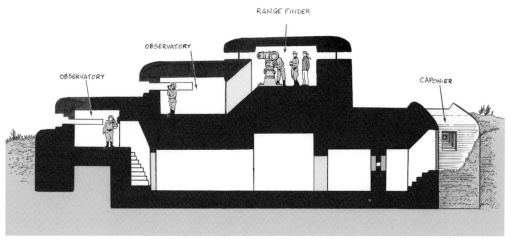

Leitstand

Ligne Maginot: See Maginot Line.

Ligne Morice: A barrier established by the French Army during the Algerian War (1954–61), named after André Morice, French Minister of Defence in 1957. The Morice Line was intended to stop infiltration by Algerian independentist combatants across the long Algerian–Tunisian frontier. Another line was constructed at the border with Morocco. By September 1957, the Morice Line was completed. It ran for 320km (200 miles) along the border with Tunisia, and was defended by some 80,000 French troops. It was composed of a lethal 5,000-volt electrified high fence, extensive barbed wire networks and highly dangerous anti-personnel minefields. It was electronically monitored with searchlights, radar sensors and artillery batteries instantly firing with pinpoint accuracy at the spot where a breach was made. The line was constantly observed from the air by spotter aircraft, and protected day and night by local patrols. As soon as a breach was made, the 'general reserve' (armoured troops, motorized infantry and helicopter-borne paratrooper units) rushed to the scene of the crossing and quickly intervened for search-and-destroy sweeps. The *Ligne Morice* (and that along the border with Morocco) proved very successful barriers, cutting off the infiltration of insurgents from Tunisia to a trickle. Both barriers enabled the French to curtail rebel movement, supplies and reinforcement, and contributed to deny the Algerian revolutionaries access to the battlefield.

Lilium: In Roman fortification, an obstacle consisting of a circular pit containing one or more sharpened stakes. The plural is *lilia*. See *Cippe*, *Trou de Loup* and Wolf's pit.

Limes: The *limes* (plural *limites*) is a Latin term designating the Roman lines of fortification built at the borders of the Empire. The Roman Empire was at its greatest extent when the emperor Trajan died in AD 117. The Romans' biggest problem was then the security of the imperial borders. Beyond the frontiers, from the Black Sea to the mouth of the Rhine, were formidable opponents. The emperor Augustus had hoped to extend the limits of the Empire to the Elbe River in the heart of Germany, but several campaigns had ended in disaster so the frontier was made along the Rhine. Because of the problems presented by the barbarian people beyond the frontier, an elaborate fortified system called *limes* was established. The first *limes* was established in Germany, along the Rhine and Danube, during the reign of the emperor Domitian (AD 81–96). The programme was continued by Trajan (97–117), Hadrian (117–138) and other succeeding emperors.

The frontiers of the Roman Empire were largely based on natural features, such as rivers (like the Rhine and Danube), mountains, deserts, marshes and forested areas. In gaps between natural obstacles, fortifications were built, including fortified towns, forts (*castra*), camps (*castella*) and watchtowers (*burgi*), linked together with ditches and earth walls (*vallum*) crowned with wooden stockades. Some of these strongholds became the sites of cities that still flourish today. Military roads ran along the *limes* so that troops could be marched quickly from one point of danger to another. The most elaborate and best developed of these artificial *limes* was Hadrian's Wall (q.v.), about 120km long, begun in AD 122 in northern Britain between the Tyne and Solway Firth. Although such defences could not (and ultimately did not) hold back any concerted invasion effort, they did physically mark the edge of Roman territory and separated two different worlds, two distinct cultures and two opposing societies. On one side of it were Roman order, law, organized markets and structured towns – in short, civilization. On the other were tribal and primitive society, technical backwardness, illiteracy – in short, barbarism. At least that was how the Romans envisioned the situation. The *limes* went some way to providing a degree of control over who crossed the border and where. Indeed, the *limites* were constructed primarily to prevent smuggling activities, attacks by small gangs of raiders or unwanted immigration from outside the Empire, not as a fighting line against a major invasion.

Line: Defensive works covering extended positions and presenting a continuous front to the enemy. Throughout history, fortresses were often combined in a series of strongholds forming a defensive linear system. Examples are numerous, the most well-known including the *limes* (q.v.) built by the Romans to defend the Empire (notably Hadrian's Wall in northern England), the Great Wall of China (q.v.), the French Maginot Line (q.v.) in the 1930s and the German Atlantic Wall (q.v.) during the Second World War.

Line of defence: An imaginary line drawn from the angle between a curtain and the flank of a bastion to the shoulder of the adjacent bastion. See Bastioned front.

List: In medieval fortification, the list (or lice) was the space between the exterior defences and the main body of the place. See Concentric castle and Lice.

Litus Saxonicum: See Saxon Shore Forts.

Lodgement: A temporary work made on a captured section of an enemy's fortified position during a siege. See Retirade.

Logistic bunkers: In modern fortification, passive works intended to support active armed combat emplacements. They form a large group, divided into troop shelters, ammunition stores, artillery garages, as well as shelters for plant, searchlights, water-supply, kitchens, dressing stations and infirmaries. Other passive bunkers are directly connected to the armed emplacements: headquarters, command stations, communication posts and observatories. Logistic and command bunkers are always camouflaged, scattered at the rear of combat units and connected to the armed bunkers by communication (roads, paths, tracks, trenches or subterranean galleries).

Longphuirt: Fortified naval base built by Viking invaders for overwintering. These bases would often be established on an island for additional security, or at the mouth of a river. They were composed of earth walls with a palisade and ditch, protecting houses, huts and sheds.

Long Walls of Athens: A fortified communication connecting Athens to its harbour Piraeus. The construction of the Athenian Long Walls was proposed by the statesman and strategist Cimon (510–450 BC). The actual building started in 461 BC when Athens was at war with Sparta (the First Peloponnesian War). Finished in 457 BC, the Long Walls provided the city with a constant link to the sea and prevented it from being besieged by land alone. The Long Walls consisted of two walls leading to Piraeus, 7km (4½ miles) long, running parallel to each other and with a broad passage between them. In addition, there was a third wall to the secondary port of Phalerum (south-west of Athens, called the Phalerian Wall), some 6.5km (4 miles) long. Between the Long Walls and the Phalerian Wall, a large secured triangle of land could be used for food production in case of a protracted siege.

Loophole: A loophole, also called an arrow loop or arrow slit, was a vertical void arranged through a solid wall for use by archers who thus remained under cover. In its simplest form, the loophole was a narrow vertical slit, perhaps 2m long, but many forms were experimented with so as to provide a broader view and wider field of fire. There was usually a splay on the inside of the wall so that the outer opening was narrower than the inner one. This provided room for the soldier and his equipment, as well as watchbanks (q.v.), as the loophole was used as an observation post too. The loophole also served to ventilate the castle and enabled a small amount of light to come inside its rather dark interior. At the base, top or middle of an arrow slit, there could be a small round opening, called an oilette, allowing a

Top row: Arrow loops adapted for firearms with the addition of a circular hole. Middle row: Early forms of gun ports. Bottom row: Embrasures for cannons.

Loophole (seen from outside).

broader view and field of fire. For the use of crossbows, arrow slits (then called crosslets) were given a cruciform shape with one or more horizontal splits, which enabled the crossbowman to aim and shoot with efficiency. When firearms were introduced, loopholes were adapted, enlarged or widened in order to allow the operation of firing weapons. In modern terminology, a distinction is frequently made between embrasures (q.v.) being used for cannons and loopholes for musketry.

Lorica: In Roman fortification, the *lorica* was a breastwork generally made of a palisade or wickerwork. It also designated the body armour worn by legionaries.

Louvre: Also called louver, this was an opening in a roof to allow smoke to escape from a central hearth. Used in medieval castles, the term Louvre also designated a royal castle/citadel in Paris, which now houses a large art museum.

Loophole (seen from inside).

Luftlandesperre: (*L-Sperre* in short) Second World War German anti-airborne landing obstacles. See Asparagus.

Luftschutzraum (LSR): A peculiarly German type of Second World War air raid shelter. It was designed to protect the population in high-density housing areas, as well as administrative centres, important archives and works of art. Made of concrete and considered completely bomb-proof, they were built upward and their structures took many forms. They usually consisted of square blocks, or low, long rectangular or triangular shapes; straight towers of a square plan rising to great heights, or round tower-like edifices, even pyramidal constructions. With the intensification of the Allied bombardments, the number and capacity of the shelters were considerably increased, allowing the protection of 500, 1,000, 2,000 or even 4,000 people. The building usually included special airtight entries, gaslocks, an independent power plant, infirmary, water supply and system, separate lavatories and washrooms for each sex and sometimes even luxuries such as telephone, air-conditioning and sleeping facilities. See *Flakturm*.

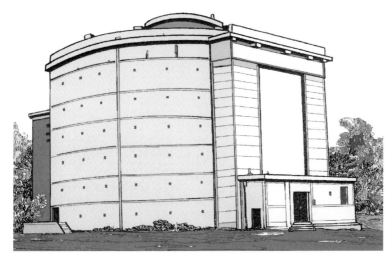

Luftschutzraum at Breslau (present-day Wrocław, Poland).

Lunette: In bastioned fortification, this term can designate two distinct works. 1) A detached and independent work placed in the glacis, generally in the form of a bastion or redan. 2) A triangular entrenched position or fortlet in the re-entering place of arms flanking the faces of a *demi-lune* or bastion.

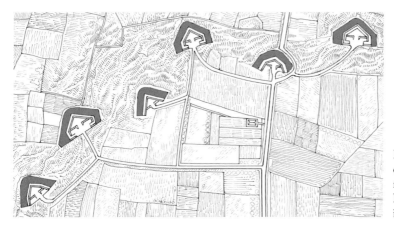

Line of Beverwijk, composed of lunettes, north of Amsterdam, the Netherlands, established in 1800.

Lunette d'Arçon: A small, standardized, detached and independent fortlet designed in 1795 by French military engineer Le Michaud d'Arçon. The *Lunette d'Arçon* was triangular in form. Its face was fitted with guns and it had a circular *réduit* tower in the gorge, which was covered by a pitch roof and defended through musketry loopholes.

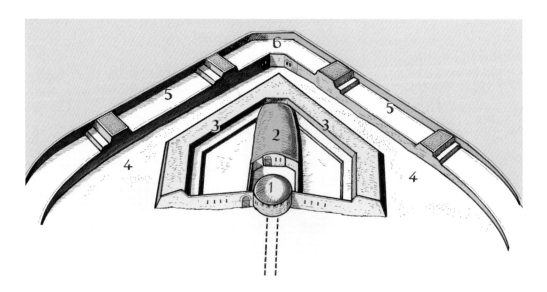

The lunette designed by Le Michaud d'Arçon was a self-supporting fortlet that included the following: a round fortified tower in the gorge (1) used as quarters for the garrison and as defence for the rear of the work; a bomb-proof vaulted ammunition store forming a traverse (2) on the *terre-plein*; two faces forming a scarp wall with parapet and barbette gun emplacements (3); a ditch (4); a counterscarp with a covered way (5) fitted with traverses; and, under the covered way in front of the salient, a flanking coffer (6) consisting of two masoned casemates for enfilading fire. Placed in the reverse slope of the ditch, these elements enabled the defenders to bring fire to bear upon attackers who had got into the ditch. They were accessible from the lunette via an underground passage.

The tower included bomb-proof quarters, stores and magazines for the garrison and was to be used for a last stand. The lunette was hemmed with a ditch and had reverse-fire casemates under the counterscarp. Possessing already most of the features of the future nineteenth-century polygonal fortification, the self-defensive *Lunette*

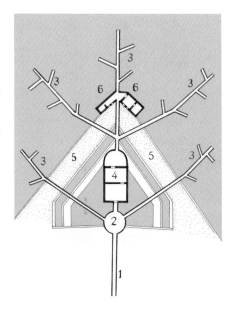

Plan of the underground passages and countermine galleries.
1: Underground passage to the main fort.
2: Flanking tower in the gorge.
3: Ecoutes and countermine galleries.
4: Bomb-proof masonry traverse (store place and quarters for the garrison).
5: Dry ditch.
6: Counterscarp casemates (coffers) for reverse fire in the ditch.

d'Arçon was a successful feature of Napoleonic fortification. Arçon's fortlets were built in Italy, Poland, the Low Countries and France, notably at Metz, Perpignan, Besançon and Montdauphin. Arçon's lunette formed the basis for Fort Tigné in Malta, designed in 1792 by French engineer Etienne de Tousard.

M

Machicolation: Machicolation (or machicoulis) was an opening made in the floor of a wall-walk near the parapet (q.v.). Placed on supporting corbels (q.v.), these voids allowed defenders to drop down rocks or other projectiles onto attackers at the base of a defensive wall. The design, developed in the Middle Ages about the end of the thirteenth century, originated from a similar temporary wooden arrangement called hoarding (q.v.). Advantages of masonry machicolations over wooden hoardings included the greater strength of stone battlements, as well as their fireproof quality. Machicoulis were placed in the parapets of walls and towers and above gates. A variant of machicolation was the murder hole (q.v.) set in the ceiling of a passage. When firearms began to play a significant role from the end of the fifteenth century, machicolation lost a great deal of its military efficiency. However, having a formidable appearance, they remained together with *echauguettes*, crenels, merlons and other medieval features, decorative elements used in residential palaces and in civilian architecture.

Machicolation. Left: Front view; Right: Cross-section.

Machine gun: A machine gun is a fully automatic weapon designed for sustained fire usually placed on a fixed mount (bipod or tripod). Combined with barbed wire entanglements, machine guns earned a fearsome reputation during the First World War. Ever since they have been standard weapons in fortifications. A machine-gun nest is a defensive combat emplacement accommodating one or more automatic weapons. See Tobruk, Foxhole, Field fortification, Trench, Sangar and Rifle pit.

Light machine gun (British Bren gun).

Magazine: A place for the storage of gunpowder, arms, ammunition or goods generally related to ordnance. See Powder house.

Maginot Line: In 1929, the French National Assembly voted on the construction of a heavily fortified line of defence along the border with Germany, a scheme proposed by

Opposite: Fort Immerhof (Maginot Line)
The small Fort Immerhof is situated near the village of Hettange-Grande, north of Thionville in Lorraine. Its task (and that of its neighbour Fort Soetrich) was to defend the main road (today's highway A31) and the railway track running from Metz to Luxemburg-City. The fort – built between 1930 and 1935 – included the following elements:
1: Entrance block. The façade was protected by a 3m-deep ditch, crossed by a movable footbridge leading to a gate reinforced with armoured doors. The block housed the telephone exchange, a supply store and ammunition store. It was defended by two armoured cupolas equipped with automatic rifles and 50mm mortars, plus one 47mm anti-tank gun placed inside a casemate.
2: Sewer for draining off infiltration and used water.
3: The totally subterranean *usine*, the heart of the unit, included a power plant, workshop, ventilation room with filters and pumping station, a kitchen, infirmary, quarters, toilets and washing facilities for troops, NCOs, officers and commander, and a headquarters with telephone exchange and map room.
4: Mixed combat block No. 3 equipped with two breech-loading 81mm mortars in an armoured turret, a firing casemate armed with one 47mm anti-tank gun (never delivered) and 7.5mm twin machine guns, two crenels for automatic rifles and an ammunition store.
5: Combat block No. 2 (western armoured turret) armed with 7.5mm Mack 31F twin machine guns, two observation cupolas armed with automatic rifles for close-range defence and an ammunition store.
6: Combat block No.1 (eastern armoured turret) symmetrically identical to the western turret.
7: Underground communication tunnel to link elements.
8: Military road to Hettange-Grande.

The fort was surrounded by barbed wire and anti-tank obstacles. Its garrison totalled 198 men, including infantrymen, gunners, electrical mechanics, telegraphists etc. Fort Immerhof was a *Petit Ouvrage* (PO, 'small work'); as a comparison, Fort Hackenberg had nineteen combat blocks and a garrison of 1,034 men. The small Fort Immerhof is perfectly preserved and open to the public from April to September.

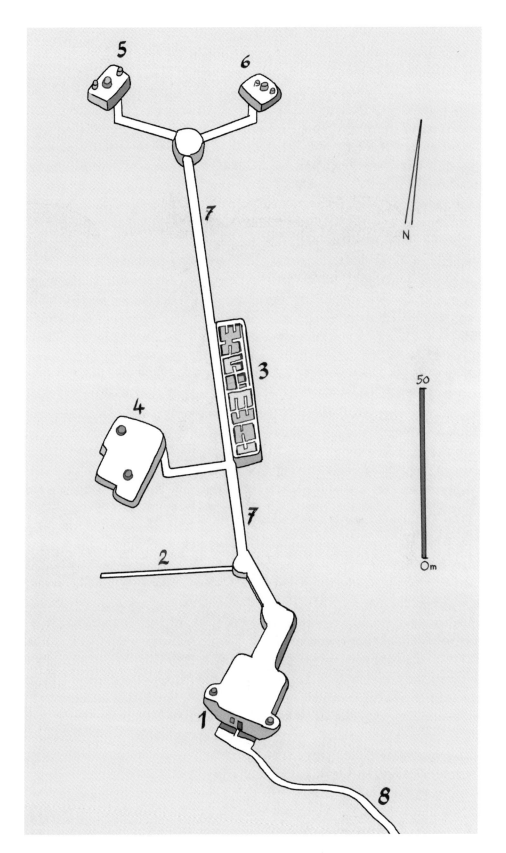

the then Minister of War, André Maginot (1877–1932). Based on earlier designs like post-1886 concrete armoured forts (q.v.) and the German *Feste* (q.v.), the line was built in two main phases. During the first phase – between 1929 and 1938 – the fortifications were designed and constructed under supervision of the Commission d'Organisation des Régions Fortifiées (CORF, the Fortified Regions Organization Committee). CORF, in order to speed up the construction, employed soldiers of the Engineering Corps, but also sub-contracted civilian companies. The CORF works included expensive, powerful and high quality forts, following a line that would take advantage of the most strategically useful natural features.

Each individual concrete fort was adapted to the topography of the terrain. On the surface, the *ouvrage* included observatories, artillery and machine-gun blocks, disappearing gun turrets, anti-tank and anti-personnel obstacles. In some sectors, the defences included flooded areas. Behind the firing zone there were fortified entrances for men and ammunition which were connected to the combat emplacements by underground passages – some wide enough to house narrow-gauge electric trains. The entrance blocks were protected by armoured doors, machine-gun posts and ditches with drawbridges. There were also false entrances designed to deceived attackers. The largest forts could house 1,200 soldiers. Between the entrances and the combat emplacements, there were underground barracks, ammunition stores, filter and ventilation rooms, emergency hospitals, telephone exchanges, command posts, power-plants, kitchens and water and food supplies. Some forts even had sun-lamp rooms. All these facilities – which were self-sufficient for about three months – were protected by thick concrete structures buried deep underground. At various positions along the tunnels, there were ambuscades and hidden mines to entomb unwary invaders, while the defenders had their own secret exits and sally ports. There were many fireproof and gastight doors, exhaust vents and air intakes fitted with anti-gas filters.

The second phase of the construction of the Maginot line was designed and completed between 1935 and 1940 by the Main d'Oeuvre Militaire (q.v.), or MOM, military manpower provided solely by the French Génie (Engineering Corps). Due to a reduction in the budget resulting from the difficult economic climate which prevailed in the late 1930s, the numerous MOM works were lighter bunkers and interval casemates of different sizes and shapes, with a reinforced field fortification character, sometimes called *camelote* (junk) fortification.

By 1939, the Maginot line was 1,500km (930 miles) long. While officially it was continuous and complete from Dunkirk (in the north near the English Channel) to Menton (at the border with Italy on the Mediterranean coast), there remained many gaps, numerous works were uncompleted and in certain sectors the 'line' was hardly even started. The defensive units were organized in twenty-five Secteurs Fortifiés (SF, fortified sectors). The line consisted of 5,800 defence works of various sizes, as follows: thirty-nine *ouvrages* (forts with artillery and entry blocks); 246 interval bunkers; fifty-two heavy artillery casemates; 205 artillery bunkers; 3,216 machine-gun pilboxes; 472 anti-tank gun bunkers; 936 combined machine-gun and anti-tank gun bunkers; 222 artillery casemates with armoured revolving turrets; and ninety-four observation posts.

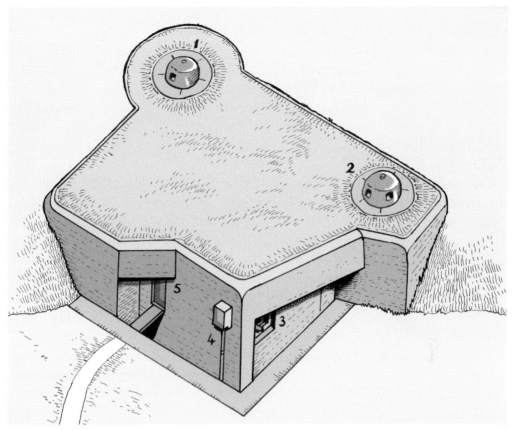

Casemate of Bois de Beuveille. Situated near Metz, Lorraine, in Sector La Crusne, the self-contained *Casemate d'Intervalle* (interval casemate) of Bois de Beuveille included two storeys. The ground floor was occupied by the combat chamber, ammunition store, ventilation and anti-gas filters. The basement included a generator, supply store (diesel-oil, drinking and cooling water, ammunition etc), crew quarters, toilet and a room for the commanding officer. The concrete walls and roof were 2.25m thick. The depicted aerial view seen from the rear included the following:

1: Fixed twin machine-gun armoured turret.
2: Mixed weapon and observation armoured turret fitted with periscope, light machine gun and 50mm mortar.
3: Flanking firing chamber armed with twin machine guns and 47cm anti-tank gun.
4: Armoured searlight.
5: Entrance with armoured door and removable footbridge over the narrow and deep concrete ditch called the *Fossé Diamant*.

The Maginot Line proper extended from Basel to Longwy, and was most powerful in the sectors facing Luxemburg and Germany (Metz, Lauter and Belfort), where the bulk of the heavy CORF *ouvrages* and forts were built. The other zones (including the extension in the Alps) were of various strengths.

The Maginot Line captured the imagination of the world in the 1930s. Several nations had been convinced of the validity of the concept, and the French fortification techniques were widely copied throughout Europe – notably in Czechoslovakia. Right until the outbreak of the Second World War, military construction was in full swing all over Europe. All those believers were fated to be disappointed. There were indeed two

Fort Fermont: Entrance block for ammunition. Fort Fermont – situated near Longwy in Lorraine – had seven combat blocks manned by 19 officers and 553 soldiers. The depicted entrance for ammunition was placed at the rear of the position, with tunnels linking it to the advanced combat blocks. Should the enemy attack from the rear, the entrance was protected by barbed wire and anti-tank obstacles and armed with a 47mm anti-tank gun and several machine guns. Note the 60cm narrow-gauge railway track used to supply the fort. The façade of the building was painted in motley camouflage colours or covered with a large camouflage net.

Maginot Lines: the real one, which was a great technical and military achievement, and another that was a myth created by optimistic apologists.

Six weeks after the start of the war in the West in May 1940, France was obliged to capitulate. The Maginot Line indeed proved impenetrable, but it has often been blamed for the collapse of France, which was caused by the defensive mentality and blindness of the French military authorities to the development of modern warfare in the late 1930s. Some sectors of the ill-fated Maginot Line – encircled and attacked from the rear – were still fighting when much of France had fallen, but their crews had to surrender after the armistice was proclaimed on 25 June.

Magistral line: The outline of a work following the scarp (q.v.).

Main d'Oeuvre Militaire: The *Main d'Oeuvre Militaire* (MOM, 'military manpower', provided solely by the French engineering corps) were concrete works built in the second phase of the construction of the Maginot Line (q.v.) between 1935 and 1940. Due to a reduction in the budget resulting from the difficult economic climate which prevailed from 1932 onwards, MOM works comprised lighter bunkers and interval casemates of different sizes and shapes with a reinforced field fortification character. They were nicknamed *camelote* ('junk').

Main enclosure: The fortified area surrounded by the main ditch.

Main line of resistance: The main line of resistance (MLR) is a military term describing the most important defensive position of an army facing an opposing force over an extended front. It may consist of trenches or a line of pillboxes, but also of a system of varying degrees of complexity with fighting positions, fortifications and obstacles intended to impede any enemy advance. See Line, Front and Trench Warfare.

Manor house: A fortified country house, which historically formed the administrative centre of a manor – the lowest unit of territorial organization in the feudal system. The term is sometimes applied to country houses which belonged to landed gentry families, as well as to grand stately homes, particularly as a technical term for minor late medieval fortified country houses intended more for civilian comfort than for military defence.

Mantenere: Italian term for keep (q.v.).

Mantrap: A device or construction (special snares, trap netting, trapping pits, fluidizing solid matter traps and cage traps) designed to entrap a person. See Booby trap and Mine.

Manueline: Architectural decorative style named after king Manuel I of Portugal (1495–1521) marking the transition from Late Flamboyant Gothic to Renaissance developed in Portugal in the sixteenth century. Influenced by Plateresque, Mudéjar, Italian and Flemish architecture, it was used in churches, monasteries, palaces, castles and fortifications, as well as in other arts such as sculpture, painting, works of art made of precious metals, faience and furniture.

March: In early medieval Europe, a march (or mark or *marcha*) was a frontier province with a primarily defensive military function. During the Frankish Carolingian dynasty (AD 751–987), the term spread throughout Europe as a barrier intended to countain hostile neighbouring peoples. Denmark, for example, was the march of the Danes, while Ostmark (Eastern march) was the name of Austria. Today in Italy there is a province called Marche (capital Ancona), which was formerly a frontier zone between the Frankish Carolingian Empire and the Papal domains. A march was thus typically a buffer zone or country with strongholds and fortified cities, and the ruler of a march was a senior feudal nobleman (appointed by the Frankish Emperor) known as the markgraf (aka margrave, marchione, marquess or marquis).

Mareth Line: A system of fortifications built by the French between the towns of Medenine and Gabès in southern Tunisia, prior to the Second World War. It was designed to defend against attacks from the Italians in Libya, but following the fall of France it fell into Axis hands and after Operation *Torch* was used by the Italians and Germans to defend against the British Eighth Army instead. The Mareth Line took advantage of natural features (the Wadi Zigzaou dry river and the Matmata hills), which were reinforced with artificial fortifications (casemates, bunkers and anti-personnel and anti-tank obstacles and mines). The Mareth Line was taken by the Allies after a ten-day battle in March 1943.

Belem Tower (aka Saint Vincent Tower) in Lisbon, Portugal. The fortified Manueline-style tower, some 30m (98½ft) high, was intended to defend the entrance to the port of Lisbon.

Martello tower: Martello towers were small independent and self-reliant defensive fortlets built in many countries of the British Empire from the time of the Napoleonic Wars and during the nineteenth century. Practically always cylindrical, a typical Martello tower stood up to 12m (40ft) high, with two floors and possibly a basement,

Martello tower at Bantry Bay, Ireland.

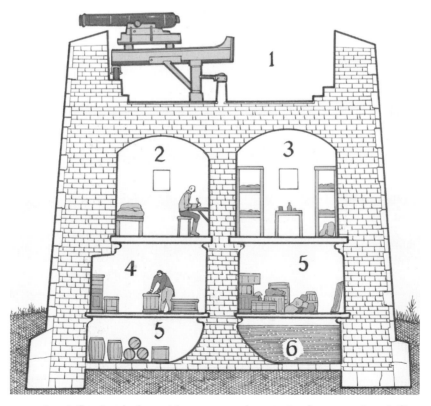

Tower cross-section. 1: Combat platform with gun mounted on rotating fortress carriage; 2: Commander's room; 3: Soldiers' quarters; 4: Ammunition store; 5: Supply store; 6: Cistern.

and had a garrison of one officer and between fifteen and twenty-five men. Its round structure and thick walls of solid masonry made it resistant to cannon fire, while its height made it a good platform for a single heavy artillery piece, placed on a rotating mount on the flat roof and thus able to traverse a 360-degree arc of fire. Some towers had a moat (q.v.) for additional defence. Martello towers became obsolete by the middle of the nineteenth century when powerful rifled artillery was developed. Many towers have survived to the present day, often preserved as historic monuments.

Masonry: Masonry is the building of structures from individual material units bound together by mortar, and the term can also refer to the units themselves. Common materials for masonry construction are brick, stone such as marble, granite, travertine or limestone, concrete or glass blocks and tile. Masonry is generally a strong and durable form of construction, often used in fortification building. Stonemasonry is the craft of shaping rough pieces of rock into accurate geometrical shapes, mostly simple but some of considerable complexity, and then arranging the resulting stones together, often with mortar. Throughout the history of fortification, the construction of castles, forts, citadels, batteries and fortresses in stone masonry always involved extremely high costs and required a large workforce and highly skilled trades using a wide variety of tools, including ditch diggers, quarrymen, sawyers and stone cutters, carvers, master and fixer masons, carpenters and engineers. It is usually assumed that bygone artisans built to last, but even the most massive castles and best-designed fortifications were always in a continual state of maintenance, dilapidation, repair, neglect or reconstruction.

Mastio: Italian term for a *donjon*, keep (q.v.), main tower or stronghold.

Materials: Materials used to build fortifications must be relatively easy to use, in good supply, durable and resistant to impact. Wood possesses a certain elasticity, particularly in combination with earth. It was used to erect fences, palisades, timber shielding etc. There was a plentiful supply since it was naturally renewed, but wood is perishable, nor is it sufficiently resistant to impact or flames. Earth is another material which is found everywhere. It is elastic, and although penetrable by projectiles, earth slows their progress, and combined with wood or stone revetment it was and still is widely used in many forms. Stone is highly resistant to compression, but less so to violent impact; it does not deteriorate significantly, but fragments could wound the defenders. The high explosive shell introduced in 1885 sounded the death knell of stone as a material. Brick is an artificial material which is relatively cheap and easy to produce. Concrete (q.v.) is a monolithic artificial material affording good resistance, particularly reinforced ferro-concrete, which contains dense layers of metal bars. Metal armour in the form of thick iron, wrought iron or steel plates, often combined with ferro-concrete, is also used as a fortification material. See Masonry.

Maunsell Sea and Army Fort: The Maunsell Sea Forts were fortified positions built in the Thames and Mersey estuaries during the Second World War to help defend the British Isles from German attack. They were named after their designer, Guy Maunsell.

Maunsell Sea Forts, operated by the Royal Navy, were planned to deter and report any German air raids following the Thames as a landmark, as well as attempts by aircraft to lay mines in this important shipping channel. There were four Thames naval forts: Rough Sands (HM Fort Roughs, or U1), Sunk Head (U2), Tongue Sands (U3) and Knock John (U4). The design was a concrete construction, with a pontoon barge on which stood two cylindrical towers, on top of which was the gun platform mounting two 3.75in guns and two 40mm Bofors guns. They were laid down in dry dock and assembled as complete units. They were then fitted out – the crews going on board at the same time for familiarization – before being towed out and sunk onto their sand bank positions in 1942. The naval fort design was the latest of several that Maunsell had devised in response to Admiralty inquiries. Early ideas had considered forts in the English Channel able to take on enemy vessels.

Maunsell also designed army forts for anti-aircraft defence. These were larger installations comprising seven interconnected steel towers with platforms: five carried guns arranged in a semi-circle around the control centre and accommodation, while the seventh, set further out than the gun towers, was the searchlight tower. Three forts were placed in the Mersey – known as Queen's, Formby and Burbo – and three in the Thames estuary – Nore (U5), Red Sands (U6) and Shivering Sands (U7). Each of these AA forts carried four QF (quick-firing) 3.75in guns and two Bofors 40mm guns. During the war the forts shot down 22 German aircraft and around 30 V1 flying bombs. They were decommissioned in the late 1950s. See Flak tower.

Maximilian tower: Named after Archduke Maximilian Joseph of Austria-Este (1782–1863), Maximilian towers were circular structures with thick masonry walls. They were self supporting, generally 80ft in diameter and 30ft high, and had three vaulted stories, with casemates for howitzers and mortars, quarters for the garrison, supply and ammunition stores, while the roof was arranged as a terrace bristling with guns. They were sunk into the ground, and so were difficult targets. They were surrounded by a narrow ditch and a screen of earth. The entrance was at the first-floor level and was fitted with a drawbridge. These works were built in the first half of the nineteenth century, for example at Linz in Austria in order to block the passage along the Danube and Traun rivers. The fortifications, however, had another aim: to protect the authorities from revolutionary citizens. Upon an initiative of Archduke Maximilian d'Este (who had to finance the enterprise himself), Linz received new defences in the form of a large fortified entrenched camp (q.v.) built between 1828 and 1836. This included a citadel on Postlingberg, a hill west of the town, where the defence's headquarters were stationed, and thirty-two large round towers blocking the passage between them not by a continuous wall but by artillery fire. Maximilian towers were also erected in Austrian possessions in Italy at Verona and Venice. Like the British Martello towers (q.v.) and the Dutch *torenfort* (q.v.) Maximilian towers illustrated the revival of the large roundish artillery tower in European fortification. This revival was, however, short-lived, and the circular masonry artillery tower fell out of favour when it was rendered obsolete by new rifled and more powerful artillery in the 1860s.

Medina: A medina (city quarter in Arabic) is a distinct urban neighbourhood found in many North African cities. The medina is typically walled, contains many narrow and maze-like streets, and was built by Arabs as far back as the ninth century AD. See Casbah.

Merli ghibellini: See Ghibelline merlon.

Merlon: The upstanding solid sections of a parapet between the crenels in a wall and embrasures in a rampart, behind which the defenders could shelter. As an essential part of a battlement (q.v.), merlons were used in fortifications for millennia. They formed the 'teeth' in crenellation, alternating with gaps or crenels (q.v.). The solid part of the parapet provided shelter whilst the void crenel permitted defenders to throw projectiles. Merlons could also be fitted with loopholes (q.v.), which provided additional firing and observation points for defenders without reducing their protection. Merlons came in various forms depending on architectural styles, as they also had a decorative function. They often had a straight rectangular shape, but many other forms were also used, including three-pointed, quatrefoil, shielded, flower-like, rounded (typical of the Islamic and African world), pyramidal or in the form of a swallow-tail (the Italian Ghibelline merlon). Merlons and crenels gradually became useless when firearms were introduced. However, they never disappeared and remained decorative features, particularly in neo-Gothic-style buildings constructed in the nineteenth century.

Merlon.

Meurtrière: French for arrow slit (q.v.). See Embrasure and Loophole.

Mezzaluna: Italian for *demi-lune* (ravelin), which was a triangular defensive outwork in a bastioned fortification. The *mezzaluna* was practically always placed in the ditch in front of a curtain between two bastions. See *Demi-lune* and Ravelin.

Michelmannstand: The *Michelmannstand*, designed by the German Colonel Kurt Michelmann – head of military engineers (Fest. Pi. Stab 27 from LXXXII Corps), stationed at Antwerp in Belgium – was a small Second World War concrete bunker made of prefabricated elements. Having the shape of a roundish hexagon, it had an open weapon emplacement (for a machine gun or mortar) in the middle and a protected shelter for the crew. See Tobruk.

Mile castle: A Roman fortlet (q.v.) also known as a *castellum*, which was used to defend part of a fortified line (e.g. Hadrian's Wall). As the term implies, it was situated every Roman mile along the length of the perimeter (approximately every 1.5km). A mile castle was usually constructed on a rectangular plan with a barrack room, store, oven and latrine.

Michelmannstand. Top left: Plan. Bottom left: Cross-section. Right: View.

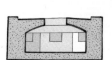
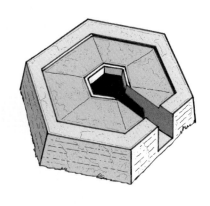

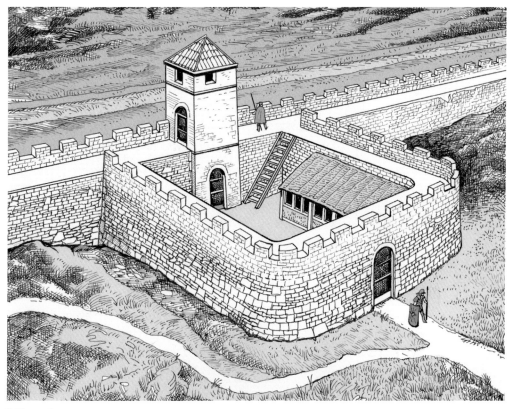

Mile castle.

Mine: An explosive charge placed underground or underwater and exploded when disturbed. The use of mines originated from the use of tunnelling and mining (q.v.) to attack under an enemy city's walls. On the whole they have the same effects as booby traps (q.v.). See Mining and Breach.

Mine chamber: The end of a tunnel gallery, under the target, where the destruction charge was placed and exploded. See Mining.

Mine clearing: Mine clearing (or demining) is the process of removing mines. Clearing off a mined zone has always been a time-consuming and dangerous task, carried out with portable electro-magnetic detectors which are sensitive enough to pick up metal objects buried in the ground. Another more violent method consists of using explosives, e.g. a bangalore charge (q.v.), or an armoured vehicle equipped with a plough or a roller fitted with chains flailing the ground ahead of the tank, provoking explosion of all the mines by shock and vibrations, thus making a safe path through the minefield.

Minefield: Zone with a heavy density of concealed mines. Mines were usually laid in checkwise rows, with 5–10 yards between rows as well as between mines. At these intervals, a minefield a mile long and 500 yards deep required some 35,000 devices. The siting of a minefield was very often co-ordinated with active armed defences. Mines do not differentiate between friend and foe, and when in the ground for a long time can deteriorate and explode by accident. To avoid lethal accidents, minefields have been signalled on the friendly side by a few strands of barbed wire or by a warning placard (often a skull and crossed bones), and are noted on maps. Mine danger signs could also be placed in a non-mined zone (a phoney minefield) to deceive an enemy who would waste valuable time searching for non-existent mines.

Mined pole: The mined pole was an extremely simple German beach obstacle used in the Atlantic Wall during the Second World War. Called *Minenpfahl* in German, it comprised a tree trunk or stake driven into the sea floor on the beach with a mine fixed on top of it.

Mined raft: A mined raft (in German *Schwimmende Balkenmine*) was another cheap beach obstacle (q.v.) used by the Germans in the Atlantic Wall (q.v.). It was composed of tree-trunks and planks to which anti-tank mines were attached. The mines were generally coated with tar so as to resist seawater attrition. These rafts, anchored by means of concrete bases and chains, represented a serious menace for landing craft as they floated about offshore.

Mining: Mining (or undermining) is a siege method used to make a breach (q.v.) in the wall of a fortified city, fortress or castle. Before the introduction of gunpowder and explosives by the end of the Middle Ages, the method consisted of digging one or more tunnels under the foundations of an enemy's walls or towers. These tunnels would normally be supported by temporary wooden props as the digging progressed. Once the excavation was complete and properly placed under the target, the mine chamber was filled with combustible material that, when lit, burnt away the props, leaving the structure above weakened, more or less unsupported and thus liable to collapse. This highly dangerous technique could not be used when the fortification was built on high and solid rock or protected by a wet ditch or a moat (q.v.). The defenders would do all they could to detect where the tunnel was dug, and then take counter-measures, notably by digging a counter-mine (q.v.). See Sapping.

The introduction of gunpowder revolutionised mining in the sixteenth century and sustained this mining as an integral part of the sophisticated art of fortress warfare. The only difference then was that instead of using fire, the attackers exploded gunpowder kegs (later high explosives) in mine chambers under outworks and bastions. If the besiegers did not surrender, then the smoking ruins of the collapsed structures were assaulted. Here again, the besiegers took counter-mine measures. When the location of a tunnel was detected, the defenders dug a counter-mine to blow up enemy sappers, for example by using a camouflet (q.v.).

From the Renaissance onwards, the dangerous and labour-intensive method of making a breach by means of mining with explosives was widely used in siege warfare. A famous instance occurred during the American Civil War at the siege of Petersburg in July 1864. Union troops dug a tunnel under the Confederate lines at Elliott's Salient and packed its end with vast amounts of gunpowder. When set off, the resulting explosion killed about 300 soldiers. This act might have been decisive if not for the faulty Union tactic of storming into, rather than around, the resulting crater, allowing the defenders to shoot down onto the attackers, who were unable to climb the steep crater sides. The action accordingly became known as the Battle of the Crater.

Mining saw a resurgence as a military tactic during the First World War when army engineers would attempt to break the stalemate of trench warfare by tunnelling under no-man's-land and laying large quantities of explosives beneath the enemy's trench, notably by the British at the Battle of Messines in June 1917, when 450 tonnes of high explosive were placed in twenty-one mines after some two years of sapping. Approximately 10,000 German troops were killed when the mines were simultaneously detonated.

As in siege warfare, mining was possible due to the static nature of fighting in the First World War. During the Second World War, however, troop movements were too fluid and tunnelling too slow, and as a result mining was not worth the effort invested. Nevertheless, mining was successfully employed by the Communist Viet Minh when they exploded the Eliane 2 stronghold during the siege of the French stronghold of Dien Bien Phu in 1954 during the First Indochina War.

Mirador: A belvedere or balcony. In military architecture, a mirador was originally a small watchtower built on top of buildings in the Spanish colonies. In the twentieth century, the term was usually associated with an observation and surveillance post placed on four high legs at the corners of a military camp or base, airfield, detention centre, prisoner-of-war camp or concentration camp.

Missile lauching site: This term is used for any base, site or facility from which rockets are launched. It may contain one or more launch pads or suitable sites to mount a transportable launch pad. It is

Mirador.

surrounded by a large safety area known as a rocket or missile range. Tracking stations, vessels and aircraft are often located in the range to assess the progress of the launches.

Moat: Synonym of ditch (q.v.). The moat is often designated more specifically as a wet ditch (q.v.), thus a ditch filled with water. The moat surrounded a castle, fortified building or town and formed a preliminary line of defence. Moats could evolve into more extensive water defences, including natural or artificial lakes, whose waters were regulated with batardeaus, dams and sluices. Moats were effective against siege engines such as siege towers and battering rams, which needed to be brought against the castle wall to be operated. They also prevented mining (q.v.). In later castles and palaces, the moat or water defence was largely ornamental and became a part of a garden or park.

Moineau: Sometimes called a *oiseau* (bird in French), the *moineau* (sparrow in French) was a small and low masonry caponier (q.v.), usually built at the foot of a tower (fifteenth century) and intended for close-range flanking fire.

Moir pillbox: Designed and patented by Sir Ernest Moir, Minister of Armaments, this was a small First World War British prefab cylindrical design based on the use of interlocking concrete blocks for extra strength. The pillbox was armed with a Vickers heavy machine gun served by two soldiers. It had a diameter of about 2.2m, and the concrete blocks were 20cm thick. Its roof included a domed armoured plate covered with a layer of concrete. The pillbox was accessible via an underground passage. It was designed for quick construction and enabled troops to rapidly establish firing strongpoints. It had an ingenious rotating steel shutter through which the machine gun could be fired, but its

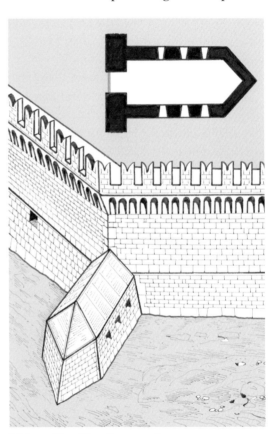

Moineau. Top: Plan. Bottom: view.

main disadvantage was the absence of a system to ventilate toxic gases caused by firing the weapon. About 1,500 of these pillboxes seem to have been built in 1918 in Belgium and France. Remains can be seen at Ieper in Belgium.

Moncrief mount: A system of disappearing gun using a counterweight designed by Captain Alexander Moncrief in the 1860s. See Disappearing gun.

Monk: An obstacle built on top of a batardeau (q.v.). The monk was very often made of masonry, given a roundish shape and topped with a spike.

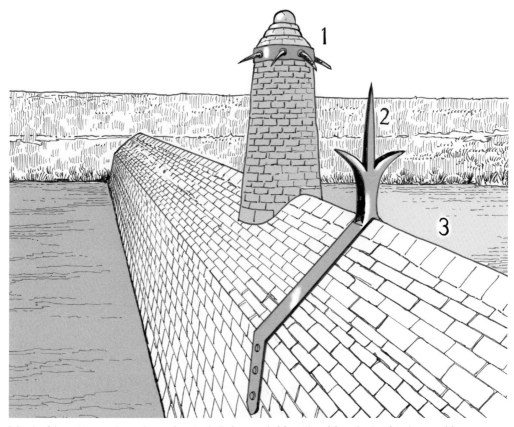

Monk. Obstacles on a batardeau often included a monk (1), spikes (2) and a knife-edge top (3).

Monte-charge: In French late nineteenth-century and Maginot Line forts, this was a goods lift used to send ammunition from magazines deep down in the ground up to the combat blocks at the surface.

Moorish merlon: A merlon (q.v.) typical of Spanish and Portuguese Mudejar architecture, characterized by a pointed apex.

Morrison shelter: Designed by John Fleetwood Baker, issued by the British Ministry of Home Security (headed by Herbert Morrison) and introduced in March 1941, the indoor Morrison shelter consisted of a heavy cage approximately 6ft 6in (2m) long, 4ft (1.2m) wide and 2ft 6in (0.75m) high. When not in use as a shelter it could be used as a table by temporarily removing the welded wire mesh sides. The Morrison shelter allowed people to crawl inside the structure, where there was sleeping space for two or three. They were especially useful in flats and in houses without cellars or gardens. The shelter was capable of withstanding the weight of debris falling on top of it. If assembled correctly, it was extremely effective and undoubtedly saved many lives.

Mortar:
1) A workable paste used to bind together construction blocks and fill the gaps between them. See Masonry.

2) A type of muzzle-loading, short-barrelled, large-calibre artillery piece introduced at the end of the fifteenth century, firing projectiles in a high trajectory – called plunging fire. Mortars used in fortifications needed adapted emplacements. This could take the form of a deep pit-like emplacement or a casemate with the port enlarged and directed slightly upward to match the high-angled trajectory of the weapon.

Mortar casemate: A firing chamber for housing one or more mortars used in eighteenth and nineteenth-century forts. It differed from a regular casemate (q.v.) by the wider embrasure that was directed in an upward direction so that the mortar could fire in safety with little prospect of being hit by return fire.

Mortar casemate (cross-section).

Motte: A motte in French is a raised mound, a small natural or man-made hill, part of a motte-and-bailey castle (q.v.). In France, some of them survive in the toponymy: La Mothe-Fénélon (Lot), La Mothe-Achard (Vendée), La Mothe-Fouquet (Orne), La Motte-Josserand (Nièvre) and La Motte-Tilly (Aube). The term gave us the English moat (q.v.), which no longer designated the mound itself but the wet ditch that surrounded it.

Motte-and-bailey castle: An early form of castle placed on top of an artificial raised earthwork (called the motte) or a natural hill. The motte was flattened at the top, and a timber tower was built at its summit. This tower was known as a keep (q.v.), although other terms were used: tower, great-tower, *donjon*, odel, dunio, domus, *domicilium* or *castellum*. The keep had both a military and a residential character. It usually had up to three storeys, including a living room, sleeping accommodation and stores for supplies, food and water. The entrance to the tower was above ground level and could be reached only by a removable ladder. The appearance of the tower is a matter for speculation, but

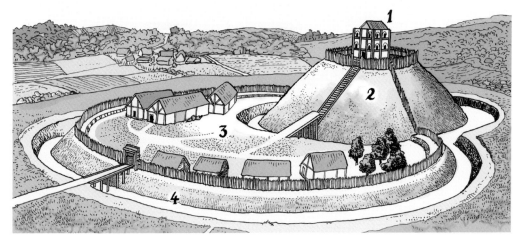

Motte-and-bailey castle. 1: Tower; 2: Motte; 3: Bailey; 4: External palisade, earth wall and wet ditch.

it is likely that there was some attempt at decoration in the form of painting, carving or sculpture as considerations of preservation, beauty, pride, ostentation and prestige are always involved in fortification. The wooden keep was surrounded by a protective palisade (q.v.) or a masonry enclosure; in the latter case it was called a shell keep (q.v.). The earth for the motte was taken from a ditch (q.v.) dug around the motte and the whole castle. The outer surface of the mound could be covered with clay or strengthened with wooden supports.

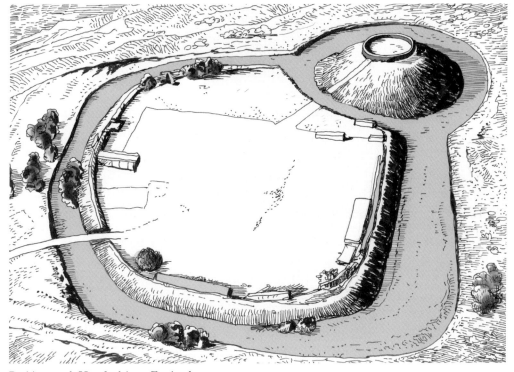

Berkhamsted, Hertfordshire, England.

The bailey was the enclosed courtyard, typically surrounded by a wooden fence called a palisade, which would be overlooked by the motte. It was usually roundish or horseshoe-shaped and used as a living area by servants and farmers who served the lord of the castle. Inside the bailey, a small community lived in autarchy, including a blacksmith, a miller and most of the necessary craftsmen of the age. The bailey would typically contain a hall, stables for the horses and cattle, a chapel, sheds and huts. A castle could have more than one bailey – sometimes an inner and an outer one. The bailey was often enclosed inside another wooden palisade and surrounding ditch, adding an extra line of defence. The bailey was connected to the keep on the motte by a timber drawbridge, which could be destroyed or dismantled in time of crisis. There was in many cases another drawbridge at the entrance into the bailey that could similarly be destroyed or raised for protection.

Many motte-and-bailey castles were built in Europe in the eleventh and twelfth centuries. They were favoured as a relatively cheap but effective defensive fortification that could repel most attackers who had no siege machines. This style of early castle could be built rapidly with readily available materials and without highly skilled labour. The simple structure of motte-and-bailey castles allowed many designs, shapes, dimensions, arrangements, groundplans and layouts, each of which was a unique system specifically intended to meet the requirements of a particular geographical or political situation. They were gradually replaced with stone towers and keeps (q.v.).

Moucharaby: In Islamic or Islamic-influenced architecture, a moucharaby (or moucharabieh or mushrabiya, also known as an oriel window) was a projecting balcony with windows of latticework. The moucharaby is a familiar feature of residences in cities of North Africa and the Middle East. It provided cool air and shadow, and was used to observe the street without being seen. This balcony had a military adaptation in the form of machicolation (q.v.) and brattice (q.v.).

Mougin turret: The Mougin turret was used in French fortifications of the late nineteenth and early twentieth centuries. It was named after the French Commandant Mougin, who designed the first turret in 1875. The armoured turret consisted of two 155mm guns under a straight or bowl-shaped armoured shield, sunk into the ground and surrounded by a thick concrete apron. See Gruson and Shuman turrets.

Multivallate: Adjective qualifying a hillfort (q.v.) with three or more concentric lines of defence. See Hillfort and Oppidum.

Mündungsgasgrube: A large and inclined concrete plate placed right under the embrasure in some Second World War German bunkers armed with artillery pieces. This arrangement was intended to deflect the fumes and gasses produced when firing the gun.

Mural gallery: A gallery (q.v.) constructed within the thickness of the wall below the parapet, which could be provided with arrow slits for reverse fire. See Gaine.

Mural tower: A tower projecting from the curtain wall of a castle.

Murder hole: In medieval fortification, a murder hole was a void in the ceiling of a gateway or above a passageway – generally in the gatehouse (q.v.) – through which the defenders

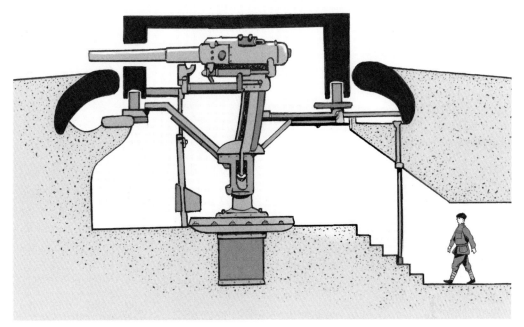

Mougin turret (cross-section).

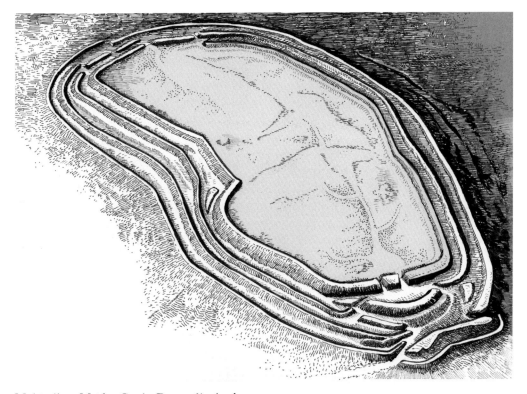

Multivallate. Maiden Castle, Dorset, England.

could fire, throw or pour dangerous or noxious substances down on attackers. When this disposition was arranged on corbels, it was called a moucharaby or a brattice (q.v.).

Murette: A temporary breastwork made of piled stones about 1 metre high, generally constructed when the ground is too hard to dig a trench. The term (meaning 'small wall' in French) was used by campaigning units of the French colonial army and the French Foreign Legion in the nineteenth and twentieth centuries to describe a temporary fortified combat positions or bivouac in the colonies, and principally in North Africa. See Sangar.

Murus caespiticius: In Roman fortification, a wall made of turf.

Murus Dacicus: Latin for 'Dacian wall'. A construction method for defensive walls and fortifications developed in ancient Dacia sometime before the Roman conquest. *Murus Dacicus* consisted of two outer walls made of stone blocks carved in the shape of a rectangular parallelepiped, the gap between them filled with gravel and rocks cemented together with clay and compacted earth. The structure was strengthened and consolidated on each layer by horizontal singed/scorched wood tie beams connected to the outer walls by means of a dovetail joint at the upper surface of the stone block. Archaeological evidence suggests that Dacian walls were topped by a wooden palisade with battlements. A properly built Dacian wall would be about 3–4m thick and 10m high.

Murus Gallicus: *Murus Gallicus* (Gallic wall) was a method of construction of defensive walls used to protect Iron Age hillforts (q.v.) and oppida (q.v.) of the La Tene period in Western Europe. The technique was described by Julius Caesar in his book *Commentaries*

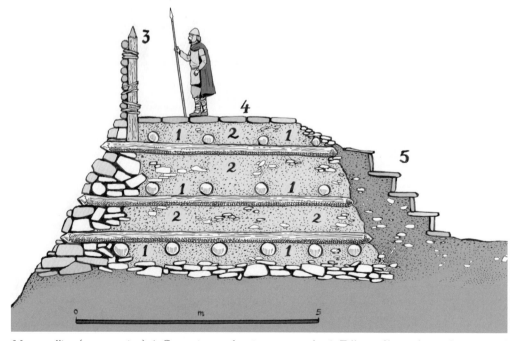

Murus gallicus (cross-section). 1: Crosswise overlapping tree trunks; 2: Filling of heaped gravel, stones and earth; 3: Stakes and wattled hurdles forming a protective breastwork; 4: Wall-walk; 5: Step.

on the Gallic Wars. Although local variations in the building methods existed, the basic distinctive features were: earth or rubble fill; transverse cross beams at approximately 2ft (60cm) intervals; longitudinal timbers laid on the cross beams and attached with mortice joints, nails or iron spikes through augered holes; outer stone facing; and cross beams protruding through the stone facing.

Mushroom pillbox: A British concrete pillbox designed and built in 1940 when Britain was threatened by a Nazi invasion. The pillbox was circular, with various diameters, and was covered with an overhanging domed concrete slab which was supported by a strong central X-shaped masonry pillar. It offered limited protection to defenders because of its large open embrasure, but allowed an excellent all-round view and defence owing to its 360-degree traverse. Mushroom pillboxes, often partially sunken into the ground, were common features in many airfields in southern England. See FW3.

Mushroom pillbox.

Musket: A muzzle-loading, smoothbore long gun intended to be fired from the shoulder. In the seventeenth and eighteenth centuries, many dimensions of bastioned fortification (q.v.) were calculated on the musket's range – between 50 and 70 yards (46–64m).

N

Nähkampfraum: In Second World War German bunkers, the *Nähkampfraum* was a small close-range defensive caponier (q.v.) jutting out of the rear façade (frontage), allowing the delivery of fire on enemies approaching doors, ventilation pipes and Tobruk (q.v.) entrances. It was pierced by a small porthole arranged as a kind of staircase in order to protect against ricocheting splinters and projectiles. The porthole had a lateral angle of fire varying from 40–60 degrees and was fitted with a sliding metal shutter.

National Réduit: A national *réduit* (or redoubt) was a general term for an area to which the (remnant) forces of a nation could withdraw when the main battle had been lost – or even beforehand if defeat was considered inevitable. Typically, a region was chosen because of its economic importance or population density. Natural conditions could also play a role, for example a mountainous area or a peninsula. The national *réduit* was intended to function as a final holdout to preserve national independence for the duration of a conflict. The national *réduit* in Belgium was the region around the port of Antwerp, while in the Netherlands it was the region of Amsterdam. The Swiss national redoubt (*Schweizer Réduit, Alpenfestung* or *Réduit suisse*) was a similar defensive plan developed by the Swiss government during the Second World War to respond to a possible German invasion.

Natural defence: Nature has played a key role in shaping and placing fortifications. In order to erect a barrier against an attacker, it is obvious to adopt, reinforce, extend and improve the defensive potential of natural obstacles. Fortifications have consequently often been erected on top of hills, mountains, cliffs or promontories, alongside marshes, in forests, rivers and islands, and at any other places where nature made the progress of an enemy difficult. An elevated position allowed a defender a panoramic view of the surrounding area and to see enemies approaching in good time. Furthermore, climbing up the hill would reduce the attacker's efficiency and place him in a disadvantageous condition compared to the entrenched and rested defender.

Naval mine: Laid offshore, naval mines represented a cheap and effective means of preventing the movement of shipping and demanded from the enemy a considerable effort in clearing them. Naval mines attacked ships at their weakest area – under the water line. There were basically two types of naval mines: controlled and independent. Controlled mines were connected and exploded by cable from an observation and control station, and used exclusively for the close defence of harbours. Independent mines were either moored or grounded on the sea bed and were actuated by contact (projecting horns passed an electric current to the detonator when struck by a ship), by magnetism (making use of the magnetic fields of a ship to trigger the firing mechanism) or by acoustic devices (using vibrations produced when a ship passed overhead). Laid near a shore, they could also be used as a beach obstacle (q.v.).

Naval turret: Armoured turrets originating from discarded ships could be recycled and installed in a fortified structure, generally a concrete bunker. They could be used as a static battery on land or as coastal defence. They had many advantages: totally rotating, the turret could fire in all directions; they were armoured and placed in a concrete bunker, giving very good protection to crews, weapons and ammunition; the weapon was generally of a large and punchy calibre with a long range and good rate of fire. Disadvantages included the extremely high costs involved in installation and maintenance, while the rotating mechanism could jam when submitted to heavy bombardment.

Naval turret.

New Dutch System: The New Dutch System was a reaction to the Old Dutch System (q.v.) of fortification. Advocated by a number of Dutch engineers, such as Hendrik Ruse, Willem Paen and more particularly by Menno van Coehoorn in his 1685 treatise, the New Dutch method reintroduced Italian elements and borrowed French features: casemates, masonry and *orillon*. The lower part of the scarp was masoned to resist erosion by water, while the curtain angle was 120 degree to ensure maximal flanking. The bastion flank was curved, fitted with two levels of gun emplacements to increase firepower and protected by a casemated *orillon*. The *fausse-braie* was discarded and replaced with a W-shaped *tenaille* and a counterguard (*couvre-face*) in the wet ditch. *Demi-lunes* and

New Dutch bastioned System (Menno van Coehoorn).

places of arms were fitted with a *réduit* (redoubt). The covered way was furnished with traverses. The counterscarp included flanking casemates and counterscarp galleries. These were important contributions to military architecture by van Coehoorn: placed in the reverse slope of a dry ditch, the counterscarp galleries enabled the defenders to bring fire to bear upon attackers who had got into the ditch, while they were accessible by underground tunnel. Advanced works (such as hornworks and crownworks) were regarded as 'useless furniture' and banned. Perhaps the most important factor was that van Coehoorn had a clear understanding of the natural conditions of the Low Countries: the use of inundation was systematically encouraged, improved and developed.

New French System: The New French System (or Modern French System) was a bastioned fortification directly based on models by Vauban (q.v.). Designed by the engineer Cormontaigne in 1728 and slightly modified by General Noizet, this method of fortification remained the accepted standard for bastioned fortifications in France until the 1870s.

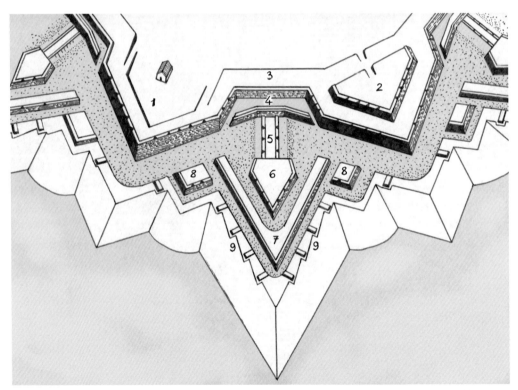

New French System (Cormontaigne). 1: Bastion; 2: Cavalier; 3: *Courtine*; 4: *Tenaille*; 5: Caponier; 6: *Demi-lune*; 7: Counterguard; 8: Lunette; 9: Covered way *en crémaillère* and Glacis.

New German System: A polygonal fortification (q.v.) method based on the work of engineer René de Montalembert. Designed and built in the first half of the nineteenth century in Germany and Austria (e.g at Koblenz, Posen, Ulm, Minden, Germersheim, Ingoldstadt and Linz), this style of fortification is referred to as the New Prussian or New German System.

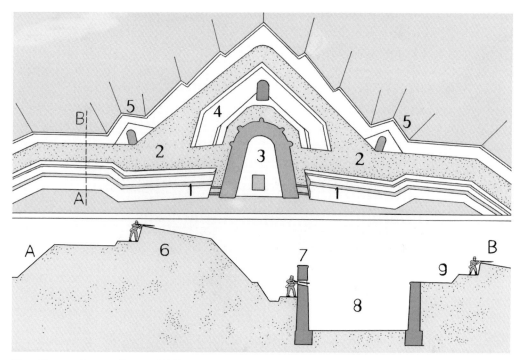

New German System (Posen, 1827).
Top: Plan with 1: Main wall; 2: Dry ditch; 3: Caponier; 4: Counterguard; 5: Covered way and places of arms.
Bottom: Cross-section with 6: Main wall; 7: Detached scarp with Carnot's wall; 8: Dry ditch; 9: Counterscarp and covered way.

New Italian System: The New Italian bastioned System was an improvement on the Old Italian System (q.v.). It largely resulted from models experimented by military engineers such as Jacomo Castriotto, Girolame Maggi and Francesco de Marchi. The bastions were larger with better-designed flanks (q.v.), fitted with cavaliers (q.v.) and spaced in such a way that each bastion could defend the curtain and the ditch, but also the adjacent face of its neighbour, thereby greatly improving flanking (q.v.) and suppressing all blind spots (q.v.). The New Italian System was further improved by the introduction of an outer work known as a ravelin or *demi-lune* (q.v.) and the creation of the covered way (q.v.), invented by the Italian military engineer Nicolo Tartaglia.

Niche: Vertical recess in a wall, often designed to take a statue or other ornament. In medieval fortifications it had a loop-hole, while in modern fortification it could designate a small ammunition store.

No-Man's-Land: A term for a zone, area or territory that is not occupied, or more specifically that is under dispute between two armies or countries. During the First World War, it was the area (usually devastated by artillery craters) between two opposing lines of trenches that neither side controlled. In a broader sense it designates a stretch of land between two borders. Although usually associated with the First World War, the term 'no-man's-land' goes back to the early fourteenth century when it was first used for a wasteland outside the northern walls of London where criminals were executed.

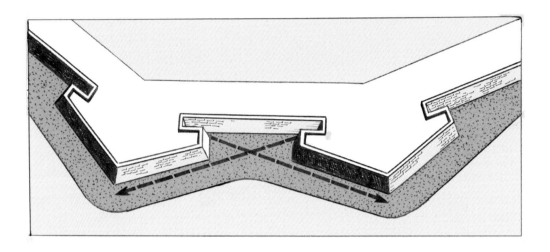

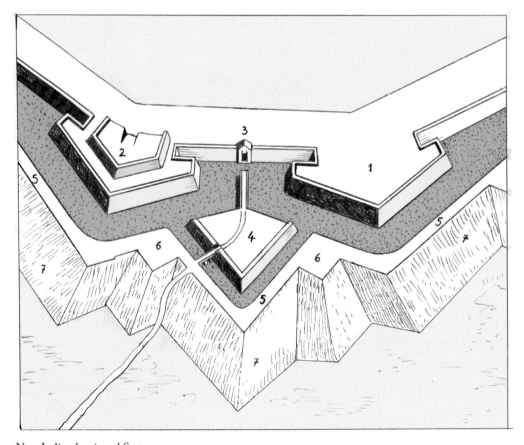

New Italian bastioned System.
Top: Schematic view of flanking both curtain and face from neighbouring bastion. Bottom: 1: Bastion with ears; 2: Bastion with ears and cavalier; 3: Gate in the middle of curtain; 4: Ravelin (*Demi-lune*); 5: Covered way; 6: Place of arms; 7: Glacis.

Norcon pillbox: The British Norcon cylindrical pillbox was named after the company that designed and produced it as a private commercial venture in 1940. It consisted of a non-reinforced concrete pipe usually 1.8m (6ft) in diameter, 1.2m (4ft) in height, 10cm (4in) thick and fitted with several cut loopholes. The original design had no cover, but later models had a roof made of timber and corrugated iron plates covered with earth. The vulnerable pillbox thus offered very poor protection, but it was extremely cheap, quick to produce and easily built. See FW3.

Norcon pillbox.

Norcon pillbox (cross-section).
1: Embrasure; 2: Earth cover; 3: Corrugated roof plate; 4: Masonry walls; 5: Entrance; 6: Additional revetment of sandbags.

Numerus: A Roman fort used to house irregular auxiliary troop units call *numeri*. An example is the *numerus* fort at Hesselbach in Germany. See Auxiliary fort and *Castrum*.

Nuraghe: Stone megalithic cylindrical tower located in Sardinia in the Mediterranean. The nuraghi's era of construction has been roughly dated from 2300–500 BC. There are about 7,000 of them (many in ruins), of which 200 have been excavated and surveyed. Their purpose remains unclear, but they seem to have had both a religious (sanctuary) and military (protecting edifice) use. Some structures consisted of a complex of several conical towers, including an outer circular stone wall with additional roundish towers enclosing a compound with accommodation buildings and huts, suggesting an early form of fortified settlement. It is generally assumed that nuraghi were fortified cores of family farmsteads, incorporating the roles of towerhouse, livestock barn and repository of valuables. See Broch.

Nutcracker mine: The German Second World War nutcracker mine (in German *Nußknackermine*) was allegedly designed by Field Marshal Erwin Rommel himself for use as an anti-landing obstacle in the Atlantic Wall (q.v.). It comprised a concrete base, inside which a heavy artillery shell or one or two mines were placed, and a stake. The mines exploded when a landing craft knocked against the pole, which worked as a detonating trigger. This system had many variants with wooden or metal frameworks, wooden or concrete lever arm and explosive charge or smoke.

O

Observation post: A covert position whose primary role is to collect information, as directed by and in support of a tactical operation. Temporary or permanent, it is a position from which soldiers can watch enemy movements, warn of hostile activities or direct

Observation bunker. (Coalhouse Fort, Tilbury, Essex).

artillery fire. An observation post is obviously better when placed on an elevated position. See Fire Control Post, Tobruk, Tower, *Hochleitstand*, and Watchtower.

Obstacle: In military terms, an obstacle is a physical and passive barrier intended to keep intruders and attackers out, block enemy action and hinder the progress of or prevent any enemy activity. The number of obstacles and the sophistication of their arrangements varies greatly. Natural obstacles include features such as woods, rivers and high ground, while man-made obstacles feature constructed elements such as canals and railway embankment. Obstacles can also be specially emplaced for military purposes, in many shapes, and with specialized objectives: against infantry (ditch, wall, palisade, fraise abatis, barbed wire); against vehicles (caltrop, fakir's carpet); against armoured vehicles (anti-tank mine, anti-tank wall, anti-tank ditch); against boats and landing ships (beach obstacles); and against gliders and paratroopers. No matter how well designed and placed, obstacles lose a great deal of efficiency unless they are fully integrated into an active defensive system. Obstacles prevent the enemy from coming to close quarters, but they must be guarded, controlled, inspected, maintained and covered by active weapons.

This massive and imposing concrete observation tower, located at Noirmont Point, St Brelade, on the south-west coast of Jersey, was built by the German occupiers during the Second World War as part of the Atlantic Wall.

Offa's Dyke: A massive linear earthwork, roughly following some of the frontier between England and Wales. It is generally accepted that much of the earthwork can be attributed to Offa, King of Mercia from AD 757–796. The earthwork originally had a length of 120 miles and consisted of a bank and ditch about 50ft (15.2m) wide – in places up to 65ft (20m) – and 8ft (2.5m) high. In certain sections, the courses of the Severn and Wye Rivers were used instead of a wall. Offa's Dyke could not possibly be continuously manned, and the thin line would never have repulsed an army, even a gang of raiders, so it was not a proper line of fortification. Its purpose in the eighth century was to express Offa's power and prestige and form a frontier delineation between the Anglian kingdom of Mercia and the Welsh kingdom of Powys, a clear warning for Welsh intruders. See Wat's Dyke.

Offener Beobachter: The German *Offener Beobachter* – literally 'open observatory', also known as a Tobruk (q.v.) – was a small open observation pit built in the thick exterior

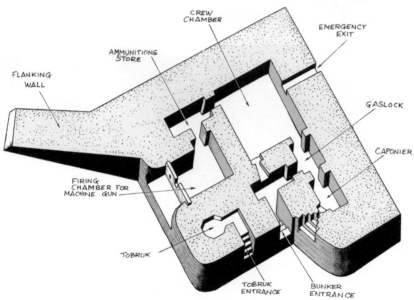

Offener Beobachter. Shown here as a Tobruk in a German type 630 bunker.

wall of many German bunkers during the Second World War. It comprised a small round or octogonal room, only accessible by a narrow door and bended staircase at the rear of the bunker.

Oilet: An oilet (or oillet) was a narrow arrow loop (q.v.) in the walls of medieval fortifications, but more strictly applied to the round hole or circle with which the opening terminated. This circular part of the arrow loop was used to give archers a greater field of fire.

Old Dutch System: During the long war of independence against the Spaniards (the Eighty Years War from 1568–1648), the Dutch evolved their own bastioned style, fully adapted to the peculiar conditions of their low and marshy land. The Dutch method,

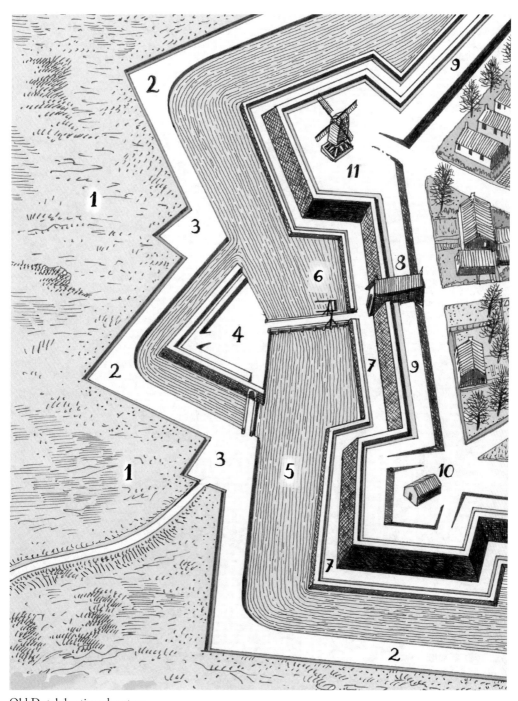

Old Dutch bastioned system.
1: Glacis (could be flooded); 2: Covered way; 3: Places of arms; 4: Ravelin; 5: Wet ditch; 6: Drawbridge; 7: *Fausse-braie*; 8: Gatehouse; 9: Curtain; 10: Hollow bastion (with powder-house); 11: Solid bastion (with windmill).

designed by the mathematician Simon Stevin and developed by the engineer Adrian Anthonisz, was characterized by extensive flooding, broad wet ditches, and bastions and curtains totally made of earth. The system often featured a *fausse-braie* (q.v.), a continuous low breastwork built at the foot of bastions and curtains. The Old Dutch System, as it became called, only made use of earth banks and ditches filled with water, was relatively cheap – much more so than bastioned systems using masonry – and was extensively exported to Scandinavia and northern Germany. See New Dutch System.

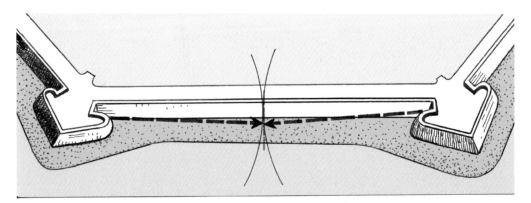

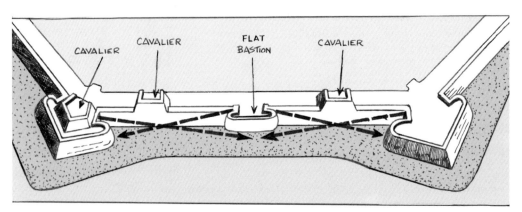

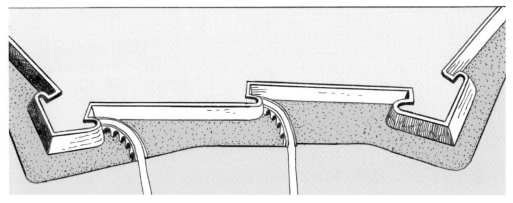

Old Italian system. Top: Basic flanking of the curtain from the flanks. Centre: Improved flanking with flat bastion in the middle of curtain and cavaliers.
Bottom: Access to the fortress either in a bastion flank or a recess in the curtain.

Old Italian system. Forte Spagnolo at Aquila in central Italy, designed *c.* 1528 by Piro Aloiso Escriba, is a good example of an early fortress in the Old Italian System.

Old Italian System: An early Italian bastioned system (q.v.) characterized by a curtain flanked by two bastions with ears, replacing medieval corner and wall towers.

Onderwal: See *Fausse-braie*.

Open fort: See American West forts.

Open work: A work open at the gorge (q.v.), thus offering no protection when captured by besiegers.

Opera coronata: See Crownwork.

Opere: Italian term for a fort or defensive work.

Oppidum: An *oppidum* (plural *oppida*) was a Celtic fortified site, a kind of entrenched camp often built upon an elevated plateau or craggy hill. Julius Caesar described the larger Celtic Iron Age settlements he encountered in Gaul as *oppida*, and the term is now used to describe the large pre-Roman fortified settlements that existed all across Western and Central Europe. Many *oppida* grew from hillforts (q.v.), and although surrounded by ditches, earthworks and palisades, it is still unclear whether they had any significant defensive function. The main features of the *oppida* were the architectural construction of the walls and gates, the spacious layout and commanding view of the surrounding area. The development of *oppida* was a milestone in the urbanization of the continent as they were the first large settlements north of the Mediterranean that

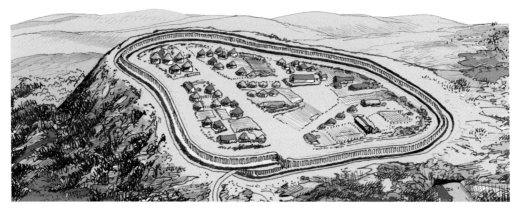

Oppidum.

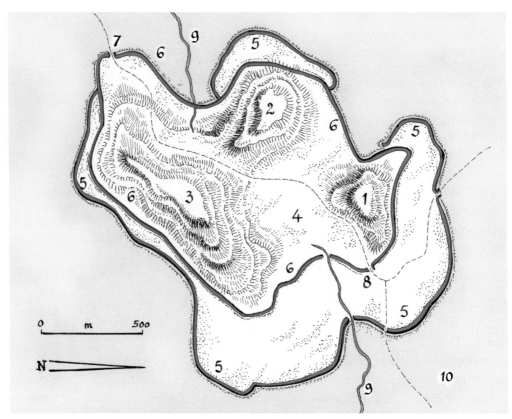

Ground plan of *Oppidum* Bibracte. Bibracte, a Gaulish *oppidum*, was the capital of the Aedui tribe and one of the most important hillforts in Gaul. Situated on Mont Beuvray near modern Autun in Burgundy, Bibracte was a fortified economic, political and religious centre. The site occupies three hills with an average height of 700m – in the north, Pierre de la Wivre (1); in the west, Theurot de la Roche (2); in the south, Le Parrey (3) – with a low central valley called Pature du Couvent (4). The *oppidum* was enclosed by a first outer wall and ditch (5) and a second inner wall and ditch (6). The perimeter was crossed by a main road with two gates: Grandes Portes (7) in the south and Porte du Rebout (8) in the north. Two small brooks (9) provided water. A necropolis (10) was placed outside the perimeter.

could genuinely be described as villages. Caesar pointed out that each tribe of Gaul had several *oppida* but that they were not all of equal importance, perhaps implying some form of hierarchy. Hillforts and *oppida*, though primitive, were often effective and required extensive siege engines and other siege warfare techniques to overcome, such as at the investment of Alesia. After they had conquered Gaul, the Romans used the infrastructure of the *oppida* to administer the new provinces of their empire, and many became Roman towns in modern-day France: Langres, Laon, Béziers, Carcassone, Uzerche and Le Puy-en-Velay.

Orechino: *Orillon* in French and 'Ear' in English. The curved or straight protruding part of a bastion screening and protecting the flank (q.v.). See Bastion, *Orillon* and Ear.

Oreilles de chat: See Cat's ears.

Orgue: French for organ. A vertical obstacle made of strong balks of wood sliding through grooves and closing the passage of a gatehouse. See Portcullis.

Orillon: Also called ear (*orecchino* in Italian). A massive screen projecting at the shoulder of a bastion (q.v.) intended to provide cover from enemy fire and protect weapons placed in the flank (q.v.). *Orillons* came into two main shapes: straight and roundish. See Ear.

Organisation Todt: The Organisation Todt (OT) originated from a conglomerate of building companies united and commanded from 1933 by the engineer Fritz Todt (1891–1942). Tightly related to the Nazi party, Fritz Todt was commissioned before the Second World War to construct Germany's *Autobahnen* (motorways) and the bunkers and obstacles of the Westwall (q.v.). In 1938, the Organisation Todt was officially created and soon militarized as a German Army auxiliary formation. During the war, the OT was led by Dr Todt until his death in 1942, and then by Hitler's architect, Albert Speer. The OT built Hitler's command bunkers, the Atlantic Wall (q.v.) bunkers, submarine bases (q.v.) and many other military constructions. As many German nationals were drafted into the Wehrmacht, and as its tasks only increased, the OT widely opened its ranks to foreign volunteers from occupied European nations. The OT also made massive use of forced and slave labour, including prisoners-of-war, political detainees, convicts, rounded up unemployed, arbitrarily displaced civilian populations, deported Jews and concentration camp inmates.

Organisation Todt worker.

Oubliette: An *oubliette* (from the French verb *oublier*, meaning *to forget*) is a pit or cellar under the floor, a form of dungeon (q.v.), which was accessible only from a hatch or trapdoor in its ceiling. The image of a dark, damp vaulted dungeon as the scene of lengthy incarceration and unspeakable cruelty is a powerful one in popular culture, but most often only a legend. It is often exaggerated (or simply invented) to arouse interest and thrill tourists. Many rooms described as dungeons or *oubliettes* (or torture chambers) were in fact only cellars, storerooms, water cisterns or even latrines.

Outworks: Various fortified elements placed into the ditch or outside the main enceinte. They were thus external and separated from the main body of the defence, but still within the glacis. In bastioned fortification they were included inside the perimeter of the covered way, and formed a tangled skein and their ditches a kind of labyrinth. Their sheer number, scale and complexity may often be as awesome to modern tourists as they were supposed to be to seventeenth-century besiegers. They were built in depth, often extending over very wide areas. They protected each other with cross-fire and made an external line of resistance. Each outwork needed a siege to be taken, or at least a fight, before the besiegers could reach the main enceinte. If the enemy managed to conquer one, he would usually find that there was another one covering it from the rear, so the time of final victory would be frustratingly postponed. Their height, outline

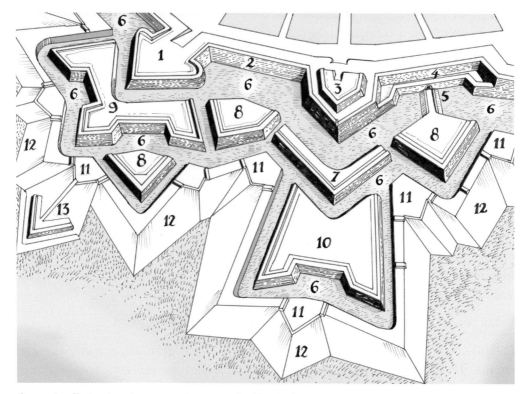

Outworks. (In bastioned seventeenth-century fortification).
1: Bastion; 2: Curtain; 3 Bastion with cavalier; 4: *Tenaille*; 5: Caponier; 6: Ditch; 7: Counterguard; 8: Ravelin (aka *Demi-lune*); 9: Crownwork; 10: Hornwork; 11: Covered way and places of arms; 12: Glacis; 13: *Flèche* (aka Arrow).

and positioning were designed so that no blind spots (q.v.) existed; their alignment was intended to create large and efficient firing lanes and killing grounds to deter attackers.

Outworks were furnished with parapets (q.v.) and ascents and surrounded by secondary moats or ditches, which were less wide than the main ditch. The gorge (q.v.) of these works was always open, which meant they were not protected by a parapet, so if an outwork was conquered it offered no protection to the besiegers. The height of every outwork was calculated in order that they command (q.v.) each other. Communication between outworks and the main body was effected through ditches when these were dry and by means of wooden foot-bridges and row-boats when ditches were wet. In bastioned classical fortification, outworks were often made of masonry and filled with earth, and generally ornamented with cordon and tablette (q.v.). Outworks included *fausse-braie* (q.v.), *tenailles* (q.v.), caponiers (q.v.), *demi-lunes* (q.v.), counterguards (q.v.) and their variations, as well as *tenaillons* (q.v.) and envelopes (q.v.).

Ouvrage:
1) In French nineteenth-century fortification, the difference between a *redoute* (redoubt) and an *ouvrage* (work) is not always clear; both were small forts or large gun batteries placed in interval between major forts, and usually manned only in wartime. The difference between a fort proper and an *ouvrage* seems to be that a fort had its ditches swept by caponiers (q.v.), and later coffers (q.v.), whereas the *ouvrage* was deprived of these flanking elements.
2) In the Maginot Line (q.v.), the term designated a collection of interconnected blocks and subterranean facilities functioning as a single unit. There were commonly two sorts: *Petit Ouvrage* (aka *Blockhaus*, armed primarily with light infantry weapons) and *Gros Ouvrage* (larger works armed with both infantry and heavy artillery weapons).

P

Palace: A large and often magnificent residence, especially a royal residence or the home of a head of state or some other high-ranking dignitary, such as a bishop or archbishop. It differs from a castle (q.v.) by the emphasis on comfort and luxury. In many parts of Europe, the term is also applied to private aristocratic mansions. Many historic palaces originate from fortified places, and many are now put to other uses such as parliaments, museums, hotels or office buildings. The word is also sometimes used to describe a lavishly ornate building used for public entertainment or exhibitions.

Palas: A residential hall (q.v.) in a German castle.

Palisade: A fence or wall composed of a row of closely aligned wooden stakes or tree trunks. The trunks would be sharpened or pointed at the top end, and be driven vertically into the ground on the other end. Coming in a variety of lengths, the stakes would sometimes be reinforced with additional constructions. As a defensive structure, palisades were often used in conjunction with earthworks. Obstacles and fortifications made of earthwork and wood were perishable. When intended to be permanent works,

Palisade.

they could not be left unattended for years, and therefore had to be constantly reviewed, maintained and renewed. See Stockade.

Palmerston forts: A group of forts and associated structures constructed around the coast of Britain. The forts were built during the Victorian period on the recommendations of the 1860 Royal Commission on the Defence of the United Kingdom, following concerns about the strength of the French Navy. The name comes from their association with Henry John Temple, 3rd Viscount Palmerston (1784–1865), who was Prime Minister at the time and promoted the project. The works were also known as Palmerston's Follies, as by the time they were completed the threat (if it had ever existed) had passed, largely due to the Franco-Prussian War of 1870; furthermore, the phenomenal advances of technology in artillery had rendered them out-of-date. The Palmerston forts were the most costly and extensive system of fixed defences undertaken in Britain in peacetime. The defences were built according to the polygonal system (q.v.) to defend a number of key areas of the British, Irish and Channel Island coastline, in particular areas around military and Royal Navy bases, including Alderney, Belfast, Berehaven, the Bristol Channel, Chatham, River Clyde, Cork, Dover, Isle of Wight, Milford Haven, North Thames and East Anglia, North-East England, Plymouth, Portland harbour, Portsmouth and Lough Swilly.

Pamart armoured cupola: See Cloche Pamart.

Panama mounting: A US emplacement for coastal batteries developed at Panama in the 1920s and later used at Corregidor, Caballo and Carabao islands in the entrance

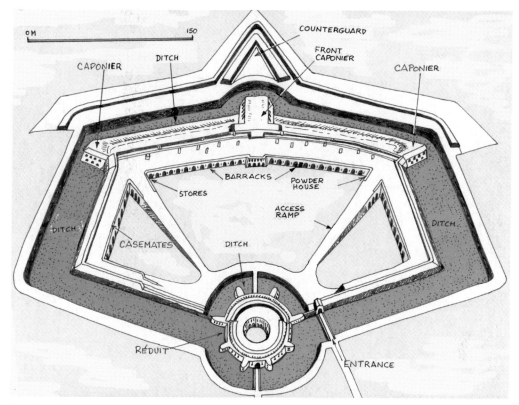

Fort Brockhurst at Gosport in Hampshire.

to Manila Bay. Typically using the 1917 French-designed 155mm Grande Puissance Filloux (GPF – a powerful 155mm gun designed by the French Colonel Louis Filloux) heavy field gun, the Panama mounting consisted of a circular concrete platform with a raised centre section, with the carriage tyres pivoting around the centre section and the split trails spread out on rails at the platform's edge.

Panzer: German general term for armour (q.v.). Panzer designates both an armoured fighting vehicle and armoured parts such as a bunker's shutters, gas-proof doors, protective plates, observations cupolas and armed turrets.

Panzergrabe: See Anti-tank ditch.

Panzergruppe: See *Feste*.

Panzerlafette: The *Panzerlafette* (armoured mounting) or *Fahrpanzer* (mobile shielding) was conceived in Germany at the end of the nineteenth century. Designed by engineer Julius von Schütz, working for the Gruson Company, the *Panzerlafette* was a small cylindrical domed armoured turret fitted with wheels. The device housed a 5.3cm quick-firing gun served by two soldiers. Lateral armour was 4mm, with 40mm on top. Like a mobile fortification, one could move the turret into any tactical position in a fort. The machine was not motorized and was moved into position behind a parapet by a party of men, or drawn by a horse, although in German fortresses it was used in special concrete

Panzerlafette. (Cross-section).

trenches with 60cm narrow-gauge railway, making possible swift movement to where they might be most needed. The mobile armoured turrets could be parked completely concealed behind part of the fortress wall and trundle into view just in time to repel an assault. Total weight in operating order was 3,600kg. This kind of machine was used in the Metz *Festen* (q.v.), but the viability of the concept was always in doubt. No motorization left the machine without autonomy, and it lacked internal ammunition reserves. The recoil of the gun also tended to severely destabilize the cumbersome machine.

Panzernest: A small armoured defensive prefab mobile pillbox made as a single block of cast steel, designed by the German Army during the Second World War and employed on the Russian Front and in Italy. A modern version of the older *Panzerlafette* (q.v.), the *MG Panzernest* (aka *Krab*) had a height of 1.8m and an average diameter of 1.6m. Armour near the firing port was 115mm, in the lower part near the hatch 35mm and in the upper part 45mm. The firing port was placed in the narrowest part of the container and featured two openings, one for observation and another for the machine gun. The size of the firing port was 160mm x 110mm, and the whole thing weighed about 3 tons. It could house two men serving a machine gun (e.g. MG 34 or MG 42) firing through a small embrasure, allowing for a 50–69-degree arc of fire. It featured a foot-operated ventilation system to extract the machine gun's fumes, and the crew had the use of two periscopes for observation. The pillbox's entrance was a small armoured hatch (50cm x 60cm) placed at the back. The *Panzernest* was mobile owing to two large wooden wheels, and was towed in inverted position by a truck. In combat the *Panzernest* was generally sunk in the ground in a prepared pit and could be easily camouflaged. It could resist enemy shellfire up to 4.7cm in calibre.

Panzerstutzpunkt: A *Panzerstutzpunkt* (armoured stronghold, abbreviated PzStP) included *Panzerwerke* (concrete bunkers armed with weapons placed in armoured turrets). The term was used in German Second World War fortification, notably in the Atlantic Wall (q.v.). It should be noted that the sonorous and impressive terms *Panzerwerke* and *Panzerstutzpunkt* sometimes designated a somewhat weak position for propaganda and deceiving purposes in order to create confusion among the Allies.

Panzerwerke: A *Panzerwerke* was a German concrete bunker with armament placed in a *Panzerturm* (armoured turret).

Parade ground (aka **Parade**): The central flat and bare square in the middle of a fort (q.v.), citadel (q.v.) or camp where troops can gather, muster and drill. See Esplanade and Place-of-arms.

Parade wall: The interior wall of the rampart, which coincided with the interior slope (q.v.). There was a continuous communication lane running parallel at the foot of the inner wall to facilitate the deployment of the garrison.

Parados: An embankment placed behind a defensive position (often a gun battery or trench). This backscreen acted as a traverse (q.v.), thus compartmentalizing a combat emplacement in order to shelter weapons and servants from reverse and plunging mortar fire.

Parallel: In seventeenth and eighteenth-century siege warfare, a trench excavated by a besieging force parallel with the attacked front in order to protect besiegers from fire from the city or fortress. Successive parallels were dug, each being nearer to the place and connected by zigzag-shaped saps, until the final parallel was close enough to take breach batteries. When the breach (q.v.) was made, the last parallel was used as starting point for the final assault. See Part 2 (Siege Warfare).

Parapet: Broadly speaking, a parapet, also called a breastwork (q.v.), is a wall-like barrier at the edge of a roof, terrace, balcony or other structure. In fortification, it designates a man-high wall, an epaulement made of earth, wooden palisade or masoned brick or stone. In permanent fortification, it was located on the exterior edge of a wall-walk on top of the wall of a castle or the rampart of a fort. In Ancient and medieval permanent fortifications, the parapet was usually fitted with crenels (q.v.) and merlons (q.v.), placed on top of towers and curtains (q.v.). In bastioned and nineteenth-century fortifications, it was a thick and massive breastwork protecting the wall-walk and often fitted with embrasures (q.v.) and a *banquette* or fire-step (q.v.). In field fortification in a trench, for example, the parapet was made of earth, sandbags (q.v.) or gabions (q.v.).

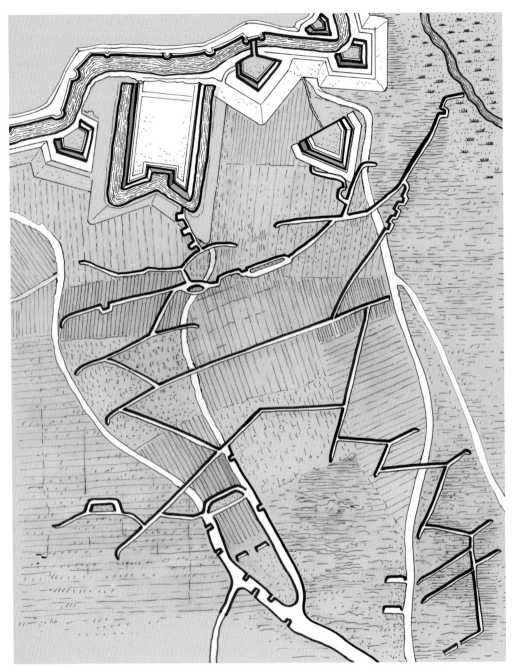

Parallel. Siege of Maastricht in the Netherlands in 1673.

Pareclat: A protective screen made of earth or formed with gabions (q.v.) or piled sandbags (q.v.) raised on the rampart, in the middle of bastions or in a trench in order to shelter the defenders from splinters of bombs and shells. It had the same function as a parados (q.v.) and traverse (q.v.).

Pas-de-souris: In French seventeenth and eighteenth-century bastioned fortification, a masonry narrow staircase placed in the counterscarp allowing soldiers to get access from

Pas-de-Souris.

the ditch to the covered way (q.v.) and the places-of-arms (q.v.). As an extra measure of security, the inferior step of the stair was often placed 1.5 or 2m from the bottom of the ditch. Therefore the defenders had to use a ladder (which in retreating they took away with them), otherwise the stair was rather difficult or impossible to use.

Passage: A passage, also called a crochet, was a narrow access built round the head of a traverse (q.v.).

Pavis: A large movable shield intended to protect an archer or arquebusier on the battlefield or in siege warfare. See *Pluteus*.

Peel tower: Peel (or pele) towers, originally palisaded courts, were small fortified dwelling keeps or tower houses, built in small settlements along the English and Scottish borders in the Scottish Marches and North of England. Built in the middle of the fifteenth century and used until the seventeenth century, peel towers also served as a temporary refuge for the local population against marauders and raiders. The pele tower often included a kind of adjoining bailey (q.v.) called a barmkin (q.v.).

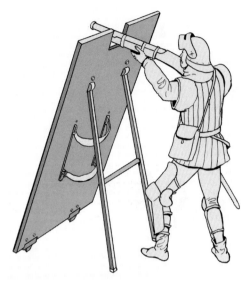

Pavis.

Peel tower.

Pen: A protected emplacement for aircraft safe parking made of blast walls on three sides.

Pen.

Pentagon: A geometrical figure with five sides and five angles. The pentagon was often used for designing the groundplan of bastioned redoubts (q.v.), sconces (q.v.), citadels (q.v.) and forts (q.v.). The pentagon offered the best proportions of internal area to length of wall with good accesss to all five bastions. In the Renaissance, the polygon's approximation to a circle was deemed to be nearing a perfect geometry.

Pentagonal fort: A fort constructed with five straight curtains and five bastions at the angles.

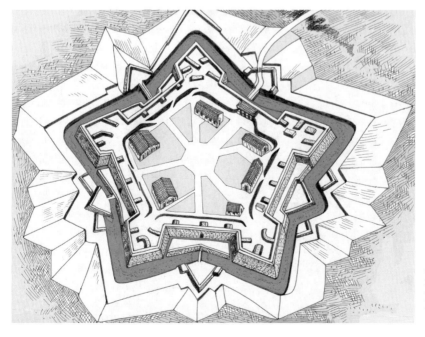

Fort of Issy-les-Moulineaux, Paris, built in 1841.

Pepper-pot tower: A pepper-pot tower was an overhanging turret (q.v.) often resting on a corbel (q.v.), and generally placed on top of a wall. It had the same observation role as an *echauguette* (q.v.) and the same flanking combat function as a tower (q.v.), but was much cheaper to build.

Periscope: An instrument for observation from a concealed position. Basically, it is intended to see without being seen. In its simplest form it consists of a tube or a long box with mirrors at each end set parallel to each other at a 45-degree angle. This form of periscope, with the addition of two simple lenses, served for observation purposes in the trenches during the First World War and in bunkers during the Second World War. Military personnel also use sophisticated periscopes in gun turrets, submarines and armoured vehicles.

Pepper-pot turret.

Permanent fortification: Military architecture is usually divided into two main branches with sub-categories.

Firstly, *permanent fortification* was designed and built mostly in peacetime with all the resources that a tribe, realm, nation or state could supply of construction and mechanical skills. It was designed with serious attention, and built with care and thought with the best-enduring materials. By nature fixed, permanent fortification was generally intended to protect the frontiers of a state or its naval and military arsenals from attack by an enemy. A sub-branch of permanent fortification was coastal fortification, which was particularly designed and built to prevent, resist and repulse enemy landing and protect military harbours and naval installations from attacks from the sea.

Secondly, *semi-permanent or siege fortification* was constructed in wartime during a siege or on the battlefield, sometimes under enemy fire. See Introduction, Part 1 (A Short History of Fortification) and Semi-permanent fortification.

Perpendicular system: A system of fortification designed by the French engineer René de Montalembert at the end of the eighteenth century, consisting of a series of *tenailles* – triangular structures with long faces, abutting each other and forming together in plan a saw-edged outline, generally with right angle of 90 degrees. Ahead of the *tenailled* front, Montalembert advocated two outer lines of counterguards fitted with musketry loopholes, walls and casemated artillery emplacements, all separated by ditches. Behind these stood strongly masoned, multistorey circular towers (generally 11 yards in diameter), each capable of firing out across the countryside for long-range defence and acting as a *réduit*. See *Tenaille* system, Prussian system and Polygonal system.

Petard: An explosive device or small bomb having the appearance of a conical metal cask filled with gunpowder and ignited by a fuse. The petard was used to blow up gates, doors or sally ports, and destroy or damage a section of a defensive wall.

Pfalz: A castle (q.v.) used as a temporary seat of power for the German Holy Roman Emperor in the Early and High Middle Ages. Etymologically, the term derived from the Latin *palatium* (in English palatinate).

Pfostenschlitzmauer: A method of constructing defensive walls protecting Iron Age hillforts (q.v.) and *oppida* (q.v.) in Central Europe. Meaning 'post-slot wall' in German, it was characterized by vertical wooden posts set into the front stone facing. The rampart was constructed from a timber lattice and transverse cross beams filled with earth or rubble. The construction method is also known as Kelheim-style, named after the extensive ramparts at the *oppidum* of Kelheim in Lower Bavaria, Germany. See *Murus Gallicus*.

Pfostenschlitzmauer (cross-section).

Philippian fortification: A system or style of castle architecture developed during the reign of King Philippe II Auguste of France (1180–1223). Examples of Philippian fortification include the Louvre castle in Paris, as well as Dourdan, Gisors and Chinon castles. Typically a Philippian castle included a regular rectangular or square plan, straight curtains with machicolation, defensive round corner- and wall-towers, a large, thick, and high circular dungeon (keep) with a conical roof placed in the middle of the courtyard, a wide moat filled with water, and usually two entrances each framed between two flanking towers fitted with drawbridges.

Piatta forma: A sort of flat bastion (q.v.) placed on a curtain halfway between two bastions in order to increase flanking. See Venitian Bastioned system, Old Italian System.

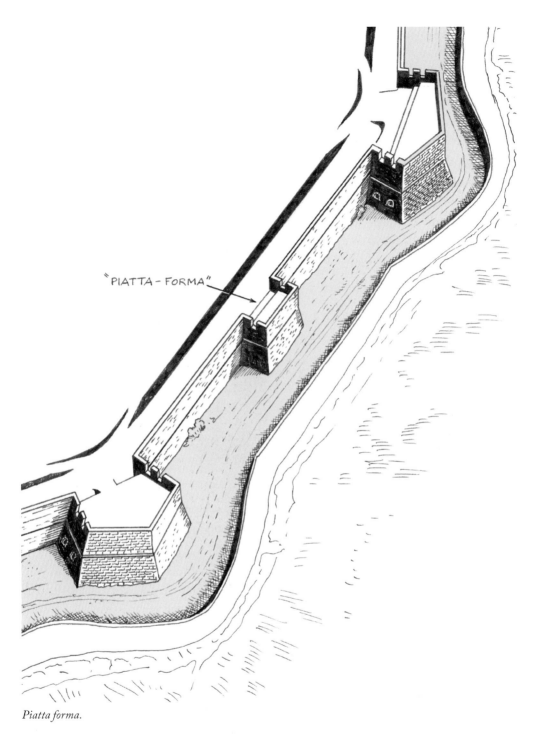

Piatta forma.

Piazza: A large courtyard inside an Italian castle or fortress which could be used as a parade ground (q.v.).

Piazza bassa: A protected artillery emplacement built in the recessed flank of a sixteenth-century Italian bastion designed to provide additional firepower. It could be screened and covered with an *orillon* or ear (q.v.). It could be casemated or simply open and fitted with a thick breastwork. It allowed defenders to enfilade both the curtain (q.v.) and the ditch (q.v.).

Picket:

1) A pointed or sharpened stake driven in the ground acting as an obstacle, generally holding barbed wire (q.v.).
2) A small advanced stronghold or post (q.v.) with a few soldiers maintaining a watch and intended to warn against an enemy attack. It could also be a stronghold of some importance acting as a base of operations or an artillery fire base. Pickets were used by the British in India in the nineteenth century and by the US Army in the Vietnam War (1955–75).

Pickett-Hamilton pillbox: The Pickett-Hamilton pillbox was designed to defend British airfields from German landing and airborne troops in 1940. As any structure built above the ground of an airfield presented a hazard to aircraft, the Pickett-Hamilton was a retractable (or 'disappearing') turret intended to pop up out of the ground only when a German paratrooper attack occurred. The cylindrical pillbox was made of concrete and was 2.7m (9ft) in diameter, with a thickness of 22–25cm (9–10in). It was buried into the ground, was manned by two or three gunners standing and serving a light machine gun, and access was via a metal hatch on the roof. The pillbox consisted of two pre-cast concrete cylinders: the outer attached to the base section and the inner, which formed the moving 'pop-up' element. The inner section was moved up and down by a compressed air-driven jack. Because it was sometimes unreliable, the jack was backed up by a hydraulic hand pump worked manually by one of the crewmen. The movement was accomplished by a double-acting pump mounted on top of a cylindrical oil reservoir, which enabled the pillbox to be raised in about eight seconds and lowered in twenty seconds. When not in use, the pillbox was totally concealed, the concrete lid of the sliding inner cylinder laying flush with the ground surface, but when brought up into action it rose some 2ft 6in above the surface to allow fire from any of its three embrasures.

Pickett-Hamilton pillbox (cross-section).

The purpose of the 'pop-up' pillbox was to maximize the element of surprise. At the start of any enemy attack on the airfield, they would rise out of the ground, with an all-round field of fire. While in theory the idea was good, it is doubtful whether these pillboxes would have been useful in practice. They were prone to flooding on rainy days, the raising mechanism was rather vulnerable, they were not large enough to accommodate heavy weapons and were cramped for the crew, and no upward view was possible (apart from cursory looks through the entrance hatch). They were, however, a very good indication of the ingenuity of the wartime British brain when it came to crisis inventions. Most of the concrete work was carried out by DWG of Barnstable in Devon, while the original castings for the raising mechanism were produced by the Cornish firm Willey and Co. Some 335 'pop-up' pillboxes were constructed, and many were installed in airfields around Britain. See FW3.

Pier: Support for an arch or vault, usually square as opposed to pillar (round).

Pila muralia: In Roman fortification, this was a wooden double-pointed beam with a central handgrip to facilitate lashing. It was used for making a palisade, a stake or an obstacle against cavalry. See *Sudis*.

Pilaster: Shallow pier used to buttress a wall.

Pillbox: English term for a bunker, a small enclosed concrete camouflaged casemate (q.v.) with loopholes through which weapons are fired. In French it is generally called a *blockhaus* (q.v.), while in German it is a *Stand* or *Kampfstand*. See FW3.

Pimple: Popularly known as dragon's teeth (q.v.), pimples were concrete pyramid-shaped blocks designed specifically to counter tanks which, attempting to pass them, would climb up and expose vulnerable parts of the vehicle or slip down with the tracks between the points. Pimples varied in size, but were typically 2ft (61cm) high and about 3ft (91cm) square at the base. They were designed and constructed by the British in 1940 when under the threat of a German invasion. There were also alternative anti-tank obstacles in conical and cylindrical form.

Pinnae: Roman battlement. See Merlon and Roman wall.

Place: Generic term used to designate a position, stronghold, fort, fortress or fortified town.

Place-of-arms:
1) The interior ground surface of a fort or citadel, which serves as a drill, ceremony and assembly area. See Parade ground.
2) In bastioned fortification, re-entering places-of-arms were set up in the re-entering angles of the covered way (q.v.), where they formed fortlets supporting the *demi-lune* and covering the glacis. Salient places-of-arms were the open spaces positioned at the salient intersection of the branches of the covered way. They were parts of the counterscarp and covered way, and formed advanced observation and combat positions.

Plane of construction: See Datum and Command.

Plan-relief: See Relief map.

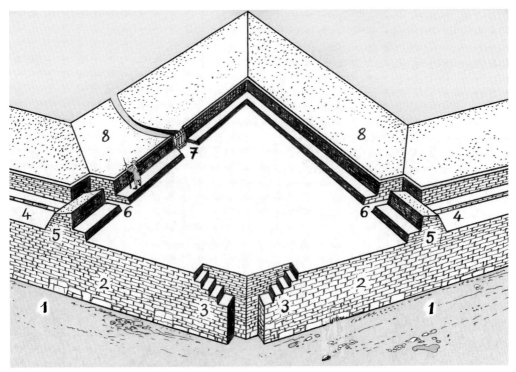

Place of arms. Seen here from the gorge, a re-entering place-of-arms included the following features: 1: Ditch; 2: Counterscarp; 3: *Pas-de-Souris*; 4: Covered way; 5: Traverse; 6: *Passage en chicane*; 7: Sortie; 8: Glacis.

Plate armour: Armour made of jointed metal plates used for protecting a medieval knight. Also used in fortification for reinforcing casemates and embrasures.

Playing card plan: Expression coined by archaeologists and historians to designate the typical shape (a regular rectangle with rounded corners) of a Roman camp or fort.

Plinth: Horizontal courses of large strong stones at the base of a wall to provide better foundation, often projecting from the wall face. The purpose of the plinth was to counter the endeavours of sappers, and also to increase the effect of machicolations (q.v.) as it deflected projectiles thrown down from the walls above. See Apron, Batter and Spur.

Plongée: In bastioned fortification, the slightly sloping top or crest of the breastwork (q.v.). See Superior slope.

Pluteus: A movable Roman screen used by archers in siege warfare.

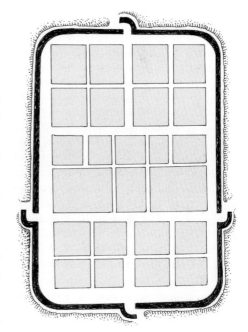

Playing card plan.

259

Poivrière: French for a small pepper-pot tower, a small turret built on top of a wall. See Pepper-pot tower and Turret.

Poliorcetics: The formal name for siegecraft or siege warfare, the art or science of laying siege to a fortification and of seizing it. In some texts poliorcetics also applies to the art of building fortification.

Polygonal fort: Fort designed according to the polygonal system (q.v.). All polygonal forts were different. Either German, Austrian, Italian, French, Dutch, Belgian, American or British, no two were the same as they were adapted to their local situation. The size varied greatly depending on their task and the terrain in which they were established. However, all of them – at least in the period from 1860–85 – had common features and consisted of the same basic elements in varying combinations. The general plan was a large pentagonal (five-sided) gun battery, in fact a large bastion composed of a front displaying two faces forming

Pluteus.

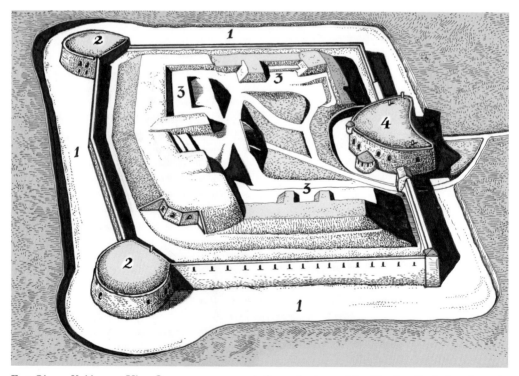

Fort Oberer Kuhberg at Ulm, Germany, was an early form of polygonal fortification displaying the main characteristics: 1: Dry ditch; 2: Flanking caponier at the front; 3: Gun batteries for long-range firing protected by traverses and breastworks; 4: *Réduit* or keep in the gorge.

Chelles Fort, France, built in 1876.

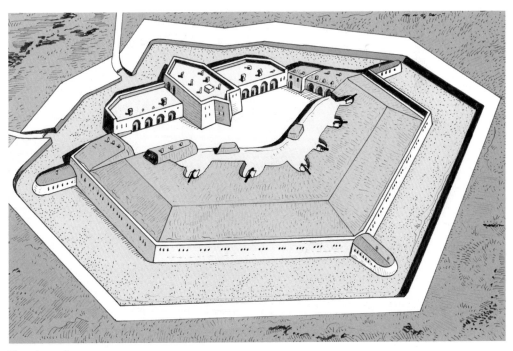

Shoreham, Sussex.

an obtuse angle turned toward the enemy and two flanks (sides). The front and flanks formed a thick rampart furnished with a wall-walk and breastwork. The combination of masonry and solid earth heaped up in front and on top of the stonework acted as a burster layer, detonating shells before they struck the fabric of the fort. Ramps gave access from the low *terre-plein* to the rampart. The gorge was generally less fortified than the front and the flanks. It had, however, to be strong enough to be defensible against an enemy attacking from the back, and if the fortress was taken it was through the gorge that it would be re-conquered. The gorge could also be a straight wall defended by a projecting caponier or was given a tracé *pseudo-bastionné* (q.v.). It could also be fitted with a *réduit* (q.v.). All forts were surrounded by a ditch defended by double or simple caponiers (q.v.), a covered way (q.v.) and a broad and bare glacis.

Each fort was a self-contained structure with everything prepared for a moderately comfortable life and survival of the community, and for operation of the armament, with bomb-proof quarters, supply store and powder magazine. The fort bristled with artillery, either sheltered in Haxo casemate (q.v.) or in the open behind thick earth parapet (q.v.), traverses (q.v.) and parados (q.v.). Infantrymen fired from a breastwork (q.v.) and could take refuge in traverse shelters (q.v.). Before 1885, the intervals between the polygonal forts was about 12–20km, the range of the rifled artillery (q.v.). According to the local situation, redoubts (q.v.) and batteries (q.v.) were built as reinforcement and additional firepower, so each fort with its annexes could cover its neighbours with its guns.

Polygonal system: A system of simplified fortification appearing in the nineteenth century based on French military engineer Montalembert's theory and German

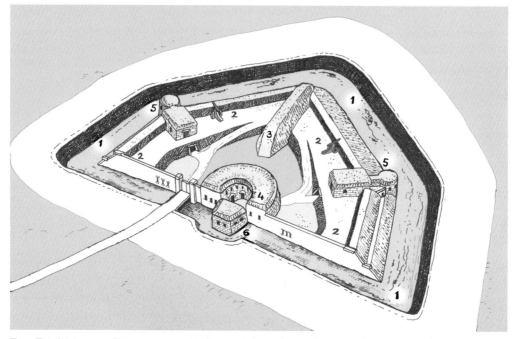

Fort Friedrichsau at Ulm was an early form of the polygonal system displaying the following basic elements: 1: Ditch; 2: Rampart with artillery emplacements; 3: Traverse; 4: *Réduit* (keep); 5: Flanking caponier; 6: Caponier flanking the gorge of the fort.

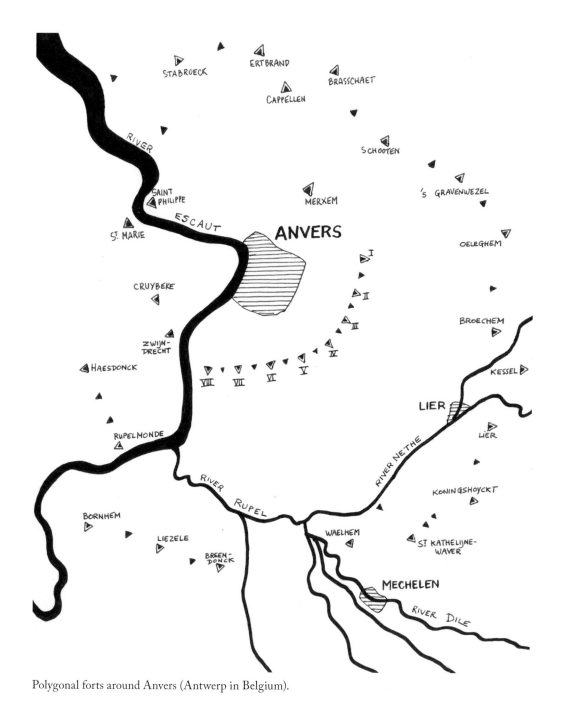

Polygonal forts around Anvers (Antwerp in Belgium).

experimentation. Given the long range and destructive power of the rifled artillery (q.v.) that appeared in the 1860s, it was henceforth pointless to protect a city at close range with ditches and continuous bastions and walls. Instead, rings of detached polygonal forts (q.v.) were established. Properly sited (on a hill for example), each fort could defend a large area and help to cover its neighbour with overlapping fields of fire. A ring of such forts could defend a city, while a line of them could protect a whole frontier. In theory there was no gap in the system, as each fort could cover its neighbours with its guns.

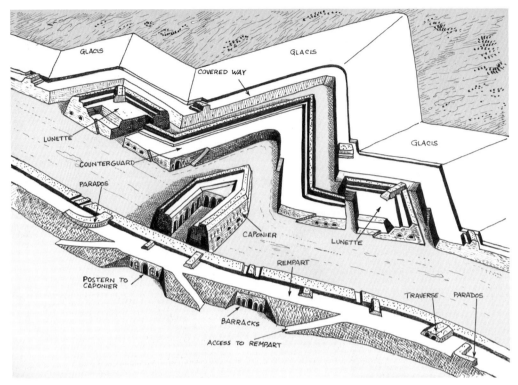

Basic elements of the so-called Prussian method.

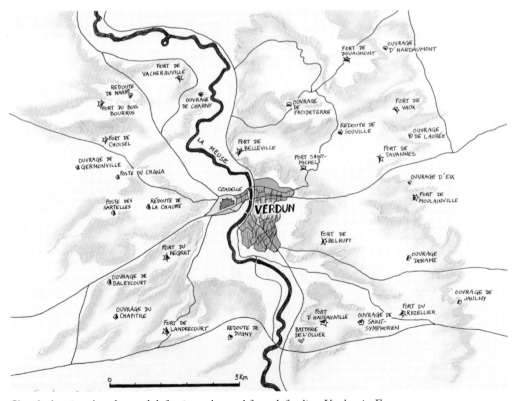

Sketch showing the advanced defensive polygonal forts defending Verdun in France.

The main characteristics of the polygonal system were the abandoning of the bastioned tracé, which was replaced with a simpler outline; a low profile; bomb-proof barracks; a ditch defended by massive flanking caponiers; masoned casemates for rifled artillery; and open gun emplacements protected by traverses. See Polygonal fort, Caponier.

Pomerium: In ancient Rome, the pomerium – from the Latin *post-moerium* ('behind the wall') – was a sacred open space located just inside the wall surrounding the four hills of the early city: the Esquiline, Palatine, Quirinal and Capitoline. Rome rapidly expanded beyond its pomerium, but the legendary date of its demarcation – 21 April – continued to be celebrated as the anniversary of the city's foundation.

In most Roman/Italian walled cities, the pomerium designated the spaces which ran along the complete length of the city walls. These strips of ground were left clear of building and planting to facilitate the manoeuvring of defenders in times of attack, and were always invested with religious significance, being dedicated to the gods in gratitude for their protection.

Port: A slit or aperture in the walls of a fortification through which weapons could be fired at an enemy force. See Arrow loop, Embrasure, Gunport and Porthole.

Porta: In Roman fortification, a gate. The Roman gate often included a single or double-span archway set in a two-storey wall flanked by round-fronted or rectangular towers. It was often a much-decorated arch of triumph, a monumental building with a strong symbolic function displaying both Rome's military strength and civilization.

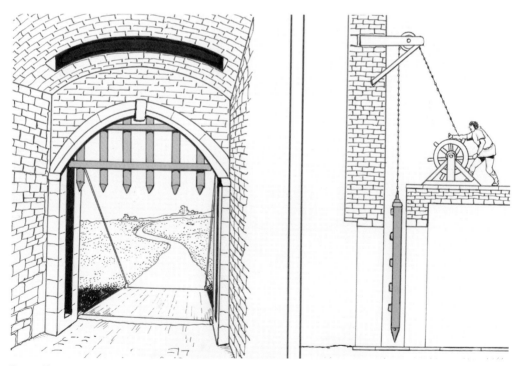

Portcullis.
Left: Seen from inside (with drawbridge down).
Right: Cross-section.

Portcullis: A heavy vertical iron grating or timber grille often shod with iron, placed above the doorway of a gatehouse (q.v.). This framework of crossed bars could be raised by a windlass placed on the first floor of the gatehouse, and in times of crisis instantly lowered by sliding along side-grooves (called coulisses), crashing down quickly owing to its own weight. Some gateways were provided with a succession of porticullises at some distance apart. See Orgue.

Porter: The porter (also called concierge, caretaker or keeper) was a governor or an officer who was in charge of the gatehouse (q.v.).

Porthole: An opening in a casemate allowing artillery to fire through. Also a split in a wall for shooting with a bow or firing a musket. In order to adapt fortifications to the use of firearms, the long narrow vertical loopholes (q.v.) in medieval towers, gatehouses and barbicans, intended to shoot with bow and crossbow, were enlarged and widened. They became full-scale embrasures or portholes, permitting the discharge of firearms. Blocked with shutters when not in use, they were of various sizes depending on the weapons used: smaller for handguns and larger for cannons. See Embrasure.

Positional warfare: A military doctrine which places emphasis on the possession of ground and its denial to the enemy, usually by static defences including fortifications and obstacles.

Position Finding Cell (PFC): A workroom, usually in a sea battery, for housing apparatus to determine the range and position of a target, usually a ship. See Firing control station and *Leitstand*.

Post:
1) A place where a serviceman is stationed.
2) A military base or installation.
3) A tactical position or a picket – a small position manned by just a few soldiers with a control, observation or surveillance mission; a sort of check point in modern parlance. The post could be a simple entrenchment such as a lunette (q.v.), *flèche* (q.v.) or redan (q.v.).

Poste: French for a small fort or small fortified camp.

Postern: A secondary small gate installed through the rampart or under a wall, giving access to the ditch and outworks. Also called a sally port (q.v.), it enabled raiding parties to launch a counter-attack or sortie, strike and then return to their fortified place.

Postern. Conwy Castle, North Wales.

Poterne: French for postern (q.v.). In Dutch nineteenth-century fortification, the *poterne* was an underground (often central) masonry passage that connected the gorge of the fort to other subterrean parts such as the barracks, armoured gun cupola and front caponier.

Poudrière: French for gunpowder magazine or powder-house (q.v.).

Powder-house: For obvious security reason, powder magazines were located as far as possible from living quarters and for tactical motives as close as possible to combat emplacements. They were therefore often placed in the protected *terre-plein* of hollow bastions. They were always guarded by sentries, with access strictly restricted to those having legitimate business. Capacity varied according to the importance of the place and several powder-houses could be scattered all over the fortress to supply a section of the defence. The building was surrounded by a palisade or a stone or earth wall. The magazine had to be protected against plunging mortar fire. Consequent measures taken included strong and highly resistant vaulted chambers covered with a bombproof roof supported by buttresses, brick and stone arches, and earth or grass cover intended to absorb explosions. Walls were very thick and strengthened by buttresses. Windows were few, small, narrow and cunningly fitted with chicanes (masonry blocks) around which air could circulate but through which sparks and missiles from outside could not pass. Inside the powder-house, kegs and barrels rested on wooden shelves and timber to ensure dryness. Nails, hinge-pins and locks were made of bronze (a metal that does not spark) to prevent accidental explosions. For the same reason, soldiers working in the powder-house were requested to wear clogs. The powder-house often included an

Powder-house.

armoury – a workshop where shells, petards, cartridges and grenades were filled. See Arsenal.

Praetorium: Commander's quarter in Roman fortification.

Pré Carré: The term *Pré Carré* (literally 'Square Meadow', to be understood as 'enclosed property') designated the double line of fortresses and fortified cities that Louis XIV's engineer, Vauban, set up during the second half of the seventeenth century along the vulnerable French north-eastern frontier, in the provinces of Flanders and Hainaut. The organization of this military network – which may be considered a forerunner of the twentieth-century Maginot Line – had two purposes. It was a deterrent and defensive line intended to protect against an invasion of France and the capture of Paris, but it also served as an offensive base to launch operations into the Spanish Low Countries (Belgium) and the Republic of the United Provinces (the present kingdom of the Netherlands). Vauban's *Pré Carré* – directly intended to cover Paris – perfectly fulfilled its role until the Allied invasions of 1814 and 1815.

Prison: Each important fortified town, fort, citadel, camp or base had a prison for undisciplined soldiers, captured deserters and criminals. When a fortress was decommissioned, it could easily be transformed into a detention centre for enemy prisoners-of-war who would be detained in spartan conditions until the end of the conflict. Being enclosed spaces with high walls and deep ditches, and guarded by an armed garrison, a fortress could easily accommodate a large number of prisoners at little additional cost to the authorities. See Citadel.

Profile: Outline of a work viewed sideways in cross-section in the vertical plane.

Promontory fort: As the name implies, a defensive settlement located above a steep river meander or rocky cliff. Thus protected on three sides by natural defences, only the (small) neck connecting with the mainland was fortified with man-made works, with consequent economy in building effort. They were numerous anywhere topography allowed such a disposition from the Iron Age onwards, and many promontory forts formed the origins of later villages, towns and cities. See Cliff castle, Hillfort and *Oppidum*.

Propugnaclum: See Hoarding.

Prussian system: A German system of fortification based on Montalembert's perpendicular system. Modern works appeared as early as 1834 at Germersheim (south of Mannheim). Eventually the system was employed at Koblenz, Mainz, Ulm and Ingolstadt, and universally adopted by all main industrial nations in the second half of the nineteenth century. The system included a front composed of a straight wall and a wide ditch covered by a powerful caponier (q.v.) reinforced by a counterguard (q.v.) and two lunettes (q.v.), a covered way and glacis. Given the long range and destructive power of the new rifled artillery (q.v.), it was henceforth pointless to protect a city at close range with ditches, bastions and walls. Instead, rings of detached forts (q.v.) were established. Properly sited (on a hill, for example), each fort could defend a large area and help to cover its neighbour with overlapping fields of fire. A ring of such

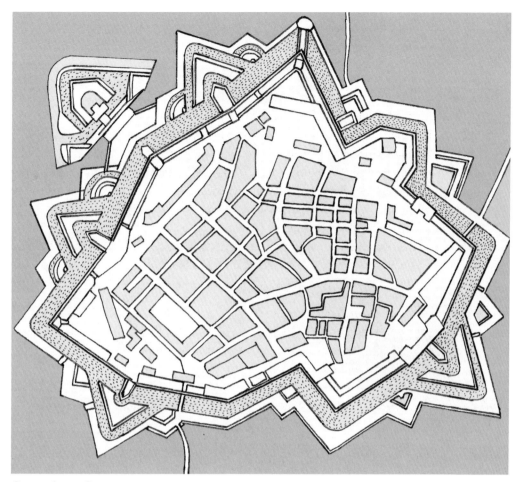

Germersheim, Germany.

forts could defend a city, while a line of them could protect a whole frontier. See Polygonal system.

Punji stick: A booby trap (q.v.) in the form of sharp iron sticks or bamboo stakes – sometimes tipped with poison – set in a well-camouflaged pit or hole in the ground. This mantrap was used in South-East Asia, notably during the Vietnam Wars. See *Trou de Loup* and Wolf's pit.

Put-log: Beam inserted into a specially prepared hole in a great tower, gatehouse or curtain to support a hoarding (q.v.). Also a short horizontal pole projecting from a wall on which a temporary scaffolding could rest for construction or repairs.

Put-log hole: Put-log holes, as the name implies, are small voids that were intended to receive the ends of logs or squared wooden beams in the walls of buildings, especially in the Middle Ages.

Pyramid:

1) A Dutch shelter officially designated *Groepsschuilplaats* (shelter for a group), nicknamed pyramid because of its sloping roof. Designed between 1928 and 1934, the shelter was roughly 8.2m long, 6.5m wide and 4.85m high. It included a single entrance with a thick armoured door and a staircase leading to a small corridor defended by a *schietgat* (rifle hole) and to the *afwachtingsruimte* (stand-by room 3.5 m x 3m) for a *groep* (a section of ten to twelve soldiers). The room was equipped with a ventilation system, telephone and a periscope for observation. The thickness of the concrete roof was 2.15m, and that of the walls was 1.8m, allowing the shelter to withstand 21cm shells. Hundreds were built before the Second World War, and many are still extant today in the Dutch countryside.

Pyramid.

2) British anti-tank concrete roadblock. See Pimple.

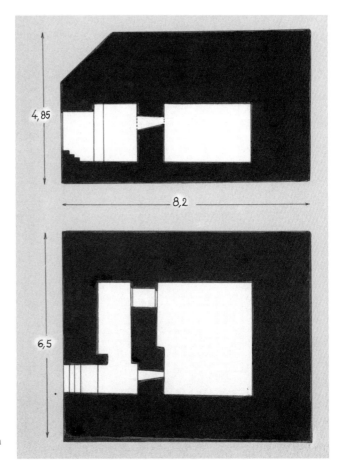

Pyramid. Profile (top) and plan (bottom).

Q

Qasr: Generic Arabic term for a castle, palace or fort. See Krak and Ksar.

Quadrangular castle: A quadrangular (or quadrilateral) castle was a type of castle characterized by buildings forming the four-winged curtains, enclosing a central courtyard or quadrangle, and typically with angle towers. There was no longer a keep in the middle of the yard, but frequently a distinct gatehouse. The quadrangular castle combined a display of strength and wealth, relative comfort and security. Built predominantly from the mid to late fourteenth century, this style of castle announced the transition from military defensive fortresses to domestic and residential-orientated palaces. See Courtyard castle and Rectangular castle.

Quadriburgia: A concentric castle in the form of two square or rectangular enclosures, generally without a keep but including projecting flanking towers.

Quatrefoil: Term used to designate a keep comprised of four interpenetrating round towers (with a clover leaf plan). Examples can be seen at the King's Tower in York (northern England) or at Etampes (France). The design was later adopted for the Tudor artillery coastal forts, such as that at Deal in Kent.

Clifford's Tower at York.

Queue d'aronde: An advanced work (q.v.) in the form of a *tenaille* (q.v.) with two wings connecting back. See Swallow's tail.

Quoin: Dressed stone at the corner of a building.

R

Radar emplacement: The electronic system Radio Detection and Ranging (Radar) was used to measure the presence, distance and direction of a flying or navigating object. Working through the broadcast and reflection of radio waves, the radar principle rests on studies made by the German scientist Heinrich Hertz in 1887 and by countless other physicists' researches. The method was experimented with and developed under conditions of great secrecy during the 1920s and 1930s, and finally greatly improved and used with much success during the Battle of Britain in 1940. Compared to modern devices, radar equipment used during the Second World War was complex, primitive, bulky and cumbersome. The device included a powerful, very high frequency microwaves generator, a highly sensitive receiver catching echoing beams, sophisticated devices translating radiowaves into visual form on a round screen, scanners, primitive

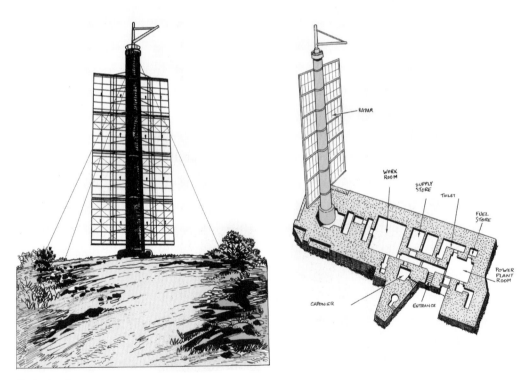

Radar bunker.
Left: Antenna.
Right: Plan of the bunker.
The Second World War German bunker type L480 was especially designed for housing a Wassermann FuMG 402 radar with a range of *c.* 200km. The radar included a large 30m-high antenna frame positioned on top of a 27m-long concrete bunker. Seven type L480 bunkers were constructed in the Atlantic Wall.

computers and calculating instruments. Waves were sent off and received back by means of a large aerial. The shape of aerial depended on the frequency which was used: they were either a rectangular flat metal frame or a parabolic round dish. Radar was costly equipment and therefore often emplaced in protective concrete structures. The size of a radar bunker/emplacement depended on the type of radar used. It generally consisted of an underground bunker with various chambers for men and equipment, computing and workrooms, ventilation system and stores. The radar aerial was fixed on one or more strong poles (or on a concrete tower) resting on the roof of the bunker. Radar stations comprised several bunkers and buildings, which were camouflaged, enclosed by a fence and defended by troops and a combat emplacement.

Rainures: Vertical slots placed in the façade of a gatehouse in which gaffs (q.v.) would fit. See Drawbridge.

Ramp: Also called an ascent or appareille, a gently sloping inclined interior roadway giving access to the *terre-plein* of the rampart or bastion (q.v.). Ramps in bastioned fortifications were usually cut obliquely in the interior slope of the rampart. In nineteenth-century forts, they were sometimes installed at right angles to the rampart then serving as a traverse (q.v.).

Rampart: The broad reveted embankment and mass of earth surrounding a fortified place. In order to protect existing fortresses when firearms were introduced, several

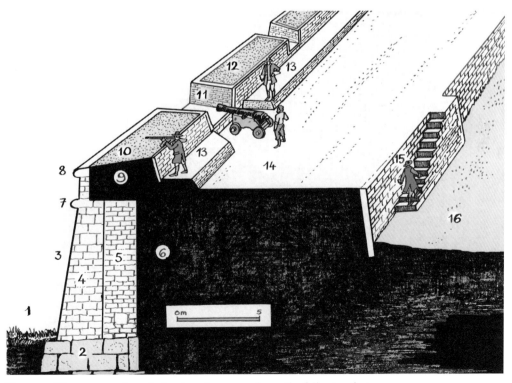

Rampart. The cross-section of a bastioned rampart shows the following features:
1: Ditch; 2; Foundation; 3: Scarp; 4: Revetment; 5: Buttress; 6: Piled earth; 7: Cordon; 8: Tablet; 9: Breastwork; 10: *Plongée* or fire crest; 11: Embrasure; 12: Merlon; 13: Firestep; 14: Wall-walk; 15: Stair; 16: *Terre-plein*.

solutions were found. Elevated towers and high walls with crenels and machicolation had become exposed targets; in reaction, the defenders gradually abandoned the benefit of height and reduced the size of their walls and towers. The tendency was to lower the works but at the same time to increase the thickness of the masonry. This proved extremely expensive and of dubious efficiency. A cheaper and more effective method was introduced: the low rampart, composed of a front and rear revetment masoned wall holding a large and thick mass of earth, absorbing the shock of cannonballs just like a pillow. The mass of earth was very often formed from the earth excavated from the ditch. The rampart, universally used in bastioned and nineteenth-century fortifications, formed the scarp or enceinte (q.v.) of the place.

Rampart street: The rampart street – also known as a parade street (q.v.) – was a continuous lane running along the foot of the inner slope of a rampart. Its purpose was to allow quick, easy and continous communication to all fronts of the fortress.

Range finder: An instrument for calculating the distance from a gun to a target. Until the development of electronic means of measuring range after the Second World War, optical range finders were large, expensive and cumbersome instruments. Some used to measure range for naval and coastal gunnery had a baseline of several metres. They were also quite vulnerable, and therefore often placed in specialized concrete bunkers when used for permanent coastal batteries. See Fire control station.

Raum: German general term for space, room or chamber (plural *Raüme*). The term can be combined to designate specific rooms in German fortresses or bunkers, such as *Bereitschaftsraum* (crew quarters), *Munitionraum* (ammunition store), *Funkraum* (wireless room), *Sanitätraum* (dressing room or infirmary) and *Maschinenraum* (engine/plant room).

Ravelin: In bastioned fortification, an outwork (q.v.) constructed in the middle of the main ditch, opposite a curtain, thus between two bastions. The ravelin, or *demi-lune* (q.v.), was often composed of two faces forming an angular work with a salient angle facing the countryside. Very often V-shaped (triangular) in plan, it always had its own

Ravelin.

Ravelin. Typically placed between two bastions.

ditch and was always open in the gorge. The ravelin was universally used to cover the curtain, gate and both adjacent bastions.

Reave: In England, a linear border wall made of stone and built in the Bronze Age (*c.* 3000–1200 BC). See Dike.

Rectangular castle: A type of castle (q.v.) built in the thirteenth and fourteenth centuries. It was a homogeneous and comprehensive sophisticated fortress composed of four straight walls with cylindrical towers at each corner and a gatehouse in the middle of one curtain. The defences were strengthened by passive obstacles (often a wet ditch), easy communications allowing rapid movement for the garrison and the positioning of war machines hurling their projectiles above the walls, efficient flanking from the corner towers, and active and efficient combat emplacements disposed in spaced outworks. These great improvements, reviving the essential principles of fortification, enabled the building of castles in sites totally deprived of natural defences. The keep became redundant and was often discarded. Ancillary buildings, residences, a hall or palace, chapel, huts for servants, quarters for soldiers, stables for domestic animals, storehouses and other elements related to the castle community's life were placed against the walls, leaving space for a central courtyard, called a bailey or basse court, and even a garden. This kind of classical regular rectangular castle was sometimes called a courtyard castle (q.v.) or quadrangular castle (q.v.)

Redan: A work or outwork (q.v.), usually triangular in shape, composed of two faces forming a salient angle and open at the rear. The redan was used in field fortification as part of a line, for example, but it could also be a part of a permanent fortification. See *Flèche*, Ravelin and Arrow.

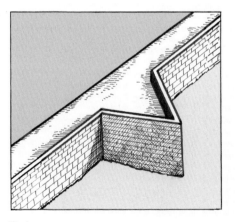
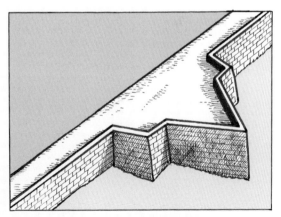

Redan.
Left: Simple redan.
Right: Reinforced redan.

Redoubt: A redoubt or redoute is a general term designating a small enclosed fortification that protected a larger fortified place but was separated from it. This small fort could be a permanent structure or a hastily constructed temporary fortification

Redoubt. (Eastbourne, Sussex, England).

of varying shape. When temporary, the redoubt could be an earthwork used in a siege, for example. When permanent, the work was made of masonry, completely self-supporting and independent, with its own ditch, a drawbridge and a covered way. In seventeenth and eighteenth-century fortification, the redoubt (also called a

In the seventeenth and eighteenth centuries, redoubts were built in various shapes, for example comprising a closed hornwork (1), *tenailled* enclosed work (2), bastioned square (3), triangle with half-bastions (4), square work with half-bastions (5) or a simple square (6).

sconce in English) was built according to a codified combination of regular bastioned forms: triangular, square or rectangular with three or four bastions or half-bastions. They could have a stellar outline when made of *tenailles* but could also, depending on natural site conditions, have a completely irregular ground-plan. When constructed inside a large fortified place, the redoubt is often termed a citadel (q.v.), *réduit* (q.v.) or keep (q.v.). See Sconce.

Redoute modèle: The French Napoleonic *Redoute modèle* 1811 was a small, simple and standardized fortlet. It was square or rectangular, and included a top terrace (serving both as an observation post and gun emplacement), musketmen galleries, quarters for the garrison and the commanding officers, stores for food, water and ammunition as well as a central yard. The redoubt was surrounded by a ditch, a covered way and a glacis, and had counterscarp coffres – vaulted casemates placed at the angles of the ditch for close-range defence. A variant existed with bastions at each of the four angles in the tradition of Vauban, Fort Liédot on Aix Island being a good example.

Réduit:

1) A *réduit* is a redoubt, a small fully enclosed work which was placed into a larger work or might stand independently. Also known as a keep (q.v.), it was a fortified structure placed in the gorge of a nineteenth-century polygonal fort (q.v.). The garrison could retire into this self-sufficient stronghold within the fort when the rest of the work was taken. The *réduit* was often used as quarters for the garrison, and headquarters and administration hub for the commander. Opinion was divided regarding the last-stand *réduit*. Some military engineers maintained that the keep stiffened resistance and allowed the garrison to withdraw to a position from which it might later sally out and eventually recapture the fort. Others, meanwhile, considered that it encouraged the idea of retreat and that the *réduit* only proclaimed the gospel of defeatism, the lurking conviction that in the long run the attack was always superior to the defence. In late nineteenth-century French forts, the *réduit* was always omitted for psychological reason: the French high command considered that without a safe place to withdraw, the defenders had no other choice than to fight to the bitter end or to abandon the work and retreat at the right time. The French were eventually proved right, for if the attacking party had got this close, the fort and its keep were as good as lost. Depending on tactical conditions, it is widely acknowledged that a withdrawal in good order and at the right time is often a better move than a desperate fight to the last man. After 1885, attached *réduits* within forts were abandoned as relics of a bygone age.
2) In a broader sense, a *réduit* could also be a complex of several defensive works, a network of strongholds or a group of bunkers to which troops could possibly withdraw. See *Kernwerk*.
3) It could also be a fortified region or defended province where authorities could withdraw and find refuge when a land was invaded. See National *Réduit*, *Vesting Holland* and Swiss National Redoubt.

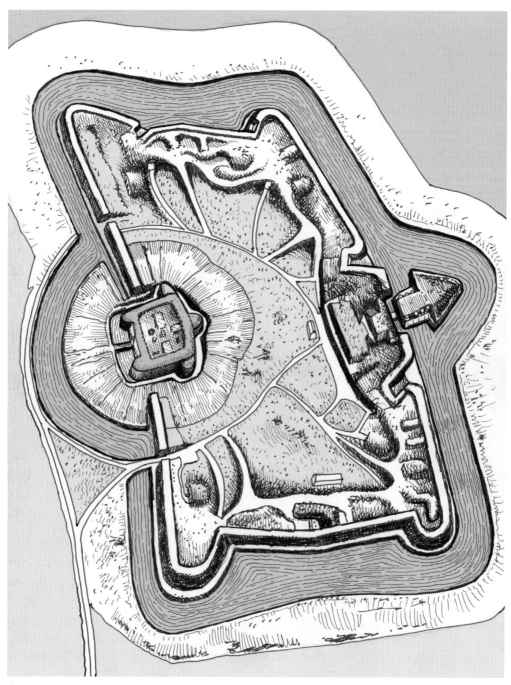

A *réduit* placed in the gorge of Fort Rijnauwen in Utrecht, the Netherlands.

Re-entering: Term denoting the movement inwards or angular projection of a trace in the direction of the centre of the fortification. The opposite, pointing outwards, is called a salient (q.v.).

Refuge: A place of safety. A refugee is thus a person who leaves their home in order to escape from danger (especially war) and looks for refuge elsewhere.

Regelbau: German system of standardized blueprint, which permitted precise planning of required materials, manpower and time of construction for Second World War bunkers.

Régions Fortifiées (RF): Fortified regions. Large areas featuring defences as part of the Maginot Line (q.v.). Fortified regions were subdivided into several *Secteurs Fortifiés* (SF), or Fortified sectors.

Reiche kazemat: A casemate characterized by small jutting-out walls protecting the embrasures. Designed by German and Dutch engineers and often used for the front caponier (q.v.) in nineteenth-century polygonal forts (q.v.).

Reinforced concrete: A concrete structure in which steel reinforcement rods ('rebars'), plates or fibres have been incorporated to strengthen a material that could otherwise be brittle. Reinforced concrete is composed of an artificial agglomeration of gravels, sand, cement, water and metal rebars. Concrete offers strong resistance to compression while the metal rebar framework opposes traction. The combination of concrete and metal forms a solid, compact, massive and monolithic material that is widely used in civilian and military architecture.

Reinforced order: A bastioned tracé with a slightly recessed outline given to a curtain (q.v.) in order to increase flanking (q.v.), believed to have been invented by the Venetian military engineer Giovanni Battista de Zanchi (1515–86).

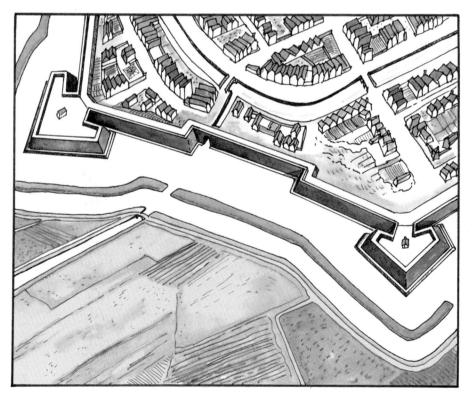

Reinforced order.

Relief: The height of any point of a work above a datum (q.v.).

Relief maps: Scale-models giving three-dimentional volume, position and extent of fortifications. For example, a French collection was created in 1668 on Louis XIV's instigation. Today about 100 plan-reliefs are preserved and a selection are exhibited in the Musée de l'Armée in the Hôtel des Invalides in Paris, and also in the Musée des Beaux Arts in Lille.

Remblai: The heap of earth that was piled up to constitute a parapet, rampart or breastwork etc. It was most of the time the *déblai* – the mass of earth excavated from the ditch. See *Déblai* and Rampart.

Remise: Bombproof vaulted masonry shelter for artillery used in Dutch forts in the nineteenth century. The remise was either sunk into the ground or covered with a thick layer of earth.

Retirade:
1) An improvised line of defence or retrenchment erected within a work, usually to act as a second line or fallback position in case of a breach being made in the main defence. The term comes from the French verb *se retirer*, which means to withdraw.
2) A small break in the face of a work of great length to provide additional emplacement for enfilading fire.

Retired flank: A flank (q.v.) protected by an *orillon* or ear (q.v.).

Reverse: A section of a work facing or commanding towards the rear. See Gorge.

Reverse fire: Firing from the rear from a fortified position.

Reverse gallery: A combat gallery or emplacement usually positioned under the counterscarp in order to fire at enemies having reached the ditch.

Revetment: A retaining wall of masonry built for the purpose of holding back a large, thick and heavy mass of earth. Revetment could be made of a facing of sandbags (q.v.), gabions (q.v.), fascines (q.v.), grass sods, mud, piled rocks, tree branches, corrugated or armoured plates, wire mesh, wickerwork, timber, planks, boards, logs, poles, railroad ties, bails of hay or straw, ice blocks and packed snow, empty wooden ammunition boxes and crates, and empty metal oil drums piled in order to protect field works (e.g. a wall, bank of earth or sides of a trench) from erosion or other damage which could cause the collapse of the sidewall.

Ribat: Arabic designation for a small fortified place or outpost built along a border during the first years of the Muslim conquest of North Africa, in order to house military volunteers. Later a term for hostels or halting places for pilgrims and travellers on important roads.

Ribat. Monastir, Tunisia.

Rideaux défensifs: The system of *rideaux défensifs* ('defensive curtains') was a French strategy advocated in the 1870 and 1880s by the French general-engineer Séré de Rivères. It was based on the use of gun batteries, rings and lines of polygonal forts (q.v.) strategically placed to defend major crossroads, passes, river valleys, railroad lines and hubs, and other weak passages or strategically important positions.

Rifled: Spiralled grooves cut into the barrel of a firearm giving the projectile a spinning movement.

Rifled artillery: Artillery pieces with spiral grooved barrels were one of the most significant innovations in firearm warfare. Introduced about 1860, rifling greatly increased penetration and stability of shells.

Rifled gun.

Rifle pit: Small excavation, especially for one infantryman, often deep enough to allow him to stand in and fire his rifle across the top edge. See Trench.

Ringfort: Circular fortified settlements that were mostly built during the Bronze Age, some being occupied up to about AD 1000. Made of large banks or piles earth and stones, they were particularly numerous in Ireland. See Hillfort and Dun.

Ringstand: See Tobruk.

Rivierkazemat: The Dutch *rivierkazemat* (river-pillbox) was a type of concrete armed bunker built in the 1930s. Specially designed to defend a bridge crossing a canal or river, it was often several storeys high and built within or near a dike.

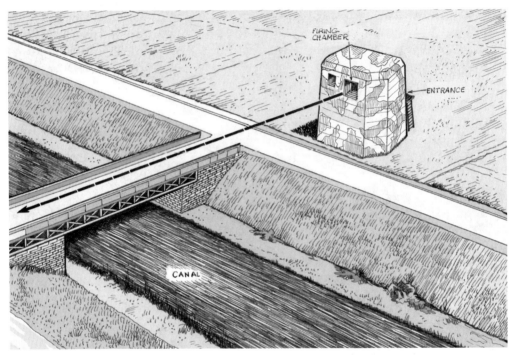

Rivierkazemat.

Roadblock: Any movable obstacle, obstruction, barrier or barricade set up by troops or police in order to control the flow of traffic. In a military context, the roadblock is intended to prevent, delay or hinder the progression of enemy vehicles and tanks. See Belgian Gate, Dragon's teeth, Pimples, Frizzy Horse, *Cheval de Frise* and Rolled steel joists.

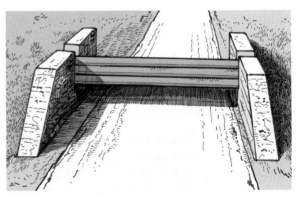

Roadblock. Movable steel beams held by concrete supports.

Rocca: Italian name for a castle, fortress or stronghold. Meaning literally 'rock', this term usually designated a stronghold located in a small town or village in an elevated place. It was the home of a local nobleman and could serve as a refuge for inhabitants in times of trouble. In a town, a *rocca* might be a citadel (q.v.), small castle or fortified house. A more extensive *rocca* would generally be referred to as a *castello*.

The Rocca at Ostia in Latium, Italy, was built between 1483 and 1487 by order of Cardinal Giuliano della Rovere, the future Pope Julius II. Designed by the engineer Pontelli, it is a fine example of Renaissance transitional military architecture.

Rollbock: See Anti-tank obstacle, *Element Cointet* and Belgian Gate.

Rolled steel joists: British removable anti-tank roadblock designed in 1940. Composed of massive concrete posts permanently installed at the roadside, they had holes and/or slots to accept horizontal railway lines or rolled steel joists (RSJs). Similar blocks were placed across railway tracks because tanks could move along tracks almost as easily as they could along roads. These blocks would be placed strategically where it was difficult for a vehicle to go around – anti-tank obstacles and mines being positioned as required – and they could be opened or closed within a matter of minutes.

Rolling bridge: A variety of bridge fitted in forts where the roadway spanning a ditch is rolled within the gates. The bridge is not hinged and remains horizontal. A rack and pinion rolling bridge is commonly used in forts. A special type named after its designer Guthrie can be found in the Portsdown Forts at Portsmouth in Hampshire, southern England. See Drawbridge.

Roman fortification: The Romans made extensive use of fortified cities, permanent fortresses and temporary fortified camps. City walls were already significant in Etruscan architecture, and in the struggle for control of Italy under the early Republic many more were built, using various different techniques. The Romans called a simple rampart wall an *agger* (q.v.). They walled major cities and towns in areas they saw as vulnerable, and parts of many walls remain incorporated in later defences, as at Cordoba in southern Spain (second century BC) and Chester (earth and wood in the AD 70s, stone from *c.* 100) and York (from the AD 70s) in northern Britain. Strategic walls and defences across open country were called *limes* (q.v.). Hadrian's Wall (from AD 122) and the Antonine Wall (from AD 142, but abandoned only eight years after completion), both on the Scottish frontier, are the most significant examples. See Playcard plan and Roman wall.

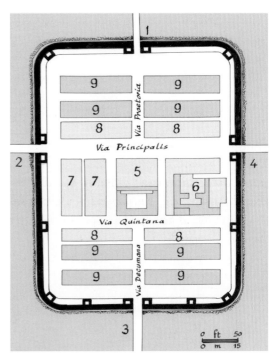

Roman fort.
1: *Porta Praetoria* (North Gate); 2: *Porta Principalia Sinistra* (West Gate); 3: *Porta Decumana* (South Gate); 4: *Porta Principalia Dextra* (East Gate); 5: *Principalia* (headquarters, religious and administrative buildings); 6: *Praetorium* (commander's residence); 7: *Horrea* (supply stores); 8: *Fabricae* and *Stabuli* (workshops and stables); 9: Troops' barracks.

Roman wall: The Romans built innumerable palisades (q.v.), combined with ditch (q.v.) and earth walls (q.v.). A favourite Roman method of constructing masonry defensive walls was to build an inner and outer masonry casing, with loose rock filling the intervening

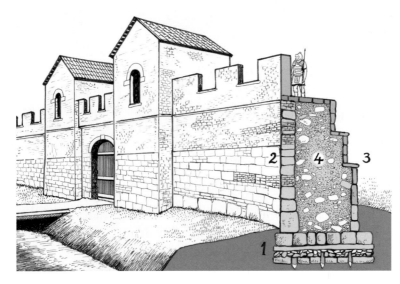

Roman wall (cross-section).
1: Foundaion; 2: Outer revetment; 3: Inner revetment; 4: Core of the wall made of rubble and mortar resting on foundations.

space. At the base of the wall, massive blocks of building stone were often keyed together with iron tie-rods and lead seals, as well as being set in mortar. The inner facing casing could have earth banked behind it, while the outer was fronted by a ditch. The top of the wall was fitted with a wall-walk (q.v.) and a head-high crenellated breastwork. This consisted of crenels (openings), which enabled the defenders to hurl missiles at the enemy, and *pinnae* (solid standing parts or merlons), which provided cover.

Roundel: The roundel (or rondelle) was an element of transitional fortification (q.v.). It was a thick artillery tower, possibly circular or U-shaped, and projecting in order to flank both curtain and ditch. It was also called a barbican, bulwark, bastei or basteja in Northern Europe, *bastillon* or boulevard in France and *torrionne* or *balovardo* in Italy. Its summit was arranged as a platform with gun embrasures, sometimes fitted with old-fashioned crenellation and machicolation as medieval traditions remained strong. The roundel was generally low but could include one or more storeys fitted with flanking casemates (q.v.).

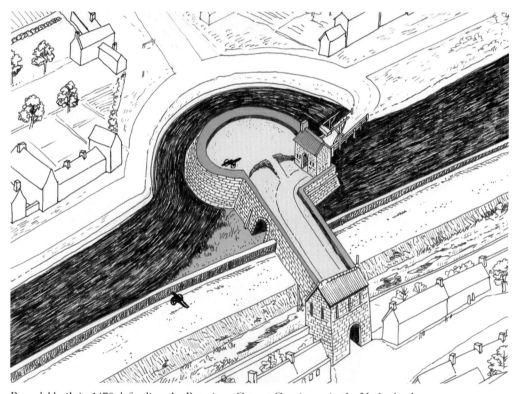

Roundel built in 1470 defending the Boteringe Gate at Groningen in the Netherlands.

Roundway: See Berm, *Chemin de ronde*, Sentry-walk and Wall-walk.

Ruck pillbox: The Second World War British Ruck pillbox (named after its designer, James Ruck) was an infantry post made from prefabricated Stanton air raid shelter sections. The segments were 20in wide and a pair of them formed an arch 7ft high, to which transverse struts were provided to ensure rigidity. These fitted into longitudinal bearers, which were grooved to receive the foot of each segment. Each pair of segments were bolted together at the apex of the arch and each segment was also bolted to its neighbour, the joints being sealed with bituminous compound. The convenient handling of these segments enabled them to be transported with ease. The pillbox, designed to be partially buried or reinforced with sandbags and piled earth, was intended for eight soldiers. Although the Ruck pillbox was said to have poor application because of its limited field of fire, Northern Command placed orders for 6,000 of them in September 1940, planning to site them at all anti-aircraft batteries, searchlight positions, airfields and other defended localities. Although 4,000 were erected in Lincolnshire and along the coast of southern England and there was an order for 2,000 more, only a few are extant. See FW3.

Rustication: A fashion in masonry (or an imitation thereof) with blocks of stone in which the centre is left rough or hewed, drilled or chiselled with profiled decorative patterns. Popular in Renaissance and Baroque civilian architecture, rustication was used in fortification principally for ornamenting gatehouses. Rustication emphasized the contrast between rough and smooth parts in the façade of a building. The purpose of this method in military architecture remains unclear. It was unlikely that it was a means of making projectiles ricochet or intended to break the point of a battering ram. The main function was probably just decorative, with a striking textural effect, and perhaps as a deterrent, giving an impression of solidity, roughness and strength.

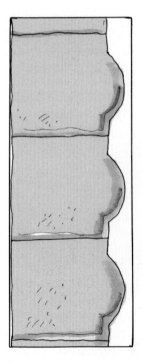
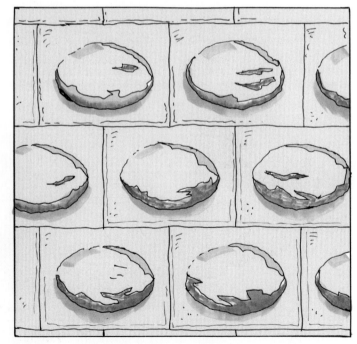

Rustication.
Left: Profile; Right: Front view.

S

Salient: The angular projection in the trace pointing away from the centre of the fortification, and therefore the point formed by two faces which projects out towards the enemy, for example the point of a bastion, *demi-lune*, redan or lunette.

Salient place of arms: See Place of arms.

Sally: In siege warfare, a sally or sortie (q.v.) was a counter-attack launched by the defenders against the besiegers. A sally was tactically important because, when successful, it could disorganize the besieger's approaches, destroy his camps and siege machines (later artillery) and thus turn the tide of the siege, particularly when the sally was made in coordination with a relief army. Psychologically, sorties and counter-attacks were also important for the defenders' morale, as they permitted an offensive role rather than the prevalent passive attitude. See Part 2 (Siege Warfare).

Sally port: A small gate, door, passage, opening or small tunnel pierced at the foot of a wall or rampart leading out of a work, by which a besieged garrison may counter-attack the besiegers. The term is also applied to the postern (q.v.) leading under the rampart into the ditch. When not in use, sally ports were closed by massive gates of timber with iron reinforcement.

Sandbag: A sandbag is a sack traditionally made of hessian or burlap (today polypropylene or other synthetic material) that is filled with sand or soil and closed with a knotted string. In military fortification, piles of sandbags provide a good form of protective revetment (q.v.), particularly when the soil is too thin or unsuited to the formation of a proper earth screen. Sandbags are also used to make breastworks (q.v.) and traverses (q.v.). Placed in

Sandbags.

courses alternate ways with headers and stretchers, sandbags have many advantages: they protect effectively from explosive blast, as well as from small projectiles and shell splinters (two or three layers are often sufficient); as burlap and sand are inexpensive, large and thick protective barriers can be erected cheaply; bags can be brought in empty and quickly filled with local sand or soil by soldiers on the spot. The most common sizes for sandbags are from 14in x 26in (36cm x 66cm) to 17in x 32in (43cm x 81cm).

Sangar: A small temporary field fortified position consisting of a breastwork made above ground level with readily available rocks and stones. The sangar is usually erected when the soil is too hard or wet to dig a trench. The term (meaning 'barricade' in Persian) was originally used by the British Indian Army on the North-West Frontier and in Afghanistan. See *Murette*.

Sap: A communication trench, often given a *cremaillère* or zigzag outline, extending forward from a parallel or a combat trench. See Boyau, Parallel and Trench.

Sap-and-parallel: System of siege warfare based on the digging of protective excavations making use of alternate saps (q.v.), parallels (q.v.) and siege batteries, allowing besieging troops to get close to the attacked place while remaining under cover from fire by the besieged. See Part 2 (Siege Warfare).

Sap-head: The end of a sap, at which point it was either extended sideways to form a fresh parallel or brought to the surface of the ground to form an exit for an attacking party.

Sapping: Sapping was a method used in siege warfare by an attacker to make a breach (q.v.). With such tactics – related to but different from mining (q.v.) – attackers would dig at the foot of a wall with various tools such as crowbars, picks and borers (q.v.), thereby destroying the base of the masonry until the structure above weakened and ultimately collapsed. Sapping was thus different from mining, which used underground tunnels. Mining and sapping were slow, laborious and dangerous operations, often costly in human life, so many commanders prefered to starve out the besieged. See Part 2 (Siege Warfare).

Saucisson: A *saucisson* (French for dry sausage) was a sort of fuse, in the form of a long and slender pipe or bag, made of cloth soaked in pitch, or of leather, filled with gunpowder. It was used to ignite mines, caissons, *fougasse* or bomb chests.

Sauveté: *Sauvetés* (also called *salvetat* or *sauveterre*, meaning safe place) were fortified villages created in Occitania (southern France) in the eleventh and twelfth centuries by the Catholic Church. The development of such safe settlements was connected to demographic growth demanding the clearing of forests and the winning of new lands for agricultural exploitation. They were also caused by the development of pilgrimages and the Crusades. *Sauvetés* were placed under the protection of the Catholic Church by the so-called Peace of God. They provided halting places and markets along the roads and tracks leading to sanctuaries and places of pilgrimage, such as Santiago de

Compostela in Spain, and along the roads going to the main Mediterranean ports for embarking to Palestine. See *Castelnaux* and Bastide.

Saxon Shore Forts: The forts of the Saxon Shore (*Litus Saxonicum* in Latin) formed a girdle of fortified ports built by the Romans along the southern coast of Britain from the current counties of Norfolk to Hampshire. The origins and purpose of the *Litus Saxonicum* were to provide powerful military and naval installations in order to protect trade and communication between Gaul (France) and Britannia and to keep watch against Saxon raiders (from northern Germany) and Frisian pirates (from the present-day Netherlands). Today, nine Saxon Shore fortified ports are preserved: Branodunum (modern-day Branscaster), Gariannonum (Burgh Castle), Othona (Bradwell), Regulbium (Reculver), Rutupiae (Richborough), Dubris (Dover), Lemanis (Lympne), Anderida (Pevensey), and Portus Adurni (Portchester).

Saxon Shore. Reconstruction of a Roman tower at Pevensey Castle, East Sussex.

S-Boote bunker: For the safekeeping of their *Schnellboote* or *S-Boote* ('fast boats' or motor boat torpedo, MBT in short), during the Second World War, the Germans built several large and thick-walled bunkers. The main harbours sheltering these fast surface units were Den Helder, Rotterdam-Hoek van Holland (sixteen pens) and IJmuiden (eighteen pens) in the Netherlands; Bruges and Ostende (four pens) in Belgium; as well as Dunkirk (ten pens), Boulogne (four pens), Dieppe, Le Havre (nine pens), Fécamp, Ouistreham and Cherbourg (two pens) in France. These ports were usually given the status of *Stutzpunktgruppe* (StPGr), 'group of strongholds' (q.v.). They were furnished with military facilities including maintenance, repair, rearmament, resupply and refuelling installations.

Scarp: The element of an enceinte on the inside of the ditch. The opposite (outer) side of the ditch is called the counterscarp (q.v.).

Scharten: German term for embrasure or gun port (q.v.).

Schartenstand: A German active casemate or bunker (q.v.) with weapon firing through an embrasure (q.v.).

Schartenturm: Armoured machine-gun turret or cupola (q.v.) fitted with one or more embrasures mounted on a German Second World War concrete bunker.

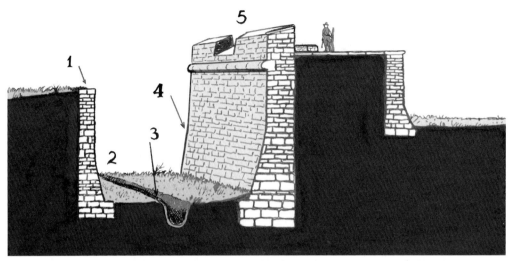

Scarp. The cross-section of a ditch shows the following elements. 1: Counterscarp; 2: Ditch; 3: Cunette; 4: Scarp; 5: Rampart.

Schildmauer: In German medieval castles, a high, strong and thick shield wall screening a vulnerable area, fitted with galleries and arrow slits. The *Schildmauer* was often built across the only line of approach of a castle built on a mountain or spur. Examples can be seen at Andlau, Bruck, Kinzheim and Wassenburg in Alsace, but also at Crest in the Rhone valley in France.

Schloss: Generic German term for castle.

Schnecke/Beobachtungsschnecke: A small observation post built in a German *Feste* (q.v.) in the period preceding the First World War. The work derives its name from its shape in plan, evoking that of a snail shell – *Schnecke* in German. It was made of a double layer of metal with a bed of sand in between. Some were made of concrete. Its roof included a 5mm-thick metal plate. It was partly sunk in the ground and offered protection against small-calibre shells, hand grenades, shrapnel and bullets. See *Feste*, Observation post and Tobruk.

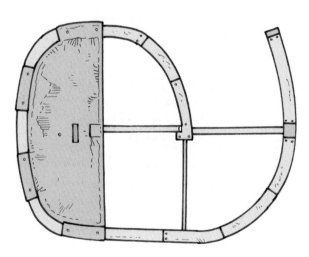

Schnecke.

Schnecke. View.

Sconce: Old English term for a redoubt (q.v.) or a small fort, generally made of earth, fitted with bastions at the angles and hemmed in by a ditch.

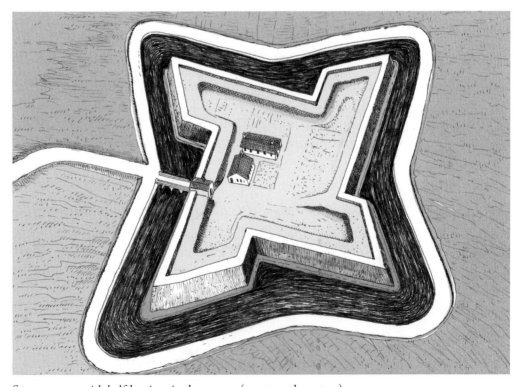

Square sconce with half-bastions in the corners (seventeenth century).

Sea fort: As the name implies, a fortified position placed not on the shore, but in the sea or in the middle of a river's mouth, usually to defend a harbour against enemy ships and later against airplanes. Famous examples of sea forts are Fort Drum (Philippines), Fort Boyard (France), Horse Sands Fort (Portsmouth) and the Maunsell forts in the Thames and Mersey in England.

Horse Sands Fort, Portsmouth.

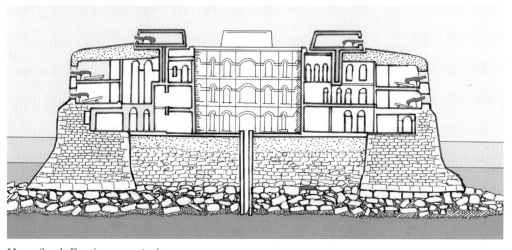

Horse Sands Fort (cross-section).

Located at the mouth of Manila Bay in the Philippines, south of Corregidor Island, Fort Drum (named after Brigadier General Richard C. Drum) is a heavily fortified concrete artillery position built by the United States in 1909.

Fort Boyard (Charente-Maritime, France). Intended to defend the naval arsenal of Rochefort on the Charente River estuary, Fort Boyard was a genuinely immovable masonry ship. It was completed in 1857.

Seafront: Term used to designate the part of a coastal battery (q.v.) or coastal fort facing the open sea where the main armament was placed. In modern fortification it designates an area where an enemy landing could occur in wartime. The seafront was frequently arranged as a defensive position with beach obstacles (q.v.), mines and armed bunkers. The sides and the rear of the seafront were covered by the so-called landfront (q.v.).

Searchlight: A searchlight is a detection and signal device, composed of a powerful incandescent filament lamp with reflectors and lenses to enhance and concentrate the beam, making it possible to see targets at night. The device was usually set on a mobile carriage. A searchlight – used to send coded messages and illuminate targets on the battlefield as much at sea as on land or in the air – has a range of several hundred metres, depending on the illuminating beam strength and weather conditions. Searchlights are fragile and expensive devices. They were stored in concrete bunkers or garages and rolled out of the shelters and deployed in special open emplacements where wheels were dismounted and the devices placed on screw-jacks. Searchlights demand a lot of energy, which can be provided by power plants either placed in garages or in special bunkers. Searchlights were mainly employed to help anti-aircraft guns and warships in the Second World War. After 1945, due to the remarkable development of radar and electronic technics, searchlights became totally obsolete.

Semi-permanent fortification: Also known as reinforced field fortification, this was hastily constructed when a danger of invasion was imminent, during the course of a campaign or during a siege when it became necessary to protect some locality, installation or position with the best imitation of permanent defences. Semi-permanent field fortification defence works were made in short time, often under great pressure with less ample resources and less skilled labour than permanent works. Consequently, reinforced fortification had much less strength than permanent works, but was more sturdy than purely temporary field fortification.

Sentry box: A small wooden, masonry or concrete shelter with roof protecting a guard from the elements. See Arkel, Bartizan, *Echauguette*, Turret and Guardhouse.

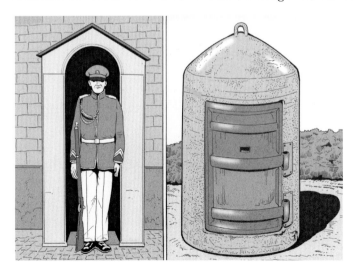

Sentry box.
Left: Made of wood;
Right: Made of concrete.

Sentry-walk: Walkway protected by a breastwork (q.v.) along the top of a wall of a castle, usually running along the entire length of the enceinte. A synonym is wall-walk (q.v.) or *chemin de ronde* (q.v.).

Séré de Rivières system: See *Barrière de Fer* and Polygonal system.

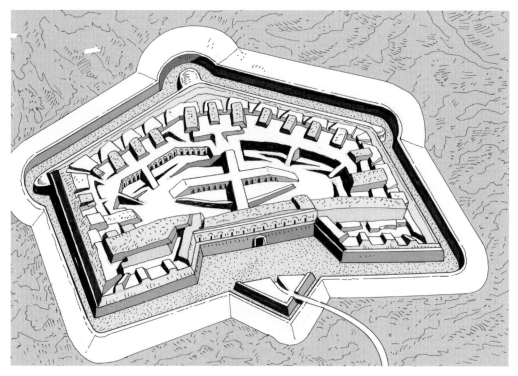

Séré de Rivières system, polygonal fort.

Serving Room: A chamber, often found in the magazine of a coastal battery, from which cartridges are issued to the guns.

Shell keep: A form of keep (q.v.) built as a circular or oval wall made of stone. Buildings were constructed against that circular wall, with the centre of the shell keep retained as an open courtyard. It was actually an improvement on the palisaded and timber motte-and-bailey castle (q.v.) as masonry rendered it much less vulnerable to fire. The defensive enclosure kept the purpose of a last refuge. Good examples are the Burcht at Leiden in Holland, Restormel Castle in Cornwall and Gisors Castle in Normandy, France.

Shifting house: Building where gunpowder was checked and prepared. See Arsenal.

Shot-hole: Opening for firearms, generally smaller than a gun port or embrasure (q.v.).

Shoulder: The junction of the face and flank of a bastion. The shoulder (or *épaule*) could be fitted with an ear or *orillon* (q.v.).

Shoulder angle: The angle formed by the intersection of a face and flank of a bastion.

Shell keep.

Shrapnel:

1) Anti-personnel hollow artillery munitions containing a large number of individual bullets, fired close to the target and thereby releasing and scattering a sudden shower of deadly missiles. Named after General Henry Shrapnel (1761–1842), the British officer who invented the projectile.
2) A collective term for dangerous shot, fragments or debris thrown out by an exploding shell or landmine.

Shutter: A hinged panel fixed on two merlons (q.v.) for additional protection of defenders when in an open crenel (q.v.).

Siege: An organized military blockade and attack of a city or fortified place to compel it to surrender. See Part 2 (Siege Warfare).

Siege battery: A number of guns placed and fired by the besiegers in order to silence the besieged's artillery and make a breach (q.v.) in their defences. See Part 2 (Siege Warfare).

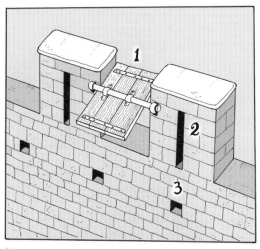

Shutter.
1: Shutter; 2: Crenel; 3: Wall.

Siege engine: A protecting device or mechanical throwing machine. See Part 2 (Siege Warfare).

Siege train: An ensemble of transportation means such as wagons and carts, carrying the equipment, provisions and other supplies for conducting a siege operation. See Part 2 (Siege Warfare).

Siege works: Fortified temporary positions established by besiegers during a siege, including gun batteries, small redoubts, parallels, trenches and saps. See Part 2 (Siege Warfare).

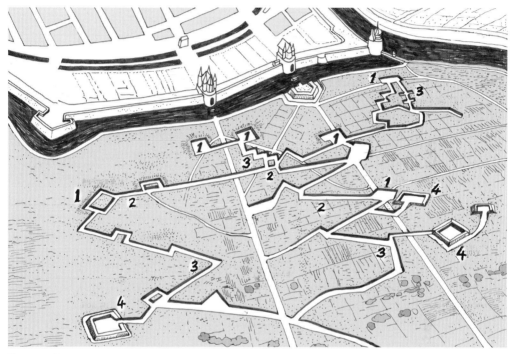

Siege works.
1: Breach batteries; 2: Parallels; 3: Communication saps; 4: Redoubts (or sconces).

Siegfried Line: Name given by the Allies to the Westwall (q.v.), a line of fortification built by Nazi Germany to defend its western border.

Siegfried Stellung: See Hindenburg Line.

Si vis pacem, para bellum: Latin tag meaning 'If you want peace, prepare for war', precisely what permanent fortification is all about.

Slit: A narrow vertical opening in a wall for admitting light and firing arrows.

Solid bastion: A bastion was called solid (or full) when its *terre-plein* was completely filled with earth. A windmill or a cavalier (q.v.) could be placed on the upper surface of a solid bastion. See Bastion and Empty bastion.

Sortie: A sortie or sally (q.v.) is a counter-attack launched by the besieged. The general objective is to thwart the advantage gained by the enemy in attack and the specific objectives are usually to regain lost ground or to destroy attacking enemy units.

Spall Skin: When concrete is hit by a high explosive, it shatters locally, and flakes or fragments of broken materials are often detached on the far side of the slab, becoming dangerous falling projectiles. A steel skin, even relatively thin, can slow or stop this scab. This spall skin was used in concrete bunkers, notably in the form of an armoured ceiling.

Spanish Main: Spain's empire in Central and South America was called the Spanish Main. The term was initially applied only to the mainland of Venezuela, but over the years it came to include Florida, Mexico, Central America, the West Indian islands and the Caribbean Sea. Due to attacks both at sea and on land by French, English and Dutch pirates, raiders, buccaneers and privateers, the Spanish authorities had to construct coastal gun batteries and forts, as well as strong urban bastioned fortifications around the most important ports, cities and harbours, for example Fort El Morro and Fort San Juan (Puerto Rico), the Fortress of the Three Wise Men (Cuba) and Castillo San Felipe (Venezuela). In addition to static permanent fortifications, the Spaniards organized an aggressive defence based on warships and mobile anti-pirate hunters patrolling the sealanes, while armed vessels escorted their treasure-laden galleons sailing home.

Spider hole: US military slang for a small one-man camouflaged foxhole (q.v.). A spider hole is typically a shoulder-deep, protective round hole, covered by a camouflaged lid so that it can be used for ambushes, in which a soldier can stand and fire a weapon. A spider hole differs from a foxhole in that a foxhole is usually deeper and its design emphasizes cover rather than concealment.

Spike-head: Obstacle, often made of sharp iron or steel, placed on top of a fence, wall, batardeau (q.v.) or monk (q.v.).

Splayed opening: A window or slit opening with tapered wide-angled sides in the thickness of a wall that allow more light to enter than is possible with straight sides. A splayed embrasure (q.v.) or loophole (q.v.) allows a broader arc of fire.

Spur:
1) In civilian and military architecture, a buttress (generally triangular) used to strengthen the bottom of a round tower by giving it a square base. See Apron.
2) An angular outwork or an arrow-like projection extending from the face of a work. See Redan.

Spur-castle: A castle (q.v.) built on top of or on the side of a spur, promontory (q.v.) or hill, making use of the existing natural and defensive features of a site.

Spreizhemmbalk: See Strand beam.

Square mine: The square mine (in German *Winkelmine*) was an underwater beach obstacle used in the Atlantic Wall (q.v.). It was composed of two balanced wooden or metal arms forming a right angle. The horizontal beam was fitted with a mine, and when the vertical arm was knocked by a passing ship, the whole device rotated upwards and the mine exploded under the hull. At low tide, the mine remained dangerous for vehicles.

Stair: In the Middle Ages, a staircase was nearly always narrow and tucked away as a purely utilitarian part of a building, and one defender could hold it against many attackers. Newel staircases taking up as little space as possible were the rule. Also known as corkscrew or turnpike, a circular staircase was the most economical method of communication between floors in a vertical keep or tower. It was not the most convenient to use, but it was easy to defend because it turned against the clock so that an aggressor had to present his vulnerable right side (the shield was commonly carried on the left arm). The last phase of the Gothic style, with its new appreciation of space, however, tried to endow staircases with spatial expression, emphasizing the delights of ever-changing axes.

Stand: The German words *Stand* and *Unterstand* (plural *Stände*) were used to indicate a passive shelter. The term *Stand* can be combined to designate specific fortified structures: *Schartenstand* (bunker fitted with an embrasure), *MG-Schartenstand* (machine-gun or MG casemate), *Geschützschartenstand* (artillery casemate), *Pak-Schartenstand* (casemate armed with an anti-tank gun), *Stand mit- 3-Schartenturm* (bunker with three MG embrasures placed inside an armoured cloche) and *Befehlsstand* (command post).

Stanton shelter: The British Second World War Stanton air raid shelters were designed and manufactured by the Stanton Ironworks Company Ltd in Derbyshire, but also built by several other companies such as Geo, Wimpey, Mowlem and Tarmac. They consisted of sections of pre-cast concrete arched-shaped sides, bolted together to form a standard Air Ministry shelter typically for fifty men. The entrance could be brick-lined and fitted with concrete steps if required. The shelter often included an emergency escape hatch at the rear. They were built above the ground or semi-sunk; for added protection and concealment purposes, blast walls were added and the shelter could be covered with soil and turf.

Star fort: A loose term wrongly referring to a bastioned stronghold. Indeed, true star forts had no bastions but generally used a stellar tracé consisting of a series of *tenailles* (q.v.) or redans (q.v.), giving in plan the shape of a multi-pointed star. Star forts were relatively rare because of the difficulty of protecting the main exterior faces. The concept was sometimes used in the design of island and coastal forts, where defence against attack by land was not a major consideration. Good examples of star fort tracé may be seen at Fort Wood on Bedloe's Island (now renamed Liberty Island) in New York harbour, at Collioure in southern France and in the English Isles of Scilly.

Stekelvarken: A small and simple Dutch trapezium-shaped rifle and machine-gun concrete bunker designed in the late 1930s. The *Stekelvarken* (meaning 'porcupine') existed in several variants according to the number of embrasures and rifle holes.

Star fort. Isles of Scilly off south-west England.

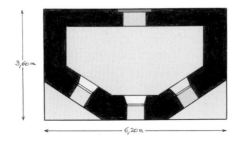

Stekenvarken. Top: Front view; Bottom: Plan.

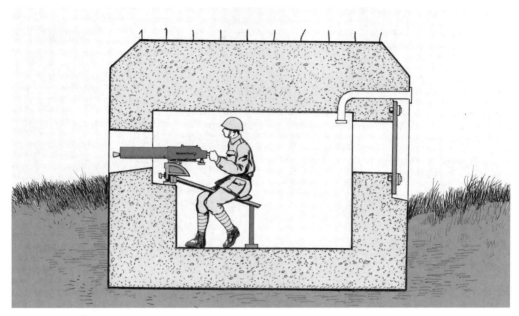

Stekenvarken. Cross-section.

Stimulus: A sharp barbed iron hook fixed on a short stake stuck in the ground. Concealed in grass and placed in great number around a position, they were intended to injure attacking enemy infantrymen and horses. Designed and used by the Romans, it was an early form of discreet anti-personnel obstacle.

Stins: See Borg.

Stockade: An enclosure of palisades and walls made of logs or stakes placed side by side vertically, with the tops sharpened. The stockade (together with the earth wall and ditch) is one of the oldest forms of fortification. Stockades were generally provided with loopholes in the upper part of the fence and a *banquette* (q.v.), fire-step (q.v.) or an elevated walk. See Breastwork, *Lorica*, Palisade and *Vallum*.

Stockade.

Stone wall: Stone walls are a masonry construction which has been made by man for thousands of years. They were first constructed by primitive farmers by piling loose field stones in what is called a dry stone wall, then later with the use of mortar and plaster, especially in the construction of city walls, castles and other fortifications prior to and during the Middle Ages. They are usually made of stone directly available in the vicinity, which could vary from limestone and flint to granite and sandstone. However, the quality of building stone varies greatly, in terms of its endurance to weathering, resistance to water penetration and ability to be worked into regular shapes before construction. Worked stone is usually known as ashlar (q.v.), and is often used for corners in stone buildings. Granite is very resistant to weathering, while some limestone is very weak. Other limestone, however, such as Portland stone, has a deserved reputation for resistance to weather erosion. See Brick, Masonry, Materials and Rustication.

Stormpole: Horizontal sharpened stakes placed in a breastwork as an anti-infantry obstacle, hindering assault operations. See Fraise.

Storm-proof: Any measure taken and any element positioned in order to prevent an enemy's assault on a fortress or other position.

Strand bars: Strand bars (in German *Hemmkurven*) were originally German anti-tank obstacles designed in 1937 to oppose 36-ton tanks. *Hemmkurven* were formed from four or five bent steel bars (or portions of rail) attached together. Each bar was about 2.3m long, supported by a strong metal framework and placed about 1.4m from its neighbour. Discarded in 1943, *Hemmkurven* were then widely used as *K-Sperre* (beach obstacles) to strand landing ships, which would be impaled on them. *Hemmkurven* were generally placed in pebble beaches, where poles could not easily be pushed into the ground.

Strand beam: The strand beam (in German *Hemmbalk*) worked like the *Hemmkurven* system. It was a cheaper version consisting of a roughly 8m-long tree trunk or concrete beam resting on supports. The beam made a 30–40-degree angle with the ground. *Hemmbalken* were placed in alternate rows on a beach and were intended to strand landing craft. The destructive potentiality was increased by the addition of sharp *Stahlmesser* (blades), which were intended to rip off the hull of landing craft like a can-opener. *Hemmbalken* could also be furnished with anti-tank mines. A variant (called *Spreizhemmbalk*) was composed of several beams, spreading over a larger position. Another more expensive variant (*Betonbock*) was made of concrete beams.

Strigae: The various rectangular spaces marked out for the erection of tents, huts or masonry quarters in a Roman camp or fort. See *Castrum* and *Castellum*.

Stutzpunkt: (*StP* in short) Created in 1942, these support points were very flexible fortified units widely used in the German Atlantic Wall (q.v.). A small *StP* could be as strong as a large *Widerstandsnest* (q.v.). The surface – enclosed by barbed wire and mines – could vary from 300–500m^2, and in some places even more than 1,000m^2. A *StP* could be occupied by a unit of more or less battalion strength. Armament was also variable: a *Stutzpunkt* could receive army units, a navy coastal battery or Lufwaffe Flak guns. Even a radar station was possible. It all depended on the strategic importance of the site.

Stutzpunktgruppe: A *Stutzpunktgruppe* (in short, *StPGr*) was a group of *StP* strongholds. In certain very important sectors, all existing units were regrouped to form a powerful continuous position spanning several kilometres of the shore. The *StPGr* generally constituted a strong multi-arm position including army *StPs*, but also navy, army and air force coastal or anti-aircraft batteries, radar stations, command posts, military hospitals, numerous stores and everything needed to withstand a siege. A *StPGr* generally maintained enough supplies to operate for about two weeks. The status of *Stutzpunktgruppe* was usually given to harbours of secondary importance.

Submarine bunker: German Second World War submarines (U-Boats) were particularly vulnerable to air strikes while they were alongside quays for resupply and repairs. Therefore submarine installations were protected by enormous concrete shelters designed by the German navy and built by the Organisation Todt (q.v.). The main Atlantic submarine bases in France were at Brest, Lorient, Saint-Nazaire, La Pallice and Bordeaux. For operations in the North Sea, the Kriegsmarine built submarine bases at Hamburg and Kiel in Germany and at Trondheim in Norway. Although incorporated into the Atlantic Wall (q.v.), the U-Boat installations had a completely different role. Instead of being defensive positions, they were offensive bases. Each of them included a vast militarized perimeter with installations and facilities. Gigantic concrete works especially designed to shelter submarines were created in docks linked to the open sea. Under thick concrete shells, various workshops, stores, pens, docks and quays were built, with cranes and other installations allowing all supply, refuel and repair operations.

Submarine bunker. Keroman at Lorient in Brittany, France.

Sudis: *Sudis* (plural *sudes*) is a Latin word meaning 'stake'. It was the name given to stakes carried by Roman legionaries for use as field fortification. Each stake was made of hardwood, usually oak, about 150-180cm (5–6ft) long and 50–100mm (2–4in) wide at the thickest point. Square in section, the shape tapered to a sharp point at both ends. The central part was narrowed in a way that strongly suggests the function of a handle, although this remains unclear. *Sudes* may have been used to form a temporary defence or barrier and incorporated into the ramparts of a Roman *castrum* (q.v.). It is also believed that *sudes* lashed in pairs at intervals along a log or beam could form a moveable *Cheval de frise* (q.v.). Alternatively, three stakes might have been roped together into a mobile obstacle resembling the Czech hedgehog (q.v.).

Südwall: 'South Wall', German Second World War fortifications along the French Mediterranean coast built after 11 November 1942, when the Germans occupied the southern part of France (the so-called 'free' Vichy State). See Atlantic Wall.

Superior slope/Plongée: The top of a parapet (q.v.) or breastwork (q.v.), slightly sloping downwards.

Swallow's tail: Also called a dovetail or *queue d'hironde*, this was an advanced work (q.v.) in the form of a *tenaille* (q.v.) with two wings swinging back. The swallow's tail differed from the bishop's mitre (q.v.) due to its two slightly re-entrant wings (q.v.).

Swiss National Redoubt: In the Second World War, the Swiss, after the fall of France completely surrounded by fascist forces (in fact, the only Axis-free country in continental Europe except for that other Swiss-guarded European state, the Vatican in Rome), took precautions to ensure national survival in case of a Nazi attack. The Swiss authorities thus drew up plans for a National Redoubt, also called the *Réduit suisse* in French and *Schweizer Réduit* or *Alpenfestung* in German. The *Schweizer Réduit* was similar in concept to other defensive lines built at that time by other European powers: the French Maginot line, the German Siegfried line and others by the Czechoslovaks, Belgians and Dutch in the 1930s. The Swiss national defence plan consisted of three stages: reinforcing the borders with new forts, preparing for a delaying war in the relatively level middle of the country and establishing an impregnable zone, the *Réduit* proper, in the high Alps. After the capitulation of France in late June 1940, Switzerland started finalizing the *Réduit*. Impressed by the German Balkan campaign of April 1941, in which the Wehrmacht conquered Yugoslavia and Greece in a mere twenty-three days, the Swiss army high command further reinforced the *Réduit* by concentrating even more troops in it – effectively giving up the middle of the country, the economically and demographically most important lower-lying areas of central Switzerland. Fortunately for the Swiss, Nazi Germany never attacked Switzerland, a country too important for international financial transactions and secret business deals.

Symbolic and aesthetic display: Essentially functional, military architecture was made of first-rate and resistant materials employing skilled craftsmanship, with the ancient Roman trilogy in mind: *firmitas* (solidity), *utilitas* (functionality) and *venustas* (beauty). Indeed, fortifications frequently possess an undeniable beauty through the ingenuity and balance of their conception, the quality of their execution, the solidity and size of their mass, the strictness of their geometry, their rigorous functionality, the sobriety of their shape and the majesty of their proportion. They often radiate an impression of quiet strength, efficiency and sculptural quality, as well as attractive grandeur, that please the aesthetic senses and delight the intellect.

T

Tablette: See Cordon.

Talus: A sloping wall, often thicker at its base for increased stability and resilience against ramming. See Apron, Batter and Plinth.

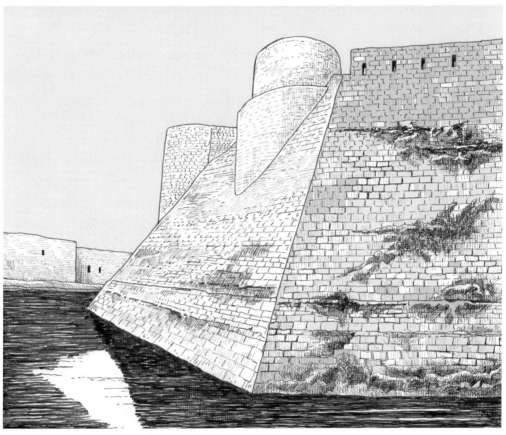

Talus. Krak des Chevaliers in Syria.

Tambour: A small defensive work defending and controlling the entrance of a nineteeth-century fort. The tambour was placed on the counterscarp in the gorge at the back of the fort, and could be hemmed by a ditch. It was either triangular or pentagonal, could feature a guardhouse, and its masonry walls were often pierced with slits for infantry weapons.

Tank shelter: Underground garage or concealed concrete shed with one or two large armoured doors and an access ramp with a slope allowing easy manoeuvre (not above 20 per cent).

Tank turret: In the twentieth century, turrets of discarded tanks were sometimes used in combination with concrete bunkers. A typical example was the German *Regelbau* (model) 687 featuring a small concrete bunker topped by a Mark V Panther tank turret.

Tank turret.

Tenaille:

1) A small and low wall located within the ditch, at the foot of the scarp between the flanks of a bastion, and in front of and along the curtain. Widely used in bastioned fortification, it is often said that the *tenaille* was created by Vauban when he had been considering the replacement of the obsolete *fausse-braie* (q.v.). The *tenaille* was an advanced work formed of two walls built in the alignment of the faces of the bastions, making a re-entrant angle. Other forms were used, for instance the shape of a bastioned front or a protuding redan placed in its middle. The purpose was to protect the base of a curtain and flanks of adjacent bastions from bombardment and to oblige the besiegers to attack the faces which were held under heavy fire from the flanks. The *tenaille* was fitted with a breastwork which contributed to the active flanking of the ditch. It could also be slightly higher than the *demi-lune* (q.v.), and infantry could fire into it should that outwork be taken. Behind the protection of the *tenaille*, a party of defenders could be regrouped for a sally; for this purpose a communication – a postern (q.v.) or sally port (q.v.) – was created under the main enceinte, allowing the garrison to move around the defences while remaining under cover from enemy sight and fire.
2) An advanced work (q.v.) having the shape of scissors, comprising two re-entrant faces with wings (q.v.) at the sides, thus the reverse of a redan (q.v.). See Bishop's mitre and Swallow's tail.

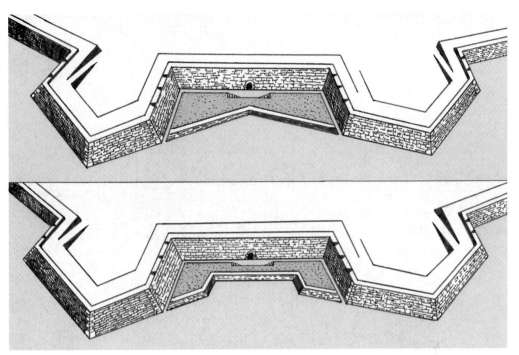

Tenaille. Top: Simple *tenaille*; Bottom: Bastioned *tenaille*.

Various forms of advanced *tenailles*.

Tenaille fort: A fort built according to the *tenaille* system (q.v.). See Star fort.

Tenaille Fort St Elmo at Collioure, France.

Tenaille front: A front built according to the *tenaille* system (q.v.) with alternate salient and re-entrant angles in a wall for flanking.

Tenaille system: The *tenaille* system was advocated by the German engineers Suttinger in 1670 and Rimpler in 1673, also used by the Dutchman Menno van Coehoorn (1641–1704) and revived by the German Heinrich von Landsberg (1670–1746) in the 1710s. It was a method of fortification characterized by the abandoning of curtains and bastions, which were replaced with a series of *tenailles* – triangular structures with long faces, abutting each other and forming together in plan a saw-edged outline generally of right angles. The advantages of this method were that it was much cheaper to build than a bastioned front, ensured very good flanking and required

Tenaille Front (Doesburg, the Netherlands).

fewer soldiers to man. The main drawback was the long faces, which could easily be enfiladed by enemy fire. The *tenaille* system was never very popular: it never supplanted the bastioned system, and only a few *tenailled* forts and lines were built in the eighteenth century. See *Tenaille* and Star fort.

Tenaillon: Small outwork (q.v.) placed along the faces of a bastion or *demi-lune* to add strength and cover the shoulders and faces of the bastion.

Terrapieno: Italian term meaning 'filled with earth'.

Terre-plein: The broad and flat surface on top of the rampart, below the level of the parapet and *banquette*, or the platform behind the parapet where guns were mounted. The *terre-plein* must be broad enough to offer room for loading and firing the guns and taking the recoil. It had also to allow the easy circulation of ammunition and gun carriages.

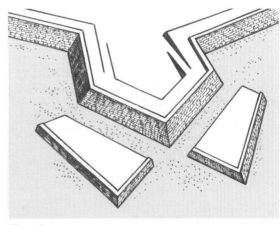

Tenaillon.

Tetrahedron: In geometry, a tetrahedron (plural: tetrahedra or tetrahedrons), also known as a porcupine or triangular pyramid, was a mobile anti-tank obstacle/roadblock of French origin used in the 1930s and during the Second World War. The tetraeder

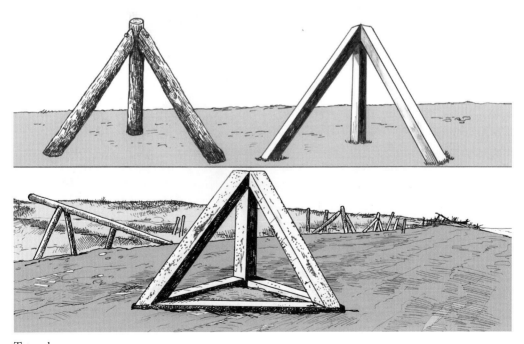

Tetraeder.
Top left: Made of wood; Top right: Made of steel beams; Bottom: Made of concrete beams.

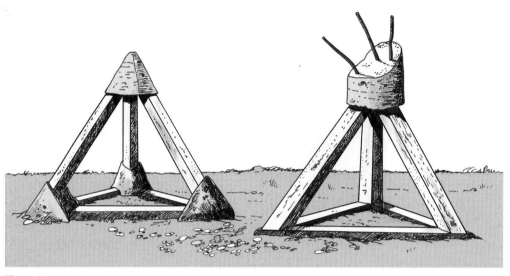

Tetraeder.
Left: With reinforced corners;
Right: With concrete block on top.

was formed of three wooden, metal or concrete pieces assembled as a pyramid. The main advantage was that it could be simply placed on hard ground where it was difficult to push in poles. Its stability and solidity were possibly reinforced with triangular wedges. Porcupines could also be fitted with one or more anti-personnel or anti-tank mines. In some cases when used as a beach obstacle (q.v.), they carried a concrete block with sharp metal rods on which landing craft would impale themselves.

Tett Turret: The Tett turret, named after its inventor and designer H.L. Tett, was a private commercial venture designed and manufactured by Burbridge Builders Ltd of Surrey in 1940. It was the same design as the Allan Williams turret (q.v.), only the

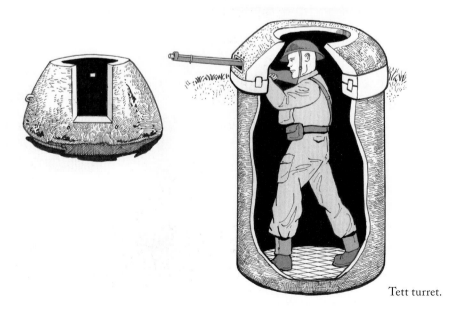

Tett turret.

cupola was not made of metal but concrete. It was thus cheaper but also much heavier, and presented the same general features and shortcomings. See Allan William turret and FW3.

Tobruk: A small German Second World War open observation and combat emplacement. Also called a *Ringstand*, the name seems to come from a similar type of position, a small Italian roofless bunker built near Tobruk in Libya during the North African campaign. It is not known if the Italian military engineers shared their designs with the Germans, so the popular name Tobruk remains something of a mystery. Approved by Hitler, the Tobruk/*Ringstand* was widely built in the Atlantic Wall (q.v.) from 1942 onwards. The Tobruk was generally built in 40cm *Verstärkt festmaßig* (*Vf*, reinforced field fortification) thickness. It was a concrete foxhole, composed of a small 1.6m-deep open pit in which a soldier could stand upright with only his head and shoulders exposed. The upper opening was 80cm in diameter, and either circular, hexagonal or octogonal in shape. A small extra space (with various dimensions) was often added to serve as an ammunition recess and shelter. The Tobruk was accessible by means of a small and narrow curved corridor/staircase. It was greatly standardized, cheap, rapidly built, easy to camouflage, adaptable and multifunctional. Tobruks existed in numerous variants, armed with a machine gun, mortar, flamethrower, light anti-aircraft gun or discarded rotating tank-turret. See *Kochbunker*, *Offener Beobachter* and *Michelmannstand*.

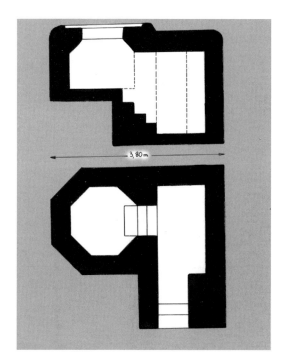

Tobruk. Cross-section and plan of a Tobruk.

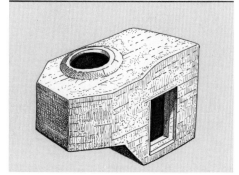

Top: Opening of a Tobruk with machine gun; Bottom: Tobruk view.

Toren: Dutch word for tower (q.v.).

Torenfort: Dutch bombproof artillery tower built in the early nineteenth century. The tower was cylindrical and made of very strong masonry. It housed quarters for the garrison, supplies and ammunition stores. Its numerous artillery was emplaced in casemates, and it was generally three storeys high and surrounded with a wet ditch and low earth walls. However, these huge towers (some could be as large as 40m in diameter) proved vulnerable when rifled artillery and new explosives were introduced

Torenfort. Top: Honswijk, the Netherlands.
Note the use of crenellation and machicolation as neo-Gothic decorative elements.
Bottom: Cross-section.

Torenfort. Muiden, the Netherlands.

in the 1860s. As a result they were lowered and encircled with a large protective screen wall made of masonry and a thick layer of earth, known as a counterscarp gallery (q.v.). Extant *torenforten* in the Netherlands can be seen at Weesp, Nieuwersluis, Honswijk, Everdingen and Vuren.

Torpedo launcher: A tube intended to fire a torpedo – a self-propelled bomb, launched above or below the water surface, propelled underwater towards a target. Torpedo tubes were standard equipment in submarines as well as in surface torpedo boats. Occasionally this kind of offensive weapon system could be part of a coastal defence system and placed inside specially designed bunkers.

Torre del homenaje: Spanish for keep (q.v.).

Torre de managem: Portuguese for keep (q.v.).

Torre Massimiliane: Italian name for Austrian Maximilian detached casemated artillery towers (q.v.) built in Italy (e.g. at Verona and Venice) and Austria (Linz) in the early nineteenth century. See Maximilian tower.

Torrione: An Italian cylindrical or U-shaped gun tower typical of Renaissance transitional fortification (q.v.), with thick walls, apron (q.v.) and casemates (q.v.), sometimes retaining medieval crenellation and machicolation (q.v.) as ornamention.

Totten shutter: The Totten shutter system was invented in 1844 by American military engineer Joseph Gilbert Totten (1788–1864). It consisted of an armoured embrasure

Torre de managem. Bragança, northern Portugal.

with hinged swinging doors installed on the cannon openings. Balanced to swing freely, the iron shutters would be forced open by the gasses expelled from the cannon and then rebound shut immediately afterwards, shielding the gunners from incoming fire, thereby offering good protection. Installed in American forts from 1846–68, the design was incorporated in such locations as Fort Montgomery (New York), Fort Delaware (Pea Patch Island, Delaware), Fort John C. Calhoun (South Carolina) and Fort Jefferson (Florida).

Tourelle: French for turret (q.v.).

Tourelle Galopin: See Galopin turret.

Tour maîtresse: Alternative French term for *donjon* (q.v.) or keep (q.v.).

Tour modèle: French Napoleonic standardized work designed by the Committee of Fortification and approved by Napoléon in 1811. Known

Torrione (Castle Roverto, Italy, *c.* 1488)

Tour Modèle. Boyardville, Oleron Island, France.

Tour Modèle. Toulinguet Battery, Brittany, France.

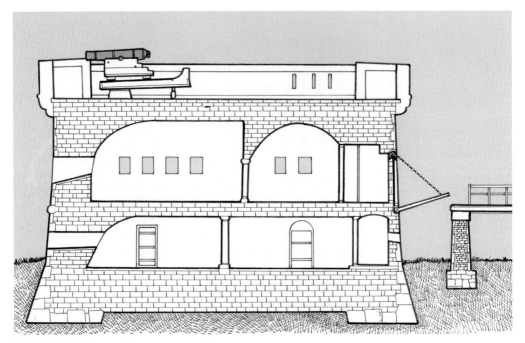

Tour Modèle. Cross-section.

as *Tour Modèle 1811*, this coastal work was a square masonry tower which existed in several variants. Intended for both a surveillance and combat role, the tower could also serve as a *réduit* for a fort or coastal battery. It had a platform armed with four guns mounted on Gribeauval carriages, and was pierced with loopholes for musketry fire. The bombproof vaulted storey contained the garrison quarters and store rooms. The tower was surrounded by a ditch crossed by a drawbridge and was about 27ft high, making it secure from escalade by an attacking party. The French *tour modèle* and the British Martello towers (q.v.) indicated the return of the tower in European fortification in the early nineteenth century. See *Redoute modèle* and Réduit.

Tower: A high, strong structure standing alone or forming part of a fortress. The tower formed one of the basic elements of fortification. Used since prehistory and Antiquity, it has always existed in numerous forms: cylindrical, semi-cylindrical, U-shaped, almond-shaped, square, rectangular or bastioned. The summit of the tower was either covered with a roof or arranged as an open crenellated terrace for observation and combat where soldiers and weapons could be deployed. The top might also be fitted with an *echauguette* (q.v.) or watch turret (q.v.), or arranged as a lighthouse. Towers varied considerably in height, strength, thickness and size, from small watchtowers to enormous forts bristling with weapons. The inside of the tower was divided into various storeys with rooms arranged as living accommodation, supply stores, arsenal and combat emplacements. Access to the rooms was by means of ladder or masonry spiral staircases, generally placed in the thickness of the walls.

Throughout the history of fortification, towers have had various functions, either a fortified dwelling place as a keep (q.v.), a permanent or temporary refuge, a stronghold arranged for active defence with combat emplacements, an isolated construction for observation, occupation, local combat and coastal defence, or even as a fire control station (q.v.) and anti-aircraft artillery position in the twentieth century.

When part of a fortified place or medieval castle, a tower projected into the ditch in order to provide flanking fire (q.v.). In this case it was called a wall tower (q.v.) or corner tower (see Rectangular castles). It was very often higher than the curtain, allowing observation and command of the curtains: if enemies conquered the wall-walk, they remained under fire from the tower. Communication between the tower and the wall-walk could be interrupted by a void that was crossed by a small drawbridge. The distance between corner and wall towers was calculated according to the range of the weapons used. Important urban towers were often given a name. See Maunsell fort, Martello tower, Maximilian tower, *Torenfort*, *Flakturm*, Tower house and *Tour modèle*.

Tower bastion: A bastion (q.v.) in the form of a defensible tower fitted with casemates intended to cover the ditch. This element was typical of Vauban's 'second and third systems'. See Bastioned tower.

Tower house: An urban fortified residence in the form of a round or square tower. Tower houses are to be found everywhere in medieval European old towns. They were built by powerful and wealthy local families as protection and places of refuge in case of riot or rebellion. Some of the best known of these 'towers of nobility' are still to be seen are at San Gemigiano in Tuscany, constructed during the internecine strife and civil war between the Guelphs and the Ghibellines. Urban fortified houses reflected both a state of constant political unrest within a city and the need for display to impress other nobles and the population at large. Simple, strong, rectangular tower houses were also built in the Scottish/English border region. See Peel tower.

Amisfield tower house (Tinwald, Scotland).

Tower houses. (San Gimignano, Italy).

Tracé à l'Italienne: Also called Tracé *Italien*. See Bastion, Bastioned system, Bastioned front and Italian system.

Tracé pseudo-bastionné: Outline sometimes given to the gorge of a French polygonal fort (q.v.). This tracé consisted of a bastioned front with small flanks from which the entrance and the rear ditch could be defended.

Traditore battery: The Italian term *traditore* means 'traitor'. In the late sixteenth century, a *traditore* battery ('treacherous battery') designated a concealed gun emplacement placed behind the ear (q.v.) of a bastion (q.v.). The term was revived in nineteenth-century Belgian and Dutch forts, when a *traditore* battery was a kind of reverse *casemate de Bourges* (q.v.) placed at the back of a fort for firing at the enemy in the flank and the rear in the intervals between forts and redoubts, so as to create a continuous belt of fire – a killing ground as it were – around adjacent forts.

Transitional fortification: Transitional fortification, developed between approximately 1450 and 1530 before the adoption of the bastioned system (q.v.), tried to conciliate two essential demands: to resist the destructive effects of heavy artillery and hand-held guns by passive means, and to use as efficiently as possible defensive firearms with active elements. See Part 1 (A Short History of Fortification).

Traverse: Verb meaning to move back and forth or sideways, or turn – for example a large gun or other device on a pivot to face a different direction. As a term of fortification a traverse is:

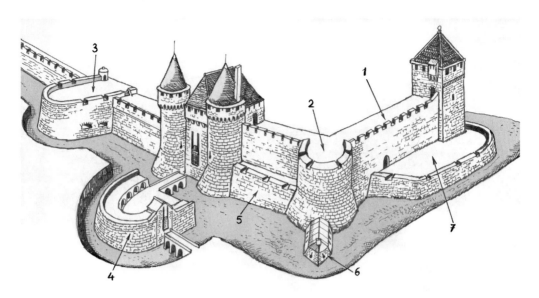

Transitional fortification. 1: Rampart; 2: Lowered tower; 3: Casemated artillery tower; 4: Advanced barbican; 5: *Fausse-braie*; 6: Caponier (aka *moineau*); 7: Bulwark (boulevard or artillery platform).

Fort built by King Henry VIII at St Mawes, Cornwall, England.

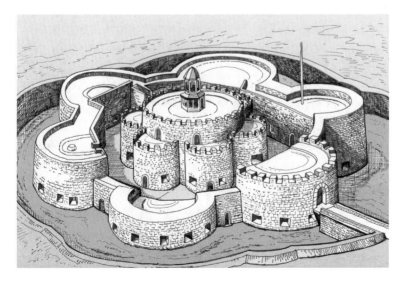

Deal Castle in Kent, England.

1) A mound of earth (often reveted with masonry) placed at regular intervals across covered ways (q.v.), *terre-pleins* of bastions and *demi-lunes* (q.v.) and curtains (q.v.) to limit the damage caused by enfilade fire. Traverses were often of equal height to the crest of the parapet and also fitted with an infantry *banquette* (q.v.), thus allowing a stepwise resistance.
2) A heap of earth or a masonry wall which protects gun emplacements, building entrances and other positions from enfilading fire.

In all cases the traverse is designed to enhance compartmentation and increase obstacles in order to prevent the effect of enfilade and ricochet fire, thereby confining the deadly effects of a bomb or shell to only a limited part of a fortified position.

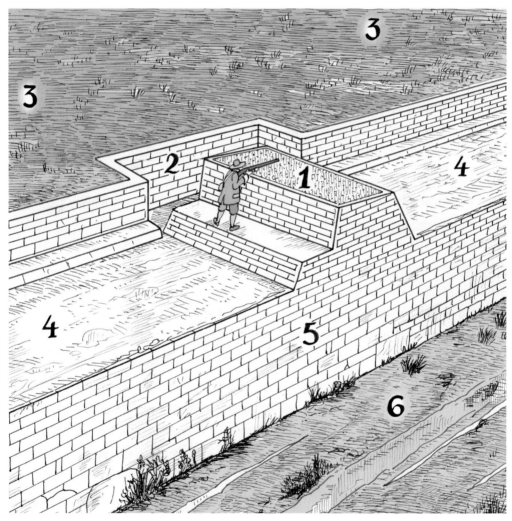

Traverse. Placed across the covered way in bastioned fortification, the traverse included: 1: Traverse; 2: Chicane passage; 3: Glacis; 4: Covered way; 5: Counterscarp; 6: Ditch.

Traversed work: Any fortified element (bastion, *demi-lune* or parapet) having its *terre-plein* divided into two or more compartments by a traverse (q.v.). Either made of thick earth or solid masonry, the traverse was generally built on the capital line (q.v.) of the work. The purpose was to protect the defenders from enemy fire. The traverse could be pierced with one or more convenient vaulted passages, which enabled the garrison to circulate from one compartment to another.

Traverse shelter: A traverse shelter, built in nineteenth-century polygonal forts (q.v.), was a protective element made of masonry covered with a thick layer of earth, inside which riflemen and gunners could seek refuge (e.g. when the fort was heavily shelled prior to an assault). The shelters, placed at regular intervals across the parapet, also provided cover against enfilade and raking fire and were used as ammunitions stores. See Traverse.

Traversing platform: A circular or semi-circular emplacement on which a gun was mounted *en barbette* (q.v.), moving on a portion of rail. This arrangement was designed to traverse (pivot) around a central point in order to have a large traversing arc of fire (or circle of traverse).

Treatise: A book or manual giving instructions or information. By the end of the fourteenth century, printing with movable type on paper bound into a book became a practical business proposition. As a result, technical, intellectual and cultural life entered upon a new and more vigorous phase, as the knowledge of reading spread swiftly. More accessible information occured just at a time when fortifications were in crisis because of the appearance of firearms when princes, architects and engineers were looking for means to counter and use artillery for defensive purposes. One consequence of printing was the appearance of an abundance of (illustrated) treatises on fortification.

Trebuchet: A medieval hurling machine working with a counterpoise. See Part 2 (Siege warfare).

Trench: An excavation or sunken path dug in the ground. As a basic element of field fortification (q.v.), the alignment of trenches was and still is an important requirement. They are always given a zigzag tracé or a broken angled layout, each section never exceeding 20 metres in order to reduce enemy enfilading fire and decrease shell shockwave. They generally include traverses (q.v.) and parados (q.v.) in order to confine shell-burst direct hits to one short section. In cross-section, a trench is narrow and unless a bomb or shell fell on it directly, relatively little damage was done. A trench often included a breastwork (q.v.), reveted sides and a fire-step (q.v.) Shelters were established at intervals made of various materials (concrete, sandbags, wooden beams and planks covered with a thick mass of earth). Pumps and a drainage system were provided when needed to keep water at bay. Parallel lines of combat trenches were connected by saps (q.v.).

Trench cavalier: See *Cavalier de tranchée*.

Trench warfare: Trench warfare was a form of warfare in which both combatants occupied static fortified lines, consisting largely of excavations in which troops were mostly immune to the enemy's small-arms fire and were relatively sheltered from artillery. Trench warfare has become a byword for stalemate in conflict, with a slow wearing down of opposing forces or attritional war. Trench warfare occurred when an important advance in firepower was not matched by a similar development in mobility, resulting

Trench (Cross section).
1: No-man's-land; 2: Barbed wire entanglement; 3: Breastwork made of sandbags; 4: *Banquette* or firing-step; 5: Drainage (for removing rain and infiltration water).

in a slow and gruelling form of warfare in which the defence held the advantage. In trench warfare, both sides constructed elaborate and heavily armed trench and dugout systems opposing each other along a front, protected from assault by barbed wire. The depth of such positions could range from several hundred to several thousand metres, and in a few cases much further. If the position was held in great depth, a screening line of strongpoints and fortified outposts – designed to slow and disorganize an enemy attack – might be constructed forward of the main line of resistance (q.v.) and a reserve line built behind it. The area between opposing trench lines fully exposed to small-arms and artillery fire from both sides was known as no-man's-land (q.v.) or the glacis (q.v.). Attacks, even if successful, often sustained severe casualties.

Periods of trench warfare occurred during the American Civil War, the Russo-Japanese War and the Second Anglo-Boer War, but it is mainly associated with the First World War, when it lasted on the Western Front from September 1914 until the summer of 1918. Trench warfare in the First World War was also conducted on other fronts, including Italy and Gallipoli. Trench warfare has become a powerful symbol of the futility of war. Its image is of young men going 'over the top' into a maelstrom of fire, leading to certain death, typified by the first day of the Somme (on which the British suffered 57,000 casualties) or the grinding slaughter in the mud of Passchendaele. To the French, the equivalent is the appalling attrition of the 'wringer of Verdun', in which they suffered 275,000 casualties.

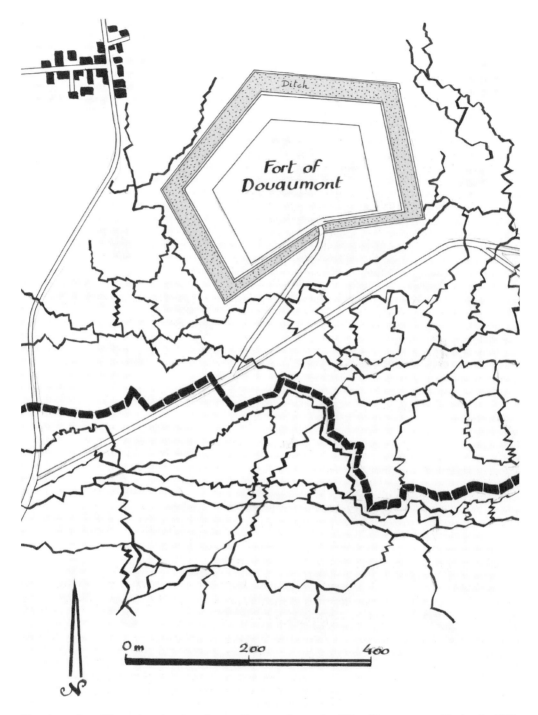

Trench warfare. Illustration showing the trench networks south of Fort Douaumont at Verdun in 1916. The thick dashed line indicates the actual front line.

Triumphal arch: A monument in the shape of an archway erected to honour a significant historical person or to commemorate an important public event such as a military victory. A triumphal arch generally included one or more arched passageways and had a tripartite division of four equal columns unequally spaced. Essentially a work of art and not intended for defence, it was always heavily decorated with reliefs, statues, carvings and dedications. Often associated with Roman architecture (in Rome the Arch of Constantine and Arch of Titus), triumphal arches can also be seen in Paris (Arc de Triomphe), at Orange in France, in London (Wellington Arch), in Bucharest (Arcul de Triumf) and in Delhi (India Gate). See Gatehouse.

Trophy: A sculpture or two-dimensional ornament carved in stone, often representing a stylized group of weapons, banners and armour – originally the captured equipment of a defeated enemy set up as a memorial of victory in Ancient Greece and Rome. In bastioned baroque fortification, it was an architectural ornament generally placed above a gate.

Trou de loup: A type of booby trap or defensive obstacle consisting of a conical pit about 2m (6ft 6in) deep and 1.2–2m (4ft–6ft 6in) wide at the top. At the bottom of the pit, a sharpened wooden stake or metal razor-edged hook would be hammered in. The pit was often concealed by a light cover of wicker and a thin layer of soil. *Trous de loup* might be found singly as a trap (in which case they were always concealed) or in a dense pattern with no gaps between pits, used as an obstacle in front of a defended position. See *Lilium*, Punji stick and Wolf's pit.

Tschechenigel: See Czech hedgehog.

Turm: German generic term for tower (q.v.). The plural is *Türme*.

Turnpike: A wooden obstacle blocking a passage or roadway as a defence against sudden attack. See *Cheval de Frise* and Frizzy Horse.

Turret:
1) A turret (from the Italian *torretta*, 'little tower', and Latin *turris*, 'tower') is a small tower that projects vertically from the wall of a building. This protective position on a fortification is situated on top of a building or wall, as opposed to a tower, which is always built with foundations on the ground. Turrets were thus much cheaper to build than towers. They were used to provide a projecting observation and defensive position allowing covering fire to the adjacent walls or curtains. Like a tower, a turret could have a circular top with crenellations, a pointed roof or other kind of apex. It might contain a staircase if it projected higher than the building. As their military use faded, turrets were adopted for decorative purposes.
2) In modern fortification (nineteenth and twentieth centuries), a turret is a combat or observation emplacement, generally rotating and protected by armour. It can be placed on top of a concrete bunker, on a ship or on an armoured combat vehicle.

See *Echauguette*, Sentry-box, *Poivrière*, Pepper-pot tower, Cupola, Eclipsing turret and Armoured turret.

Turret cap: Steel-plated covering in the shape of a skullcap that protects the gun and those inside the gun chamber of an armoured turret. The rounded shape of the cap was intended to deflect enemy projectiles.

Turris: A Roman watchtower.

Tutulus: In a Roman camp, a *tutulus* (plural *tutuli*) was a free-standing length of bank and ditch working as a screen, constructed directly in front of the opening of a gate in order to prevent a direct approach. An alternative disposition was the *clavica* (q.v.).

Twydall profile: Typical profile (q.v.) given to some polygonal forts (q.v.) in Britain in the nineteenth century. The profile – intended to replace a vertical scarp and deep ditch – consisted of a simple sloping earthen rampart, built as low as possible. At the foot of the slope was an unclimbable palisade made of angled steel palings, referred to as Dacoit fence (q.v.) with a recommended height of 9ft 6in (2.9m). The main advantage of this arrangement was that defenders could clearly see what was going on in the ditch from their position on top of the wall.

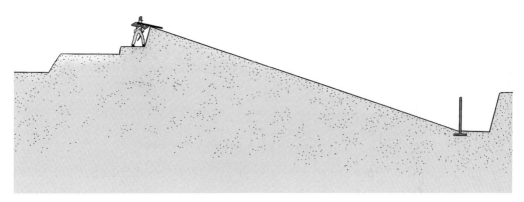

Twydall profile.

U

U-Boat bunker: See Submarine bunker.

Unterstand: This generic term (plural *Unterstände*) designated a German Second World War concrete shelter (q.v.). See Stand.

Unterstellraum für Kampwagen: See Tank shelter.

Usine: In the French Maginot Line (q.v.), the *usine* (literally 'factory') was the power plant facility, equipped with diesel engines, which produced and converted alternating current. In certain cases the *usine* could also convert high-voltage current provided by the French national power grid.

V

Vallum: In Roman fortification, the *vallum* usually comprised an earth or turf rampart (*agger*) with a wooden palisade on top, with a deep outer ditch (*fossa*). The name is derived from *vallus* ('stake'), and properly designated the *lorica* ('palisade'), which ran along the outer edge of the top of the *agger*, but is usually used to refer to the whole fortification.

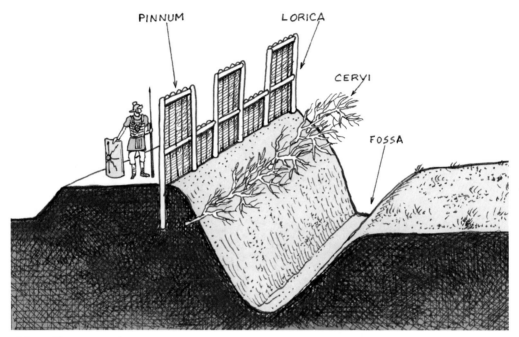

Vallum. (Cross-section).

Vamure/Vauntmure: A parapet or breastwork erected on the outer side of a rampart, or an advanced wall or earthwork built in front of the main fortification. See *Fausse-braie*.

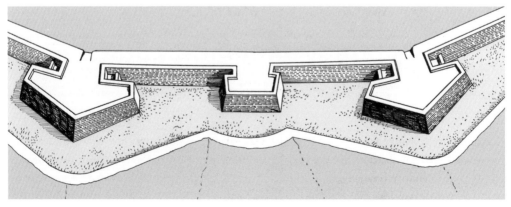

Venetian fortification.

Venetian fortification: An early form of sixteenth-century Italian bastioned fortification characterized by a curtain, two bastions with ears, a ditch and frequently a flat bastion (q.v.) called a *piatta-forma* (q.v.) in the middle of the curtain, increasing firepower and flanking of both the wall and ditch.

Vesting Holland: The *Vesting* Holland ('Fortress Holland') was an ensemble of Dutch fortifications and military flooding built and established between 1922 and 1940. They stretched from Naarden near the Zuiderzee in the north, passing Utrecht and ending near Moerdijk in the south. Fortress Holland was a National *Réduit* (q.v.) intended to defend the Randstad (the most populated and industrialized part of the Netherlands). In May 1940, the use of paratroopers opening the way to tanks and infantry, and a devastating terror bombardment by the Luftwaffe on the port of Rotterdam, resulted in the rapid surrender of the small Dutch Army.

Villa: A Roman self-contained agricultural domain, actually a large farm. It comprised a house for the owner, his family and his retinue, quarters for the labourers, various farm and service buildings and stables for livestock, and around the settlement were meadows, fields, orchards, vineyards and woods. The living accommodation of the *dominus* (the lord or master, who was often a retired military man) could be fortified with a *vallum* (earth wall), palisade or stockade and a *fossa* (ditch).

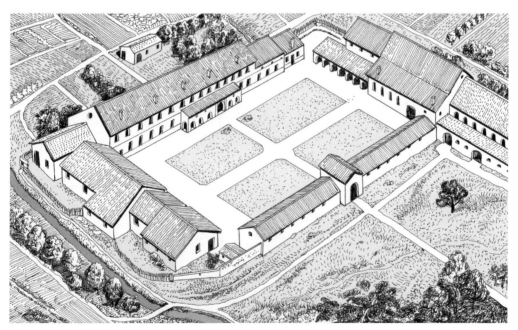

Villa.

Village perché: *Village perché* (literally 'perched village' in French) designates a fortified village in southern France. In the ninth and tenth centuries, the Provençal peasants had to build their villages (e.g. Grasse, Mons, Eze, Seillans, Venanson, Castellane and Sisteron) perched on isolated hilltops like eagles' nests and surrounded them with ramparts as a precaution against North African Moorish raiders.

Void bastion: A bastion was said to be void (or empty) when it was terraced only along its revetments. This hollow and protected *terre-plein* was suitable to place a powder-house or an ammunition store, for example.

W

Wagenburg: See Wagon fort.

Wagon fort: A mobile fortification made of wagons or vehicles arranged into a rectangle, circle or other shape, possibly joined with each other, in order to make an improvised military camp or temporary entrenched bivouac (q.v.) for defence against surprise night attack. The term was mentioned as early as in the fourth century AD by a Roman army officer in reference to fortified camps of the Goths. Notable historic examples include Hussite camps and battle formations known under the German word *Wagenburg* (wagon castle), as well as *tabors* in the armies of the Polish-Lithuanian Commonwealth and Cossacks, *laager* of South African colonists and defensive enclosed encampment formed of wagons of early American settlers known as corrals.

Wall: A defensive wall is the basis of fortification. It is an obstacle used to enclose and defend a settlement, camp, castle, fort, city etc from potential aggressors. Generally, these are referred to as curtain (q.v.), city or town walls, although there were also walls – such as the Great Wall of China, Hadrian's Wall and the Atlantic Wall – which extended far beyond the limited perimeters of a place and were used to enclose regions or mark and defend territorial boundaries. The practice of building massive walls had its origins in prehistory, and was further developed and refined in the Fertile Crescent of the Middle East, the Indus Valley, Egypt and China. This was continued by the Greek city-states, then in the Roman and medieval periods. Beyond their defensive utility, many walls also had important symbolic functions, notably representing the pride, status and independence of the communities they embraced. The city wall also formed a fiscal barrier, enabling the city to levy taxes. Ancient and medieval walls were often masonry structures, although brick, palisade, earth and timber-built variants were also widely employed. A classical method of constructing defensive walls consisted of an inner and an outer masonry casing (revetment, q.v.) with loose rock, mortar, earth or sand filling the space between.

Outer walls and flanking towers (q.v.) were initially regarded as accessory defences, but there was a gradual tendency toward the strengthening of curtain walls and a reduction in the role of the keep (q.v.) in both a military and residential context. Depending on the topography of the area surrounding the castle, camp, fort, city or settlement the wall was intended to protect, natural elements of terrain (e.g. rivers or coastlines) could be incorporated in order to make the wall more effective. Walls included an elaborate system of strong appended defences. They could only be crossed by entering the appropriate gate (q.v.) and were often supplemented with elements such as wall towers, a ditch, gatehouse and parapet, as well as additional obstacles and outer works. In the

Middle Ages, the right of a settlement to build a defensive wall or a castle was a privilege granted by a lord-suzerain – the so-called 'right of crenellation'.

The introduction of firearms resulted in the abandonment of the high vertical stone wall and its replacement with a thick rampart (q.v.) filled with earth. Walls and fortified wall structures were built in the modern era too, such as the Berlin Wall or the Belfast Peace Line in Northern Ireland. They did not, however, have the original purpose of being a structure able to resist an assault, a prolonged siege or bombardment, but worked as a separative border. See Barrier, Curtain, City wall and Dike.

Wall tower: A tower (q.v.) of varying strength and shape built along a wall or curtain (q.v.) in a castle or fortified town. Wall towers (also known as mural towers) were strongholds arranged for active defence, with the summit either covered with a roof or arranged as an open crenellated terrace.

The wall tower almost always extended outwards slightly, so as to enable soldiers to observe and flank the exterior of the wall on both sides. With enfilade or flanking fire nearly parallel to the wall, a few crossbowmen and archers placed inside or on top of the tower could thus observe and defend a whole length of curtain on both sides. Towers were placed at varying distances (about 60–70m) from one another. The distance was always

Wall tower.

calculated according to the range of weapons used: the effective range of a crossbow was about 100m. Wall towers rose higher than the wall itself, providing maximum visibility for the defenders, who normally used the towers as their principal bases for defence. A wall tower also provided shelter against the weather, an important consideration to maintain the morale of the guards, since rain lessened the effectiveness of the defenders' bows. From the wall-walk there was a door which gave entry to the tower. This passage could be defended by a small drawbridge or a brattice (q.v.). The base of the towers could be strengthened by a thick sloping apron, a spur (q.v.) or a buttress, providing stability and protection against ramming.

The inside of the tower was divided into several storeys arranged for various purposes, including supply-store, shelter and quarters for the guards. The storeys were linked by staircases or ladders and their walls furnished with narrow arrow-slits or loopholes (q.v.), through which guards could observe and shoot at enemies with bows during a siege. Wall towers were often given a name, at least the strongest of them. They could be fitted with hoarding (q.v.), later with machicolation (q.v.), and could be topped with an *echauguette* (q.v.) or a watchtower (q.v.). A corner tower – as the name implies – was a wall tower placed at an angle of two walls in a castle or an urban enceinte.

Wall-walk:

1) In Ancient and medieval fortifications, the wall-walk, also known as the rampart walk, was a continuous path and combat emplacement protected by a crenellated parapet (q.v.) installed on top of a wall (q.v.) or curtain (q.v.). Not infrequently, the wall-walk had a rear- as well as a fore-parapet, with crenels and merlons, so that the curtain wall could be held even when the enemy had penetrated inside the castle's courtyard. The wall-walk often had openings between supporting corbels, through which stones or other projectiles could be dropped on attackers, known as machicolation (q.v.). The wall-walk might be covered with a timber structure or even with a permanent tiled roof in order to shelter sentries from cold and rain and protect combatants from enemy projectiles.

2) In bastioned fortification it was a continuous and rather broad alley or a terrace arranged on top of curtains and bastions (q.v.). Its purpose was to provide an observation post, uninterrupted communication and combat emplacement suitable for artillery protected by a thick breastwork (q.v.). The rampart walk was much larger than in preceding eras because it had to allow the circulation of troops, guns and supply carts. It also had to allow the firing of cannons, which meant including sufficient room for muzzle loading and space behind the gun for recoil. The wall-walk was paved with tiles or made of stamped earth, as it was observed that, when heavily bombarded, masonry gave off dangerous stone splinters. Access to the wall-walk was by ramps or ascents (inclined planes), whose angle of slope and width were calculated to enable the mobility of guns and supply carts. Ascents were placed in the gorge of bastions to facilitate movement. Foot-soldiers reached the wall-walk by means of staircases arranged in the inner slope of the wall.

Ward: A courtyard or bailey (q.v.) in a medieval castle.

Wasserburg: German term for a medieval castle built on a bank or island of a river, or making use of a ditch filled with water for its defence.

Watchbank: In medieval fortification, stone seats placed in the thickness of wall near a loophole (q.v.) providing a resting place for the guard. See Window.

Watchtower: A watchtower is a type of small tower (q.v.) used everywhere in the world, throughout the history of fortification. Often but not necessarily a freestanding structure, its main purpose was to provide a high and protected place from which a sentry or guard

Watchtower. (Roman *Turris*)

might observe the surrounding area. Observation towers or observatory posts are similar constructions. See *Echauguette*, Pepper-pot tower, Mirador and Observation post.

Waterburcht: Dutch term for a medieval castle surrounded by a large defensive wet ditch.

Waterburcht. Montfoort, the Netherlands.

Water castle: A medieval castle in which natural or artificial water was part of the defences. See Ditch, Flooding, *Wasserburg* and *Waterburcht*.

Watergate: When a fortified place was established on both banks of a river, defences were adapted. Riverbanks were reinforced by dikes, while running water was impeded by batardeaus (q.v.) or retained by dams. To maintain access, a watergate was arranged in the middle of a curtain. It could take the form of a masonry gatehouse (q.v.) with one or more arches to allow the passage of inland boats. In time of crisis, the watergate could be blocked by sliding down one or more porticullises (q.v.).

Waterlinie: Dutch system of national defence based on the use of inundations (flooding) and fortifications. The Old Holland Waterline, intended to protect the western part of the United Provinces, was established in the seventeenth century from Muiden in the north to Gorichem in the south. The New Holland Waterline was established in 1871 from Naarden in the north to Gorinchem in the south, but made a wider arc in the east in order to include the important city of Utrecht within the defended area. The *Grebbelinie*, established east of the Utrecht ridge, ran from the Zuiderzee in the north to Rhenen on the River Rhine. The *Zuiderfrontier* (Southern Border) was another

Watergate. Amersfoort, the Netherlands, completed c. 1450.

waterline running from Willemstad in the west to Grave and Cuijk in the east, leaning on the Meuse, Waal and Rhine rivers. See Flooding and *Vesting* Holland.

Water supply: Throughout the history of fortification, water supply has been a matter of major concern to any garrison. A besieged place without sufficient water was doomed to rapid surrender. Each castle, fort or citadel was equipped with a well. Given its essential importance, the well was commonly protected by a bombproof roof resting on strong pillars, or even included inside a fortified vaulted building. The well was guarded by a sentry and fitted with a hoisting wheel. When a well was not available, water tanks and cisterns were arranged to collect rain. In the nineteenth and twentieth centuries, water was indispensable for the men but also as cooling for machinery and weapons, so specialized concrete bunkers and underground shelters for water supply were designed.

Wat's Dyke: An earth wall and ditch running from the Dee estuary to south of Oswestry in England, a distance of some 35 miles, more or less parallel to, and to the east of, the northen part of Offa's Dyke (q.v.). King Wat was a predecessor of Offa of Mercia, and his (uncompleted) work was intended to perform the same function as his successor's: a physical mark of his realm's border.

Wellblech Unterstand: A cheap German twentieth-century personnel shelter. It had a semi-circular roof made of corrugated plates, above which a layer of concrete was poured. It was usually sunk or dug into the ground for camouflage purpose and additional protection.

Wellington Barrier: A defensive scheme based on fortified cities in southern Belgium, partly financed by Britain and supervised by Arthur Wellesley, 1st Duke of Wellington (1769–1852). The Wellington Barrier, developed after the Napoleonic Wars in 1815, was intended to create a buffer zone that would prevent future French aggression on the continent. It included a series of twenty-five city fortresses spreading across and along the Scheldt and Meuse rivers, notably the main strongpoints of Antwerp, Ghent, Liège, Huy and Maastricht.

Westwall: The name of the German pre-Second World War defence line, which stretched along the German western border running from Kleve near Nijmegen (Netherlands) in the north to the Swiss border in the south. Built by the Organisation Todt (q.v.) between May 1938 and August 1939, it consisted of some 14,000 defensive constructions, including bunkers, shelters, anti-tank obstacles and ditches. With an average of twenty-three bunkers per kilometre, the defensive line was garrisoned by only 200,000 soldiers in September 1939, allowing the German armies to engage most of their strength and efforts against Poland. By then the Westwall was called the Siegfried Line (q.v.) by the Franco-British Allies.

The Westwall played no military role during the first years of the Second World War and was totally neglected at the expense of the Atlantic Wall (q.v.). However, by the end of 1944, with Allied forces nearing the border, the retreating Germans rearmed the Westwall. In February 1945, the line was attacked by the Allies, and the hastily refortified and obsolete Siegfried Line could not seriously impede their progress.

Wicket: The wicket (also called guichet) was a small door allowing the passage of only one person at a time without having to open the main portal of a fortified city or castle. The wicket could be made inside the main door, but it could also be independent from the main portal and fitted with its own narrow drawbridge moved by its own gaff (q.v.) and windlass, protected by its own portcullis (q.v.).

Widerstandsnest: Generic German term meaning resistance nest. During the Second World War, a *Widerstandsnest* (in short *W, WN* or *Wn*) in the Atlantic Wall was a fortified position called a defence post by the Americans. These defensive positions were composed of several armed bunkers and shelters, surrounded by barbed wire and anti-personnel mines and generally placed on heights overlooking approaches and beaches. See Atlantic Wall, *Stutzpunkt*, *Stutzpunktgruppe* and *Zwischenwiderstandsnest*.

Window: In medieval fortification, windows were few in number, only being set up in dwelling rooms in domestic buildings. The window openings could be covered with a grid for security, or with oiled linen or canvas to keep out draughts without entirely excluding light. At night they were closed with wooden shutters. In stone buildings like the keep (q.v.) or the hall (q.v.), windows were splayed so that the outer opening was narrow and the inner one at least twice the width in order to let in light. It was usual to have stone seats called watchbanks (q.v.) along the thickness of wall in the window opening where a guard could sit and watch, or ladies could do embroidery, read or chat.

Wing: Ramparted wall connecting a crownwork (q.v.), hornwork (q.v.), *tenaille* (q.v.) or bishop's mitre (q.v.) to the covered way (q.v.).

Wing-wall: A term often designating a palisade placed on the slope of a motte (q.v.) to protect the stairway leading to the upper terrace and the main tower. See Motte-and-bailey castle.

Widerstandsnest. The beach facing the sea was protected by various obstacles (1) and enfiladed by concrete casemates (2). Infantry and anti-aircraft guns were placed in open pits (3), and an observatory conducted fire (4). Shelters for men (5) and ammunition stores (6) were scattered all over the *Wn*. The rear of the position (the landfront) was defended by trenches (7), Tobruks (8), barbed wire and mines (9).

Winkelmine: See Square mine and Beach obstacle.

Wolf's pit: The wolf's pit – also called pitfall, *trou de loup* (in French) or *Wolfsgrube* (in German) – was a mantrap obstacle consisting of concealed interlocking excavations (about 2m in diameter and 2.5m deep) in which one or more deadly sharpened stakes

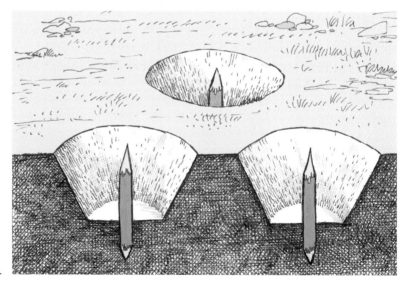

Wolf's pit. Cross-section.

or spikes were placed. The opening was camouflaged and covered with a light layer of vegetation, which gave way under the weight of any enemy soldier passing over it. First used by the Romans, it was usually positioned in advance of or in the glacis (q.v.). The wolf's pit was discarded and replaced by barbed wire entanglements in the nineteenth century. It still exists as a modern variant in the form of a highly dangerous mantrap and booby trap (q.v.) known as a punji stick (q.v.).

Woolsack: Mobile and folding screening breastwork sometimes used by infantrymen, principally in siege warfare in the seventeenth and eighteenth centuries. See Mantlet.

Work: A general term for a defensive structure or a military construction or fortification, such as siege work, field work, temporary work or outwork. See *Ouvrage*, Fort, Citadel and Fortress.

Wrought iron: A tough, malleable, relatively soft iron used to make armour in fortification in the second half of the nineteenth century.

Y

Yard castle: See Rectangular castle.

Yett: A gate or grille of latticed or crossed wrought iron bars used for defensive purposes in castles and tower houses (q.v.). Predominately found in Scotland.

Z

Zemlyanka: In the Second World War, a type of dugout (q.v.) or partially underground timber-made earth-house with a flat roof covered with branches or grass sods. It provided shelter and a hiding place to partisans or armed resistance fighters in the Soviet Union and Eastern Europe. In Poland it was called a *ziemianski*.

Zériba (plural zéribas): Originally designated an enclosure or a corral for animals (or a small hut) in the Maghreb (North Africa). In the First Indochina War (1946–54) it was a defensive network or fence made of sharp bamboo surrounding a French military post or fortlet. See Punji stick.

Zigzag: Tracé (q.v.) with alternate straight lines and sharp turns. This outline is often given to approaches (q.v.), saps (q.v.) and trenches (q.v.) in order to reduce the amount of exposure to enfilading enemy fire.

Zone de servitude: An off-limits zone, an open and bare area in the countryside beyond the glacis (q.v.). The construction of civilian buildings and the planting of vegetation was restricted or forbidden there, the purpose being to deny enemy besiegers any cover whatsoever.

Z-plan towerhouse: A fortified residence built in northern Britain and Scotland in the sixteenth century. It was characterized by a rectangular main residential block, with

Z-plan. Claypotts Castle, Dundee, Scotland, built between 1569 and 1588, is a good example of a Scottish Z-plan fortified house with asymmetrical square chambers corbelled out over two circular towers at diagonally opposite corners.

two additional protruding towers, either round or rectangular, placed at two diagonally opposite corners. Each jutting-out tower provided flanking fire (q.v.). Examples of Z-plan towerhouses can be seen in Scotland at Castle Menzies in Perthshire, Glenbuchat Castle and Castle Fraser in Aberdeenshire, Claypotts Castle in Dundee and Hatton Castle in Angus. See L-plan castle.

Zuda: Fortified Moorish palace. See Alcazar.

Zwischenwerk: German for 'interval work', a small fortified position generally intended to fill a gap between two main forts.

Zwischenwiderstandsnest: A *Zwischenwiderstandsnest* (in short *ZWN*, meaning 'interval resistance nest') was a Second World War German interval stronghold created to fill the gaps between existing *Widerstandsnesten*, notably in the Atlantic Wall (q.v.). These additional positions enabled defenders to increase firepower and provided extra interlocking firing for mutual flanking. See *Stutzpunkt*, *Stutzpunktgruppe* and *Widerstandsnest*.

Bibliography

Books and articles on fortification are extremely numerous. Only those which have been relevant to the writing of this dictionary are listed below. It is the author's hope that they may provide sources of reference for readers wishing to study further. The internet, notably Wikipedia, also provided much useful information, but always required circumspection, close inspection and careful control about sources.

Association des Amis de la Maison Vauban, *Vauban, sa vie, son oeuvre* (Saint-Léger-Vauban, 1984).
Augusta, Pavel, *Encyclopédie de l'Art Militaire* (Paris: Ars Mundi Editions, 1991).
Benevolo, Leonardo, *De Europese Stad* (Amsterdam: Agon BV, 1993).
Berhow, Mark (ed.), *American Seacoast Defenses: A Reference Guide* (Bel Air, MD: Coastal Defense Study Group Press, 1999).
Bertin, François, *14–18: La Grande Guerre* (Rennes: Ouest-France, 2006).
Blockmans, Willem, *Oorlog door de Eeuwen heen* (Hilversum: HD Uitgeverij, 1977).
Böhme, Horst Wolfgang, Friedrich, Reinhard and Schock-Werner, Barbara, *Wörterbuch der Burgen, Schlösser und Festungen* (Stuttgart: Philipp Reclam jun. GmbH & Co., 2004).
Bon, Antoine, *Forteresses Médiévales de la Grèce Centrale* (Bulletin de Correspondance Hellénique, 1937).
Bragard, Philippe, *Dictionnaire Biographiques des Ingénieurs des Fortifications. Pays-Bas Espagnols, Principauté de Liège, Franche-Comté 1504–1713* (Liège: Les Amis de la Citadelle de Namur, 2011).
Bragard, Philippe, Termote, Johan and Williams, John, *A la Découverte des Villes Fortifiées (Kent, Côte d'Opale et Flandre Occidentale)* (Dunkirk: Syndicat Mixte de la Côte d'Opale, 1999).
Braun, Georg and Hogenberg, Franz, *Civitas Orbis Terrarum (Steden van de Wereld, Europa – Amerika reprint)* (Amsterdam: Atrium, 1990).
Breasted, James Henry, *Ancient Time. A History of the Early World* (New York and Chicago: Ginn & Company, 1916).
Brochard, Philippe, *Chevaliers et Châteaux Forts* (Paris: Poche Nathan, 1985).
Brodie, Bernard and Brodie, Fawn, *From Crossbow to H-Bomb, the Evolution of the Weapons and Tactics of Warfare* (Bloomington: Indiana University Press, 1973).
Brøndsted, Johannes, *The Vikings* (Baltimore: Penguin Books, 1960).
Buisseret, David, *Ingénieurs et fortifications avant Vauban* (Paris: Editions du CTHS, 2000).
Camon, Hubert, *La Fortification dans la Guerre Napoléonienne* (Paris: Editions Berger-Levrault, 1914).
Campbell, Duncan and Delf, Brian, *Roman Legionary Fortress 27 BC–AD 378* (Oxford: Osprey Publishing, 2006).
Casado, Antonio, *Castillos y Fortaleza* (Junta de Comunidades de Castilla-La Mancha, 1989).
Claudel, Louis, *La Ligne Maginot, Conception–Réalisation* (Association Saint-Maurice, 1974).
Copeland, Peter F., *Historic North American Forts* (Mineola: Dover Publication Inc., 2000).
Corvisier, André, *Dictionnaire d'Art et Histoire Militaires* (Paris: Presses Universitaires de France, 1988).
Crefeld, Martin van, *The Art of War* (London: Smithsonian Books-Cassell, 2002).
Cruickshank, Daniel, *Invasion: Defending Britain from Attack* (Basingstoke and Oxford: Boxtree Pub., 2001).
Diderot, Denis, Le Rond d'Alembert, Jean and De Jaucourt, Louis, *Encyclopédie, Arts Militaires* (eighteenth-century originals republished by Interlivre Editions Paris, 1986).
Dropsy, Christian, *Les Fortifications de Metz et de Thionville* (Metz: self-published, 1998).
Dupuy, Trevor N., *The Evolution of Weapons and Warfare* (New York: Da Capo Press, 1984).
Falls, Cyril, *De Grote Veldslagen* (London: Weidenfeld Ltd, 1964).
Faucherre, Nicolas, Mesqui, Jean and Prouteau, Nicolas, *La Fortification au Temps des Croisades* (Rennes: Presses Universitaires, 2004).

Fields, Nic and Spedaliere, Donato, *Rome's Saxon Shore. Coastal Defences of Roman Britain AD 250–500* (Oxford: Osprey Publishing, 2007).

Fischer, H.A.L., *A History of Europe* (London: Edward Arnold & Co, 1938).

Fleischer, Wolfgang, *Feldbefestigungen des deutschen Heeres 1939–1945* (Wölersheim-Berstadt: Podzum-Pallas Verlag, 1998).

Floriani, P.P., *Difesa et Offesa delle Piazze* (Venice: 1654).

Gay de Vernon, F. de, *A treatise on the Science of War and Fortifications* (trans. Captain J.M. O'Connor) (New York: J. Seymour Publication, 1817).

Génicot, L. and Houssiau, P., *Le Moyen Age* (Paris: Casterman, 1959).

Gille, Bertrand, *Les Ingénieurs de la Renaissance* (Paris: Herman Collection Point, 1964).

Gravett, Christopher and Hook, Adam, *Norman Stone Castles (1): The British Isles 1066–1216* (Oxford: Osprey Publishing, 2003).

Gravett, Christopher and Hook, Adam. *The Castles of Edward I in Wales 1277–1307* (Oxford: Osprey Publishing, 2007).

Hamilton-Thompson, A., *Military Architecture in England during the Middle Ages* (Oxford: University Press, 1912).

Harding, D., *Weapons: An International Encyclopedia from 5000 B.C. to 2000 A.D.* (London: Diagram Visual Information Ltd, 1980).

Harmand, Jacques, *La Guerre Antique* (Paris: Presses Universitaires de France PUF, 1973).

Hart-Mahan, D., *A Complete Treatise on Field Fortification* (1836).

Heer, Friedrich, *The Medieval World, Europe from 1100 to 1350* (London: Weidenfeld & Nicolson Ltd, 1961).

Hogg, Ian V., *Fortress: History of Military Defence* (London: McDonald & Jane Pub., 1975).

Kamps, P.J.M. (ed.), *Terminologie Verdedigingswerken, Inrichting, Aanval en Verdediging* (Utrecht & Zutphen: Stichting Menno van Coehoorn- De Walburg Pers, 1999).

Krahe, Friedrich-Wilhelm, *Burgen des deutschen Mittelalters, Grundriss-Lexikon* (Würzburg: Flechsig, 2000).

Hale, John Rigby, *Renaissance War Studies* (London: The Hambledon Press, 1983).

Haslinghuis, E.J. and Janse, H., *Bouwkundige Termen* (Leiden: Primavera Pers, 2005).

Hughes, Quentin, *Military Architecture* (Hants, UK: Beaufort Pub. Ltd, 1974).

Keegan, John, *A History of Warfare* (London: Hutchinson Publications, 1993).

Koch, H.W., *Het Krijgsbedrijf in de Middeleeuwen* (Amsterdam: Elsevier BV, 1980).

Koenigsberger, Helmuth Georg, *Medieval Europe 400–1500, A History of Europe* (Harlow: Longman Group UK Limited, 1987).

Lebas, G., *Places Fortes* (Paris: Editions Payot, 1923).

Le Hallé, Guy, *Précis de la Fortification* (Paris: PVC Editions, 1983).

Lendy August, Frederick, *Treatise on Fortifications or Lectures delivered to Officers reading for the Staff* (London: W. Mitchell Stationer, Printer, Engraver and Bookbinder, 1862).

Lepage, Jean-Denis, *Castles and Fortified Cities of Medieval Europe* (Jefferson, NC: McFarland & Company Inc. Publishers, 2002).

Lepage, Jean-Denis, *The Westwall (Siegfried Line) 1938–1945* (West Chester, OH: The Nafziger Collection, Inc., 2002).

Lewis, Emanuel R., *Seacoast Fortifications of the United States* (Annapolis: Naval Institute Press Maryland, 1979).

Lewis, Michael J., *City of Refuge* (Princeton: Princeton University Press, 2016).

Libal, Dobroslav, *Châteaux Forts & Fortifications en Europe du Ve au XIXe Siècle* (Paris: Ars Mundi, 1993).

Lippmann, Harry, *Heeres-Regelbauten* (Cologne: Interessengemeinschaft für Befestigungsanlagen beider Weltkrieg, Sonderheft 30, 1995).

Lippmann, Harry and Delefosse, Yannick, *Panzersperren und andere Hindernisse* (Cologne: Interessengemeinschaft für Befestigungsanlagen beider Weltkrieg, Sonderheft 13, 1987).

McGovern, T, Smith, B. and Bull, P, *American Coastal Defenses 1885–1950* (Oxford: Osprey Pub., 2006).

McInnes, C. and Sheffield, G.D., *Warfare in the Twentieth Century: Theory and Practice* (London: Unwin Hyman Ltd, 1988).

Martini, Francesco Gorgio, *Trattate dell'Architectura civile e militare* (reprint) (Turin: Saluzzo & Promis Publishing, 1841).

Merian, Matthaeus, *Deutsche Städte* (Hamburg: Hoffmann & Campe Verlag, 1963).
Merian, Matthaeus, *Die Schönsten Europäischen Städte* (Hamburg: Hoffmann & Campe Verlag, 1963).
Meurer, Peter H., *Das Festungsbuch des Nicolas Person* (Bad Neustadt: Verlag D. Pfähler, 1984).
Mohr, A.H., *Vestingbouwkundige Termen* (Utrecht: Stichting Menno van Coehoorn- De Walburg Pers, 1983).
Monnier, Gérard, *Histoire de l'Architecture* (Paris: Presses Universitaires de France PUF, 1994).
Montanelli, Indro, *Histoire de Rome* (Paris: Editions Mondiales, 1959).
Montgomery, Bernard, Law, *A Concise History of Warfare* (Ware, Herts: Wordsworth Editions Limited, 2000).
Moore, David, *A Handbook of Military Terms* (Solent Papers & Victorian Forts Publications, 2011).
Neumann, Hartwig, *Festungbaukunst* (Bonn: Bernard & Graefe Publishers, 1988).
Nossov, Konstantin, *Ancient and Medieval Siege Weapons* (Staplehurst: Spellmont Limited, 2005).
Paluzie de Lescazes, Carlos, *Castles of Europe* (Barcelona: EGC S.A., date unknown).
Parker, Geoffrey, *Cambridge Illustrated History of Warfare* (Cambridge: Cambridge University Press, 1995).
Pedretti, Carlo, *Léonard de Vinci Architecte* (Milan–Paris: Electra Moniteur, 1988).
Peyen, Paul, *Middeleeuwse Kastelen* (Bussum: Uitgeverij van Dishoeck, 1965).
Phillips, Ellen, *The Enterprise of War* (Time-Life Books BV, 1991).
Poppema, Simon and Lepage, Jean-Denis, *Historische Verdedigingswerken* (Amsterdam: Stichting Open Monumentendag, 1995).
Potter, David, *Renaissance France at War: Armies, Culture and Society* (Woodbridge: The Boydell Press, 2008).
Potter, David, *War and Government in the French Provinces, Picardy 1470–1560* (Cambridge: Cambridge University Press, 2002).
Rocolle, Pierre, *2000 Ans de Fortification Française* (Paris: Editions Lavauzelle, 1989).
Rolf, Rudi, *Armour Forts and Trench Shelters – German Imperial Fortification 1870–1918* (Middelburg, Netherlands: PRAK Publishing, 2017).
Rolf, Rudi, *Atlantikwall, Batteries and Bunkers* (Middelburg, Netherlands: PRAK Publishing, 2014).
Rolf, Rudi, *Die Deutsche Panzerfortifikation – Die Panzerfesten von Metz und ihre Vorgeschichte* (Osnabruck: Biblio Verlag, 1991).
Rolf, Rudi, *Torens, Wallen en Koepels* (Middelburg, Netherlands: PRAK Publishing, 2007).
Ropp, T., *War in the Modern World* (London: Duke University Press, 1959).
Rorive, Jean-Pierre, *La Guerre de Siège sous Louis XIV* (Brussels: Editions Racine, 1998).
Sailhan, Pierre, *La Fortification, Histoire & Dictionnaire* (Paris: Tallandier, 1991).
Sakkers, Hans, *Generalfeldmarschall Rommel* (Koudekerke, Netherlands: Uitgeverij Zeelucht, 1993).
Saunders, A., *Fortress Britain: Artillery Fortification in the British Isles and Ireland* (Beaufort Publishing Ltd, 1989).
Sheffield, Gary, *Forgotten Victory – The First World War: Myths and Realities* (London: Headline Publishing, 2001).
Siegner, Otto, *Frankreich ein Bildwerk* (Munich: Verlag L. Simon, date unknown).
Soudagne, Jean-Pascal, *L'Histoire de la Ligne Maginot* (Rennes: Editions Ouest-France, 2006).
Specklin, Daniel, *Architektur von Vestungen* (Strasbourg: 1589; reprint Unterschneidheim: 1979).
Stier, Hans-Erich, *Grosser Atlas zur Weltgeschichte* (Braunschweig: Georg Westermann Verlag, 1956).
Strayer, Joseph R., *Feudalism* (London: Van Nostrand Company Ltd, 1965).
Tardi, Jacques, *Loopgravenoorlog* (Paris: Casterman, 1993).
Thevenot, Emile, *Les Gallo-Romains* (Paris: Presses Universitaires de France PUF, 1978).
Treu, Herman and Sneep, Jaap, *Vesting Vier Eeuwen Vestingbow in Nederland* (Zutphen: Stichting Menno van Coehoorn/Walburg Press, 1982).
Vérin, Hélène, *La gloire des ingénieurs. L'intelligence technique du XVIe au XVIIIe siècle* (Paris: Éditions Albin Michel, 1993).
Viglino, Davico, *Forteresse à la moderne et ingénieurs militaires du duché de Savoie* (Turin: Editions Celid, date unknown).
Villa, G., *Pier Francesco da Vitterbo e l'architettura militare italiana del primo cinquecento* (Rome: Edizioni Kappa, 2009).
Viollet-le-Duc, Eugène, *Histoire d'une Forteresse* (Paris: Berger-Levrault Editions, 1978).
Virilio, Paul, *Bunker Archéologie* (Paris: Editions du Demi-Cercle, 1996).

Visscher, Corrie and Bullinga, Nicki, *Kastelen Vanuit de Lucht* (Hoogeven, Netherlands: Slingenberg BV, 1997).

War Department (U.S. Army), *Handbook on German Military Forces* (TM E-30-451, March 1945).

Warry, John, *Oorlogvoering in de Klassieke Wereld* (Helmond, Netherlands: Uitgeverij Helmond BV, 1980).

Wells, H.G., *A Short History of the World* (Harmondsworth: Penguin Books, 1938).

Wenzler, Claude, *Architecture du Bastion* (Rennes: Editions Ouest-France, 2000).

Westermann, Georg, *Grosser Atlas zur Weltgeschichte* (Braunschweig: Druckerei und Kartographische Anstalt GmbH, 1956).